Volume Two

Trends in Corrections

Interviews with Corrections Leaders Around the World

Interviews with Global Leaders in Policing, Courts, and Prisons Series

---

International Police Executive Symposium Co-Publications

Dilip K. Das, *Founding President-IPES*

PUBLISHED

Trends in the Judiciary: Interviews with Judges Across the Globe, Volume One
By Dilip K. Das and Cliff Roberson with Michael Berlin, ISBN: 978-1-4200-9978-2

Trends in Policing: Interviews with Police Leaders Across the Globe, Volume Four
By Bruce F. Baker and Dilip K. Das, ISBN: 978-1-4398-8073-9

Trends in Policing: Interviews with Police Leaders Across the Globe, Volume Three
By Otwin Marenin and Dilip K. Das, ISBN: 978-1-4398-1924-1

Trends in Policing: Interviews with Police Leaders Across the Globe
By Dilip K. Das and Otwin Marenin, ISBN: 978-1-4200-7520-5

Trends in Corrections: Interviews with Corrections Leaders Around the World
By Jennie K. Singer, Dilip K. Das, and Eileen Ahlin, ISBN: 978-1-4398-3578-4

Trends in Corrections: Interviews with Corrections Leaders Around the World, Volume Two
By Martha Henderson Hurley and Dilip K. Das, ISBN: 978-1-4665-9156-1

FORTHCOMING

Trends in Policing: Interviews with Police Leaders Across the Globe, Volume Five
By Bruce K. Baker and Dilip K. Das, ISBN: 978-1-4822-2449-8

Trends in the Judiciary: Interviews with Judges Across the Globe, Volume Two
by David Lowe and Dilip K. Das, ISBN: 978-1-4822-1916-6

Volume Two

Trends in Corrections

Interviews with Corrections Leaders Around the World

Edited by
Martha Henderson Hurley
Texas A&M Commerce
Sociology and Criminal Justice Department
Commerce, Texas, USA

Dilip K. Das
International Police Executive Symposium
Guilderland, New York, USA

International Police Executive
Symposium Co-Publication

CRC Press is an imprint of the
Taylor & Francis Group, an **informa** business

CRC Press
Taylor & Francis Group
6000 Broken Sound Parkway NW, Suite 300
Boca Raton, FL 33487-2742

Printed on acid-free paper
Version Date: 20140728

International Standard Book Number-13: 978-1-4665-9156-1 (Hardback)

Visit the Taylor & Francis Web site at
http://www.taylorandfrancis.com

and the CRC Press Web site at
http://www.crcpress.com

Contents

Series Preface

The International Police Executive Symposium, in collaboration with CRC Press/Taylor & Francis Group, has launched a series entitled *Interviews with Global Leaders in Policing, Courts, and Prisons*. The objective is to produce high-quality books aimed at bringing the voices of leading criminal justice practitioners to the forefront of scholarship and research. These books, based on interviews with leaders in criminal justice, are intended to present the perspectives of high-ranking officials throughout the world by examining their careers, insights, vision, experiences, and challenges, the perceived future of the field, and related issues of interest.

The literature is replete with scholarship and research that provides academic interpretation of the field, its practices, and future. However, these are often published in journals that are difficult to access and are written from the perspective of the academic, with little interpretation or feasible action items for those professionals working in the field. A comprehensive work discussing the on-the-ground, day-to-day understanding of how police, courts, and prison systems work, do not work, and need to be improved, is lacking. This series provides "inside" information about the systems as told to respected scholars and researchers by seasoned professionals. In this series, the dialogue between scholar/researcher and practitioner is opened as a guided, yet candid, discussion between the two professionals. This provides the opportunity for academics to learn from practitioners, while practitioners also learn from an outlet for the expression of their experiences, challenges, skills, and knowledge.

Throughout the world, the criminal justice field is at juxtaposition and the time is ripe for change and improvements. Many countries throughout the world have long-standing policies that have been successful for their culture and political climate or are in need of serious revamping due to budgetary concerns or corruption. Other countries are at a precipice and are beginning to establish new systems. In all of these situations, the international criminal justice field stands to benefit from an accessible, engaging, and enlightening series of frank discussions of the leaders' personal views and experiences in the field.

The current volume, *Trends in Corrections: Interviews with Corrections Leaders Around the World*, Volume Two, sets the stage to enhance readers' understanding of correctional programming and management styles used throughout the world from an insider's perspective. The correctional leaders interviewed in this volume represent a variety of cultures, political environments, and economic systems. Representatives from the Americas (Mexico, United States), Asia (Singapore, Thailand), and Europe (Ireland, Northern Ireland, Slovenia, Slovakia, France, Spain, Switzerland) are interviewed. The introduction familiarizes the reader with the issue of international corrections and the need for a forum to discuss corrections from the perspective of noted corrections officials. Chapters 1 through 12 each provide the transcribed interview of the corrections leader as conducted by the scholar/researcher. A brief portrait of the corrections system in each jurisdiction is also provided. The final chapter is a reflection on the interviews and summary of common themes evident throughout the book.

Thus, *Trends in Corrections: Interviews with Corrections Leaders Around the World,* Volume Two, continues the work of the IPES and CRC Press series *Interviews with Global Leaders in Policing, Courts, and Prisons* by advancing knowledge about the corrections system, examining comparative corrections from the perspective of correctional leaders in a variety of countries, and opening a dialogue between scholars/researchers and practitioners. It is anticipated that this addition to the series will facilitate discussions within and between countries' correctional systems to add value to their current operations and future directions. It is hoped that this series will also bridge the gap of knowledge that exists between scholars and researchers in academia and practitioners in the field. I invite correctional scholars, researchers, and practitioners across the world to join in this venture.

Dilip K. Das
Founding President, International Police Executive Symposium,
www.ipes.info
Series Editor for
Advances in Police Theory and Practice
Interviews with Global Leaders in Policing, Courts, and Prisons
CRC Press/Taylor & Francis Group
PPR Special Issues as Books
Routledge/Taylor & Francis Group
Founding Editor-in-Chief
Police Practice and Research: An International Journal, PPR
http://www.tandfonline.com/GPPR

Acknowledgments

The publication of this volume could not have occurred without the support of numerous individuals who contributed time and effort. We would like to thank the authors Claudia Campistol, Srisombat Chokprajakchat, José Cid, María Contreras, Natalia Delgrande, Pascal Déscarpes, Deirdre Healy, Dominic Kelly, Pavol Kopinec, Attapol Kuanliang, Gorazd Meško, Brian Norris, Jacqueline Rhoden-Trader, and Susan Sim for their submission of chapters to this volume.

We also want to express our sincere thanks to the correctional leaders who graciously gave of their time in interviews conducted around the world: Keith Deville, Michael Donnellan, Eduardo Enrique Gomez García, Jaroslav Jánoš, Gary D. Maynard, Sue McAllister, Ramon Parés, Philippe Pottier, Ayuth Sintoppant, Walter Troxler, Dušan Valentinčič, and Soh Wai Wah. This book could not have been completed without them taking time out of their very busy lives to have conversations about their life experiences and perceptions.

The editors, authors, and interviewees wish to express our thanks and appreciation to Carolyn Spence, senior acquisition editor at CRC Press/Taylor & Francis Group, for her unwavering editorial support of this series.

Editors

Martha Henderson Hurley is department head and professor in the Department of Sociology and Criminal Justice at Texas A&M University–Commerce. Dr. Hurley is a native of South Carolina and received her undergraduate degree from Furman University. She earned her PhD in criminal justice from the University of Cincinnati. Her specific areas of research and teaching experience include criminal justice ethics, risk assessment and classification, analysis of performance measures, organizational change, prisoner reentry, special populations, and implementation of evidence-based practices in corrections. She has also worked as a senior researcher for the Ohio Department of Rehabilitation and Correction and served as a research analyst and facilitator of group sessions in a community-based juvenile program. Dr. Hurley published *Correctional Administration and Change Management* with CRC Press, and her new book, *Aging in Prison: The Integration of Research and Practice*, was released by Carolina Academic Press in November 2013.

Dilip K. Das has years of experience in criminal justice practice, research, writing, and education. After obtaining his master's degree in English literature, Dr. Das joined the Indian Police Service, an elite national service with a distinguished tradition. Dr. Das is a professor of criminal justice, a former police chief, and a human rights consultant to the United Nations. He is the founding president of the International Police Executive Symposium (IPES), where he manages the affairs of the organization in cooperation with an appointed group of police practitioners, academia members, and individuals from around the world. Dr. Das is also the founding editor-in-chief of *Police Practice and Research: An International Journal*. He is author, editor, or coeditor of more than 30 books and numerous articles. Dr. Das has received several faculty excellence awards and was a distinguished faculty lecturer.

Contributors

Claudia Campistol is a researcher at the Autonomous University of Barcelona, Spain, and visiting researcher at the University of Lausanne in Switzerland. After her studies at the University of Barcelona (MA Psychology) and postgraduate certificate in family and systemic psychotherapy, she worked for 4 years in the juvenile justice department of Catalonia, Spain. She later moved to Lausanne where she obtained a master of arts in criminology and is preparing her PhD. Her main field of interest is the analysis and comparison of juvenile justice systems. In addition, she is a member of the European Sourcebook of Crime and Criminal Justice Statistics group. She participates as an independent expert to several projects of reform of the Tunisian prison system and the International Committee of the Red Cross. Claudia also works as a consultant in juvenile delinquency and juvenile justice at the Open University of Catalonia.

Srisombat Chokprajakchat is currently an associate professor in the doctoral program in criminology, justice administration, and society in the Department of Social Sciences, Faculty of Social Sciences and Humanities, Mahidol University, Thailand. She also serves as a member of the Mahidol University Institutional Review Board and the Committee for Research Ethics for Social Sciences, Program B, Mahidol University. She is currently assigned by the National Anti-Corruption Commission Thailand as a member of the National Strategic Steering Committee (private sector) on Anti-Corruption. Srisombat Chokprajakchat has authored a book on anti-corruption policy in Thailand and is the coauthor of a book on victimology. She is currently drafting the Third Human Rights Plan of Thailand on a grant funded by the Department of Rights Protection and Liberties, Ministry of Justice, Thailand.

José Cid is associate professor of criminal law and criminology at the Autonomous University of Barcelona in Spain, where he coordinates the degree program in criminology. He teaches Introduction to Criminology, Theories of Crime, and Comparative Penology. He has been director of the research group in applied penology (criminologia.uab.cat), a team that has been conducting research on prisons and alternatives since the early 1990s. His research has been devoted to analyzing the use of discretion by judges, comparing the effectiveness of prison and suspended sentences, analyzing the effectiveness of parole, and understanding the process of desistance. Some of his research has been published in the *Probation Journal* (2005), *Punishment and Society* (2005), and the *European Journal of Criminology* (2009 and 2012). At present, he is conducting research on the process of desistance of young offenders in the transition to adulthood.

María Contreras lectures penology in the undergraduate degree program of criminology at the Autonomous University of Barcelona in Spain. After obtaining her degrees in law and criminology, she completed one master's degree in penology and another one in applied social research. After some years of practice, she joined the university where she coordinates the practicum program for undergraduate students of criminology and took up the course of penology. She has conducted research on the effectiveness of community service orders, social networks of juvenile offenders, implementation of safety local audits, and effectiveness of community prevention programs. She is currently preparing her PhD research on the involvement of the community in the supervision of offenders, taking into account supervision programs carried out in Chile that she studied as a visiting scholar at the University of Chile in 2013.

Natalia Delgrande is research associate and part-time lecturer in penology at the Institute of Criminology and Criminal Law, University of Lausanne, Switzerland. She has two master of arts degrees: the first one in history and psychology and the second one in criminology. Her core activities relate to the analysis of the trends in corrections across Europe. She has several publications on the typology of penal populations and on the functioning of the penal institutions in the member states of the Council of Europe. She contributes to research on institutional adjustment and primary desistance from crime. From an international perspective, Natalia participates as an independent expert in projects launched by the Council of Europe and the International Committee of the Red Cross. She has some experience of volunteering in launching a nonprofit project in probation as well as a program of social support to the families of prisoners.

Pascal Déscarpes is research associate at the chair of criminology under the direction of Professor Dr. Frieder Dünkel at the University of Greifswald in Germany. Since 2007, he has been working for the European Commission in Brussels as an expert on the program "Prevention of and Fight against Crime (ISEC)," evaluating research projects and action plans in the field of criminality and criminal justice. He worked from September 2011 to May 2012 for the United Nations Development Programme in Romania as an expert consultant on European criminal systems and social inclusion of offenders. He also worked as an expert advisor to the Algerian and Jordanian prison services (respectively spring 2010 and winter 2012–2013) in a project financed by the European Union. In 2010–2011, he worked as a scientific consultant for the Hessen Ministry of Justice in Germany. He is deputy secretary-general of the French Society of Criminology.

Robert Hanser is the coordinator of the Criminal Justice Program and the director of the Institute of Law Enforcement at the University of Louisiana at Monroe (USA). In addition, he is the director of offender programming for LaSalle Corrections and is responsible for overseeing inmate reception, drug rehabilitation, and inmate reentry. Dr. Hanser serves as the board president for Freedmen, Inc., a faith-based organization that provides reentry services for offenders in Louisiana. He also serves as the board president and CEO of North Delta Human Services Authority, which is a nonprofit organization that provides contract therapeutic services for the 4th Judicial District Adult Drug Court and DWI Court in northeast Louisiana. Lastly, he is the lead facilitator for the 4th Judicial District's Batterer Intervention Program and serves as the president on the board of directors for the Louisiana Coalition Against Domestic Violence for the State of Louisiana.

Deirdre Healy is a lecturer at the University College Dublin Sutherland School of Law (Republic of Ireland). Before taking up this position, she completed a 2-year postdoctoral research fellowship at University College Dublin that was funded by the Irish Research Council for the Humanities and Social Sciences. During this time, she conducted the first prospective study of desistance from crime among adult male probationers in Ireland. Her research interests include desistance, reintegration, community sanctions, and victims and the criminal justice system. She has a track record of high-quality publications in peer-reviewed international and Irish journals and her work has attracted interest from policymakers and practitioners as well as academics. She has published two books: *The Dynamics of Desistance: Charting Pathways Through Change* (Routledge, 2012) and *Rape and Justice in Ireland* (with Conor Hanly and Stacey Scriver; Liffey Press, 2009) and is currently editing the *Routledge Handbook of Irish Criminology* (with Claire Hamilton, Yvonne Daly, and Michelle Butler; Routledge).

Dominic Kelly received his master of social science degree in criminology from the Institute of Criminology and Criminal Justice within Queen's University Belfast, Northern Ireland (United Kingdom), having previously completed a bachelor of science degree in psychology. Dominic is currently a doctoral candidate at this university in the School of Law and also serves as a teaching assistant in this faculty. His current project explores the reactions of prison officers to planned organizational reforms. He has a particular interest in establishing an understanding of the trauma associated with prison work and its effect on prison staff change responses. His wider research and teaching interests include the history of Northern Ireland prisons, penal policy, punitiveness, and social research methods. Dominic is currently on a career break from the Department of Justice in Northern Ireland.

Pavol Kopinec is a researcher at the Institute of Social Studies and Curative Education at the Comenius University in Bratislava in Slovakia. His main subject of interest is migration and the human rights protection of vulnerable groups. He has worked as a program manager for refugee camps in Slovakia and with the Separated Children in Europe Program as a coordinator of support to unaccompanied children coming to the Slovak Republic. He has participated in international teams monitoring the living and care conditions of children in the asylum process and detention centers in various European countries. From 2011, he worked as a consultant for the International Organization for Migration in the capacity-building field. He has published two books on working standards and provision of high-quality services to refugees and vulnerable groups.

Attapol Kuanliang is an associate professor, graduate program coordinator of criminal justice, and director of the Institute of Corrections and Juvenile Justice at the University of Louisiana at Monroe. He is also a faculty member in a doctoral program in criminology and criminal justice administration at Rangsit University, Thailand. His primary interests include juvenile justice and delinquency, corrections, drug use and abuse, quantitative methods and analysis, and program evaluation. He has published several book chapters and articles in peer-reviewed journals. He is also a consultant to and member of the advisory board of the Juvenile Justice Reform Project operated by the Department of Juvenile Observation and Protection, Ministry of Justice, Kingdom of Thailand. His current projects include a federal-funded project on Alzheimer's and missing person cases.

Gorazd Meško is professor of criminology and dean in the Faculty of Criminal Justice and Security, University of Maribor (Slovenia). He has been a visiting scholar at the University of Cambridge (1995, 2011–2014) and Oxford (1996, 1999) as well as a visiting professor at Grand Valley State University, Michigan (2000). He conducted postdoctoral research (Open Society Institute/Higher Education Support Program) on crime prevention at the Institute of Criminology, University of Cambridge, UK, in 2001. In addition, Gorazd Meško is a member of the scientific board of the international PhD in criminology at the Catholic University in Milan, Italy. He also serves as the editor-in-chief of the *Journal of Criminal Investigation* *and Criminology* (originally *Revija za kriminalistiko in kriminologijo*) and a member of the editorial board of *Policing: An International Journal of Police Strategies and Management*. His research fields are crime prevention and provision of safety/security, policing, comparative criminology, fear of crime, and crimes against the environment.

Brian Norris is assistant professor in the Criminal Justice Department at The Citadel, Charleston, SC. He holds a PhD in international relations from the Johns Hopkins University, a master's degree in Latin American studies from the University of Texas at Austin, and a bachelor's degree in business administration from the University of Texas at Arlington. He has a background in social work, having lived and worked for 5 years with the rural poor in Bolivia and El Salvador in need of water and sanitation services. Norris has worked on projects to strengthen the administration of justice in Latin America, including enforcement offices for judicial codes of ethics, criminal code and criminal procedural code reform, strengthening of prosecutors' offices to investigate white collar crime, and anticorruption initiatives. Since 1997, he has made 20 research and work trips to the region. He is a board member with the World Affairs Council of Charleston and lives in Charleston with his wife and three daughters.

Jacqueline Rhoden-Trader is an assistant professor at Coppin State University in Baltimore, Maryland. She is an applied social science researcher and policy analyst in the field of criminology. Having worked in both the private and public sectors, Dr. Rhoden-Trader brings creativity, sensitivity, and a wealth of experience in the areas of policy analysis, research and evaluation, systems and program development, and training. She is passionate about enhancing the life opportunities of children, youth, and women and has over 20 years of direct service and leadership experience working with and on behalf of those deemed "disadvantaged." In addition, she has conducted qualitative and quantitative research on disadvantaged populations, written several articles that were published in scholarly journals, and trained thousands of individuals nationally and internationally. Specific research interests include human trafficking, race and gender disparities across the globe, at-risk/disadvantaged youth, crime and delinquency prevention through the use of geospatial analysis, and youth development policy.

Susan Sim is consulting editor of the *Home Team Journal*, a publication of the Home Team Academy, a multiagency training facility of the Singapore Ministry of Home Affairs. A graduate of Oxford University, she has been a senior police officer, intelligence analyst, and diplomat working for the Singapore government and currently serves as chair of the Research

Committee of the National Crime Prevention Council, a volunteer group that works closely with the Singapore Police Force. She has written on the Singapore Home Team approach to homeland security, crime prevention and policing, suicide bombing, countering violent extremism, and terrorist rehabilitation. She is also vice president for Asia at the Soufan Group, an international strategic consultancy with offices in New York, Doha, London, and Singapore.

Interviewees

Keith Deville is a past warden of Richwood Correctional Center, a medium-security prison owned by LaSalle Corrections in the United States, which houses nearly 1200 inmates in northeastern Louisiana. After providing his interview, Warden Deville was promoted to a larger and more complicated assignment as warden of the Madison Parish facilities, which is a multisite post that includes Madison Parish Correctional Center, Madison Parish Detention Center, and Madison Parish Louisiana Transitional Center for Women. Prior to joining LaSalle, Deville served 33 years with the Louisiana Department of Public Safety and Corrections. He has received many awards throughout his career, most notably the Secretary of Corrections Award of Excellence, Lawman of the Year (which included nominees from corrections and local and state police), and Honorary Senator. He is a member of the American Correctional Association, Louisiana Association of Wardens, National Association of Wardens, and Southern States Correctional Association.

Michael Donnellan was appointed director general of the Irish Prison Service (Republic of Ireland) by the Minister for Justice and Equality in December 2011. Prior to his appointment as director general, Michael served as director of the probation service from 2005. Before this, he served as director of two children's detention schools in Dublin. He has previous experience in health and social services in Ireland and London. Michael spent his early career working within adult psychiatry before specializing in child and adolescent psychiatry. He worked in inner-city London as a social worker and then as manager of Brixton Child Guidance Unit, before returning to Ireland in 1994.

Eduardo Enrique Gomez García is the commissioner of the Independent Office of Social Prevention and Rehabilitation (OADPRS), the entity responsible for the administration of federal penitentiaries in Mexico. As a young man, Gomez studied in the military educational system (*castrense*), and in the 1960s he attended Mexico City's University of Anahuac, a Catholic university founded in 1964 offering classes in business administration, public administration, psychology, law, architecture, and the humanities. Gomez served 32 years in the Mexican military and retired with the rank of general. After 2000, Gomez served in the Mexican Attorney General's Office (PGR) of President Vicente Fox (PAN party) where he led initiatives to improve coordination across different ministries within the executive branch and helped create Metropol, a unified municipal police force in northern Mexico. In 2008, he was appointed to head the OADPRS under the Felipe Calderón (PAN party) administration.

Jaroslav Jánoš is a prison governor in Hrnčiarovce nad Parnou (Slovakia; 2010) responsible for management and security of the prison. Dr. Jánoš started as a regime officer in the prison for women in 1988. After 11 years in frontline service, he was offered policy work at the directorate general. He authored a significant part of Act No. 475/2005 on serving of prison sentences and helped to outline new directions of the prison system in Slovakia. He successfully defended his PhD dissertation in 2004 and is continuing in academic activities in the field of penitentiary and postpenitentiary work. He is an expert member of various interministerial groups, for example, on discrimination, drug abuse and addiction, prevention measures in prisons, and education of prisoners.

Gary D. Maynard brings more than 30 years of extensive correctional administrative experience to the job of secretary of Maryland's Department of Public Safety and Correctional Services. Prior to his appointment, he served as director of the Iowa Department of Corrections. Maynard's professional experience includes serving as director of the South Carolina Department of Corrections, the Corrections and Public Safety Programs at the University of Oklahoma, and the Oklahoma Department of Corrections; regional director and assistant director for the Oklahoma Department of Corrections; and warden at both the Oklahoma State Penitentiary and the Joseph Harp Correctional Center in Oklahoma. Maynard's professional activities include serving as president of the American Corrections Association (ACA). He also has served as a commissioner and, since 1980, an auditor/consultant for ACA's Commission on Accreditation for Corrections. Maynard is the author of the 15th edition of *Correction Officer* (Thomson, USA).

Sue McAllister has been the director general of the Northern Ireland Prison Service (UK) since July 2012. She has held management positions within the prison services in England and Wales for 25 years, rising through the ranks from assistant governor and in-charge governor postings in a number of prisons, to the head of security for England and Wales, to the area manager for West Midlands. She has also been head of the Police Performance Unit in England and Wales. Before taking up her current post, she was responsible for the Public Sector Bid Unit. Sue has a bachelor of science from the Open University and a master of arts (honors) from University of St. Andrews, Scotland.

Ramon Parés studied law at the University of Barcelona, Spain. After finishing his degree, he was involved with Catholic church–related organizations that helped disadvantaged groups, and he worked in community prevention in relation to gangs. He contributed to the creation in Catalonia of a new juvenile system based on community control made by juvenile probation officers. In the early 1990s, he moved to the prison system as prison inspector, where he developed a tough mission not always well understood by prison staff. After spending some years as a director of the Centre for Legal Studies and Specialized Training, a training and research center of the Catalan Justice Department, he took on heavy responsibilities as director of the Catalan correctional system (2001–2003) and director of the Catalan prison system (2010–2012).

Philippe Pottier has been director of the National School of Prisons Administration (France) since January 2013. As a head officer of the prison services, he was director of the probation unit in New Caledonia from 2012 to 2012, in charge of the development of community sentences and new types of intervention and organization of probation services in the Oceania zone. Prior to this mission, he was deputy director of the central prison unit. He obtained a master in social sciences at the University of Paris 13 (1992) and a master in anthropology at the University of French Polynesia. He is vice president of the French Society of Criminology and was its president from 2005 to 2007, succeeding Pierre V. Tournier and preceding Alain Blanc (2013, the current president). He is member of the think tank DES maintenant en Europe and was general secretary of a prison union (SNEPAP-FEN) between 1978 and 1988.

Ayuth Sintoppant is currently a prison commander (prison warden) at Thonburi Remand Prison, Thailand. He received a bachelor of laws from Dhurakij Pundit University, a master of arts in criminology and justice administration and a PhD in criminology, justice administration, and Society from Mahidol University, Thailand. He has close to 30 years of correctional experience. Some of his most important research is on public–private partnership in correction. He has initiated several correctional programs such as a correctional call center, gender equality in organization, prison classification among high-risk offenders, and scorecards for correctional officers. He is also a guest lecturer for numerous universities and agencies in Thailand.

Walter Troxler is a graduate of the University of Freiburg in Switzerland and the Center for Therapie ZAK, Basel. From 1980 to 1992, he was the deputy governor at the Penitentiary Center Wauwilermoos. From 1992 to 2004, he served as the director of the Young Offender's Institution Jugenddorf. Since 2004, he has served as the head of the Federal Office of Justice, Execution of Sentences and Measures Unit in Switzerland. He has served in leadership positions with several significant organizations such as Integras, the Swiss

Association for Social Education, the Swiss Training Center for Prison Staff, and the Federal Office of Justice, Committee on Pilot Projects. Troxler is also the Swiss representative on the Council of Europe, PC-CP, and CDAP.

Dušan Valentinčič is the director general of prison administration of the Republic of Slovenia. He studied sociology at Ljubljana University where he graduated in 1981. He started as a prison officer in Koper Prison and then continued as a pedagogue, assistant governor—head of the treatment service and the economic unit—and governor for 6 years (1983–1997). From 1997 to 2006, Dušan Valentinčič was the director general of the prison administration of the Republic of Slovenia. Since 2006, he has been the director of Koper Prison. In 2009, the government of the Republic of Slovenia nominated him as director general of the prison administration of the Republic of Slovenia again. He is a member of the Middle Europe Roundtable of Directors General of Prison Services. He is the representative of Slovenia in Europris, the European Organization of Prisons and Correctional Services. He is the author of several articles in the field of enforcement of prison sentences.

Soh Wai Wah, the commissioner of prisons in Singapore, was second in command and the chief of staff of the Singapore Police Force until 2009. He holds a bachelor of arts (economics) degree from the University of Cambridge, UK, and a master of science (criminal justice) degree from Michigan State University, USA. He was awarded the Public Administration (Silver) medal in 2000 and the Public Administration (Gold) medal in 2009.

Introduction

Throughout history, nations have struggled with what to do with those members of society who violate the social contract and must be relegated to some form of punishment. Early correctional reformers such as John Howard (1777), Benjamin Franklin, Benjamin Rush, and many others all compared their punishment systems with those of other countries and found them lacking (Friedman 1993; Allen et al. 2013). Their use of the comparative perspective to assess correctional operations and implement more effective policies led to major transformations in correctional practice such as the radial design, better and more sanitary living conditions, and separation of male and female prisoners (Friedman 1993; Allen et al. 2013). These early reformers embraced the cultural differences and used this knowledge to improve practice. Despite evidence suggesting that comparative analysis can be used to improve correctional policy, few scholars have examined the cross-cultural context of corrections.

Numerous scholars have detailed the punitive policy agendas that have driven correctional policies in Western industrialized nations for the last 40 years (Garland 2001; Irwin and Austin 1994). Yet, questions about how we punish remain. Regardless of whether a correctional leader supports a punitive regime, the public unfailingly calls for rehabilitative programming as well (Cullen et al. 2000, 2007). Consequently, correctional leaders are often faced with competing demands. On one hand, they are expected to punish those who violate the law, and on the other hand they are tasked to implement programs that will reduce recidivism, all the while facing an ever-shrinking budget and external calls for procedural change (Hurley and Hanley 2010). Perhaps, as administrators face such daunting tasks, it would be helpful for correctional leaders around the world to be afforded an opportunity to "walk a mile in someone else's shoes," that is, to hear how others in similar positions address challenges. This point is particularly salient given the perception that there is a widening divide in correctional practices between the United States and the rest of the world (Whitman 2003).

In *Trends in Corrections,* Volume One, we introduced readers to the importance of understanding the perspective of correctional leaders. By viewing corrections through the lens of its international leaders, we were exposed to the great diversity that exists cross-culturally in the political, social, and economic context of the correctional system. The general conclusion drawn from the first volume was that the 12 correctional leaders interviewed exhibited "striking similarities" despite vast differences in the social and political climates in which they worked. They all appeared to struggle with some of the same issues.

With this in mind, Volume Two has several goals. First, we seek to extend the reach of the interviews by incorporating leaders from other countries such as Slovenia, Slovakia, Northern Ireland, Switzerland, and France. Second, we expand the knowledge base by asking specifically about the impact of the economic downturn on corrections in each country. Third, we continue just as in *Trends in Corrections,* Volume One, to explore the changes in correctional practice experienced by each leader. Across all volumes, the themes identified in the book afford an opportunity for you to have a candid conversation in your part of the world about corrections and correctional leadership.

This current volume provides rare, first-hand accounts of correctional practices from the viewpoint of 12 correctional leaders from 10 countries throughout the world. Each chapter contains an in-depth interview with a correctional official with major administrative responsibilities for a department or agency related to the field of corrections. The interviews are conducted by scholars or practitioners with intimate knowledge of correctional practice and who are familiar with the correctional system under discussion. The interview is designed to solicit and explore the views, experiences, and thought processes of the correctional leader. Particular emphasis is placed on exploring how correctional leaders throughout the world think about and evaluate trends and developments. This series affords correctional leaders an unprecedented opportunity to express their views on current practices and the future of corrections in their country.

In Chapter 1, Philippe Pottier, the director of the National School of Prisons Administration in France, is interviewed. Pottier began his correctional career as a probation officer for juvenile offenders. He notes that French prisons have changed significantly over the last 40 years, primarily as a result of the European Court of Human Rights and the European Prison Rules law of 2009. He discusses the need for criminology programs at universities in France to help address prison problems. Also detailed in this chapter is the roughrider program, where violent inmates work to tame wild horses and learn to control themselves.

In Chapter 2, Michael Donnellan, director general of the Irish Prison Service, talks about the impact of the Children's Act of 2001. Donnellan details how this act reduced the number of children below the age of 10 who were incarcerated and increased the number of community interventions. He points out that the Irish correctional system has not joined the "massive bandwagon of punitiveness" (see page 24). Donnellan believes that an effective prison system has to be built on trust, mutual respect, and dignity.

He believes that the Irish correctional system is impacted by other countries such as the United States and England, but the system should look at the best of what others are doing in corrections and then reshape Ireland's correctional system.

Jaroslav Jánoš, the prison governor in the Corps of Prison and Court Guards in the Slovak Republic, began his correctional career as a regime officer in a prison for women. In Chapter 3, Dr. Jánoš discusses how the Leopoldov prison riot of 1991, when five members of the prison staff and a cellmate were killed, transformed correctional policy in the country. Slovakia is currently dealing with the major issue of overcrowding in the prison system. The lack of fiscal resources and prison programs in the country is also discussed.

Dušan Valentinčič, the director general of the Slovenian prison administration, became employed by the prison system by accident and never imagined that one day he would become a correctional leader. In Chapter 4, he discusses the shift in management philosophy from a sociotherapeutic (democratic, horizontal model) to the current hierarchical, pyramidal style of management. Director Dušan Valentinčič states that "ensuring the respect of human rights" and successful reintegration of prisoners into society represent the basic mission of prisons. Furthermore, he stresses the importance of prison employees maintaining "fair" relationships with the offenders they supervise. The development of solutions to address overcrowding, provide funds for replacement prison construction, and employ more correctional workers are tasks that would improve prison conditions in Slovenia.

In Chapter 5, Ramon Parés, the former director of the Catalan prison system in Spain, discusses the changes in correction over the last two decades. In Spain, rehabilitation appears to be the goal of the prison system, but more work needs to be done on alternatives to incarceration. While in other countries there have been discussions on evidence-based practices, the evidence-based approach has not gained momentum in Spain. As in other countries, Parés states that policies aimed at reducing prison populations are a must.

In Chapter 6, Walter Troxler, head of the Unit for the Execution of Sentences and Measures at the Federal Department of Justice and Police in Switzerland, discusses the federal prison system. He details the need to identify inmates with mental disorders, place them in separate forensic facilities, and better train staff on how best to work with this special population. Switzerland has embraced evidence-based corrections and has supported projects to develop protocols for the assessment and supervision of dangerous offenders. Moreover, he believes that Switzerland serves as a model for corrections in Europe and discusses the fact that Russia is now copying the Swiss juvenile justice model.

In Chapter 7, Susan McAllister, the director general of the Northern Ireland Prison Service, discusses the role of prison officers and assesses the level of service provided to prisoners in the correctional system. She stresses the fact that more rehabilitation interventions that focus on practical life skills such as finance are needed. She believes that the Northern Ireland Prison Service should examine the education courses provided and determine whether reorganization is necessary. Director McAllister readily admits that, as in other correctional organizations around the world, collaboration between academics and practitioners has been sparse.

General Eduardo Enrique Gomez García is the head of the OADPRS, the unit responsible for operational policy in federal prisons in Mexico. General Gomez was tasked with improving the Mexican prison system. In Chapter 8, he discusses the improvements to the system that are needed: an increase in resources, merit-based recruiting, and better management practices such as the creation of the National Registry of Penitentiary Information. According to General Gomez, rehabilitation is the dominant correctional philosophy. A major concern for corrections discussed by General Gomez is the need for Mexico to develop better postincarceration institutions such as monitoring systems for sex offenders and halfway houses. General Gomez states that Mexican federal prison officials can learn from outsiders, and he has visited Singapore, Chile, France, England, Italy, and Germany for that purpose.

In Chapter 9, Keith Deville, warden of Richwood Correctional Center in Louisiana, discusses the use of technology to help administrators make decisions. Warden Deville believes that more should be done to help offenders become productive citizens upon release from prison and states that the warehousing of inmates in prisons without self-help programs is a major problem. He worries that the current budget crisis will reduce the number of programs provided to inmates and increase recidivism rates. Warden Deville discusses the importance of research and provides examples of areas where more research is needed.

In Chapter 10, Gary Maynard, Secretary of Public Safety and Correctional Services, Maryland, discusses the level of inmate-on-staff violence in prisons. He notes that rates of inmate-on-staff violence have dropped 65% in recent years. He believes restorative justice programs and community-based programs have reduced the recidivism rates in his state. A major problem facing corrections in Maryland and elsewhere is the handling of inmates with mental health problems. Secretary Maynard believes that we need to do more to address the needs of mentally ill inmates by providing treatment programs. He also discusses the need for the correctional system to partner with other agencies such as the Department of Labor, Mental Health, and Veteran's Administration to address offender needs.

In Chapter 11, Soh Wai Wah, the commissioner of prisons in Singapore, began his career as a police officer but is now in charge of more than 12,000 prisoners in eastern Singapore. Commissioner Wah believes that correctional officers must focus on rehabilitating prisoners despite the dangers associated with their jobs. He is very proud of the fact that he has doubled the number of counselors on his staff, but this has not alleviated the severe shortage of resources.

Warden Ayuth Sintoppant (Chapter 12), of the Kingdom of Thailand's Department of Corrections, oversees the Thonburi Remand Prison in Nonthaburi Province, Thailand. This prison leader provides a discussion that supports the use of selective incapacitation as a primary correctional philosophy. From this interview, it is clear that the Thai prison system has a very disproportionately large of drug offenders. The provision of treatment along with the need for more intermediate sanctions and programming, outside the prison walls, is made apparent in this interview. Warden Sintoppant also noted that in Thailand, there is an increased emphasis on professionalizing correctional staff throughout the Department of Corrections. This includes both training and education. In fact, Warden Sintoppant has, himself, mirrored this effort, having received a doctorate degree in criminology. Thus, Warden Sintoppant is very supportive of furthering the skills, training, and education of personnel in the department and provides an optimistic outlook on the field of corrections in Thailand, in terms of both organizational operation and opportunities for employment, for future years.

Europe

I

1 Philippe Pottier, Director of the National School of Prisons Administration, France

PASCAL DÉSCARPES

Contents

Overview

The French prison administration is divided into nine regional sectors (*direction interrégionale*) with a central unit in Paris. A formal classification process for prisons identifies the prison security level. In France, *maison centrale* (MC) and *quartier maison centrale* (QMC) are prison facilities designed to provide the highest level of security and a very strict prison routine (to Article D.71 Code of Criminal Procedure). Detention centers (CD) are defined under Article. D.72 Code of Criminal Procedure as prisons with less security and focus on reintegration and preparation for release. Community-based prisons (CPA) are transition-based prison facilities with daily routines designed for inmates with less than 1 year to serve before their release (Article D.72-1 Code of Criminal Procedure). The criteria for placement in each facility vary. Gender, age, penal status, remaining years to serve, physical and mental health condition, reintegration prognosis, and so on, are all taken into consideration when determining which type of prison facility to assign an offender to serve out his or her prison sentence.

On May 1, 2012, there were 191 prisons in France, including 115 remand prisons housing 77,752 persons. There were 16,773 remand inmates (22% of the total), 50,300 sentenced inmates, and 9,467 persons sentenced to electronic monitoring. The total number of inmates detained in prison facilities was 67,073. During the last 30 years, the average length of detention increased from 4.7 months in 1977 to 8.3 months in 2005 and 9.8 months by 2010. In 1984, about 55% were serving a sentence of more than 3 months and by 2005 this figure had increased by more than 70%.

As a result, prisons are vastly overcrowded with the number of prisoners exceeding the number of places by 12,600. Overcrowding exists despite placing thousands of offenders on electronic monitoring in the community.

Additional data gathered in 2012 reveal several trends. Women and juveniles comprised 3.4% and 1.1% of the prison population, respectively. Interestingly, foreigners were overrepresented at 17.6% of the total prison population. In 2012, the average age of prisoners approached 35. Because of the size and scope of the prison population, there were 35,420 employees in prison administration. Of these, 26,100 were prison wardens and 4,100 were probation officers. The annual operating budget was 2.4 billion euros in 2012. Consequently, the challenges associated with the prison population in France mirror the challenges and issues that exist for other Western nations.

Introduction

In the following sections, I present the responses from my interview with Philippe Pottier, Director of the National School of Prisons Administration (ENAP) in France. Director Pottier generously agreed to share his perspective and insights into corrections. During the interview, I asked several questions about his career, the changes he has experienced, his personal correctional philosophy, the problems he has experienced, and his overall perspective concerning the system of corrections in France. Director Pottier openly responded to the questions asked.

Career

Q: Tell me a little bit about your career: length, organizations worked in, movements, specializations, trajectories in your career that might differ from those expected, etc.

A: I started my career in prison administration in 1975 as an educator, which fits the description for a probation officer (PO) today. Between 1975 and 1986, I worked as a PO, mostly in Fleury-Merogis with juvenile inmates. After that, I became head officer at the National Centre of Orientation (CNO) in Fresnes. I was placed in charge of the multidisciplinary team addressing the concerns of inmates who went through the CNO. In 1989, I began work at the Bureau of Reintegration as the director of Prison Administration (DAP) where I supervised the activities of educational staff. I then moved to the Inspection Prison Service from 1990 until 1994. After this period, I went to French Polynesia where I launched the first probation service. We were a kind of pilot project and experimented with probation concepts. We developed over time a manual for probation operations. I came back to France from Polynesia in 2000 and worked for 2 years at the ENAP (National School for Prison Administration) as a lecturer and researcher in the research department (the Interdisciplinary Research Center Applied to Prison—CIRAP). From 2002 to 2005, I was the head officer of the SPIP (probation services unit) of La Charente for 3 years. This is during the period that France started to experiment with PPR—what we call the Programs of Reoffending Prevention and their discussion groups. After La Charente, I became the head officer at the SPIP of Essonne.* In 2006, I was assigned as a deputy of the head officer at PMJ (the offender supervision unit). In 2010, I became head officer of the SPIP in Nouméa.

Q: What motivated you to enter the field of corrections?

A: Actually, it was a mixture of hazard and circumstances. I never dreamed that I would work for the prison services. After high school graduation, I studied law. It is a discipline that can lead to that kind of job [prison job]. During my studies, I had no idea what I wanted to do. Between 1972 and 1974 (I passed the exam† in 1974), there was much discussion in the country about prisons. With revolts in prisons, the publication of *Discipline and Punish* by Foucault (1977), there was pandemonium around prisons. Then, President Valérie Giscard d'Estaing created the state secretary for prison conditions position. With all this and having come from an activist milieu, to work as a probation officer with the prison services at that time was intellectually something that I found could be exciting and interesting on an intellectual level.

Q: Did the way your career developed surprise you, or do you consider it logical and coherent?

A: I'm not sure that it is logical but at the same time I can't separate things. I was a member of the SNEPAP (National School Prison Union). I'm still in this union. This union is for prison educators, so it is a union made

* Local probation services.

† To enter the National School of Prison Administration (ENAP).

out of people who tend to reflect on ideas. For example, we thought a lot about the definition of our work. In 1982, at the general assembly meeting of the SNEPAP union, we set the premises of the SPIP (probation services) with a text creating the first local probation services unit that integrated the closed-sector prison with the community sector. So I think that we had an influence on the evolution of probation and it has marked me. I'm one of those persons belonging to a generation who thought about the future of probation and prison services. Thus, this opportunity [working in corrections] has served me well because I was identified as someone who was able to bring things forward.

Q: Were you always able to decide upon your career yourself?

A: In this regard, I was actually fairly fortunate because when I decided to become head officer at the CNO (National Center of Observation) it was my decision. It was a position I was interested in along with my position at the central administration unit in Tahiti.* There were of course opportunities that have impacted my career. It is this initial opportunity [CNO] that lured me into this work. I worked on the probation project and I was interested in it [probation]. So no, there was no position imposed on me that I didn't want to have. Now, I couldn't have foreseen all that [the changes in career], Tahiti was for instance completely unpredictable, still I was lucky to have interesting positions, even if I did not always get what I wanted.

Q: And what are the positions you would have liked to obtain?

A: When I got the position in Angoulème,† I went there because I knew that they were working on the [offender discussion probation] support groups and I wanted to participate with that and to develop it. Though, at that time, I would have rather targeted a bigger SPIP like the one at Lille. Or for instance, although I was glad to go there in 2000, when I left the ENAP in 2002, I did it voluntarily because I did not agree with what was being done and it did not fit me. [As a result] I took a vacant position in Angoulème. It was a free decision, even if I wish I had a more important position at the SPIP. Still, I do not regret it at all because thanks to this position and a very good performing team, I was able to reflect and focus more on my work.

Changes Experienced

French prisons have changed considerably since the 1970s. Prisoners have more freedoms and rights, and since the 1990s they can challenge prison

* French Polynesia.

† As a director of the local probation services of La Charente.

decisions before a court. Under pressure due to the importance of the European Court of Human Rights' decisions (ECHR, based in Strasbourg) and the 2006 actualized Council of Europe, the 2009 prison law was passed to establish standards and avoid as far as possible further condemnations from the ECHR. However, prisons remain a sensitive political issue and each director of the prison administration has to work with "cautious" ministers of justice who might be reluctant to engage in necessary prison reforms.

Q: What do you see as the most important changes that have occurred in the field of corrections over the course of your career?

A: The first most important changes were those regarding daily life (initiated by Robert Badinter in 1982–1983) along with the development of inmates' rights. It was the beginning of deep reflection on what happens in prison and what we do there. After that, to me, the SPIP reform [connecting closed and community sectors] was the next essential development. [SPIP reform] was validated as an orientation in 1993 and achieved in 1999. It was hard and long work for the prison administration but provided probation with a certain relevance that it had not had before. Before 1999, there were probation committees deep inside courts but the prison administration didn't deal with it. In 1982, I was involved with proposed changes and establishing probation services. The SPIP evolved in the 1990s because of the development of alternatives to imprisonment, the development of sentence management like conditional release, and the creation of control by courts* of sentence management. There was step-by-step a change, with all the possible difficulties. In 1982, we were a small number of persons, a minority saying "stop, we can't go on this way" [focusing primarily on prison]. At that time, we were less than a minority, people looked askance at us. [At the same time] one had to take into account what happened abroad, criminological knowledge about evaluation processes [best practices] had started in the 2000s thanks to practitioners.

In 2006, Claude d'Harcourt was head officer of the prison administration and asked me to take the position of deputy at PMJ (the only position I didn't ask for). He invited me for a meeting but I didn't know why he wanted to see me. He told me then that an SPIP officer was needed for this position and we talked for one hour. When I entered the position, it was as a practitioner. I had with me the criminological knowledge and the need to develop programs. Programs didn't exist in France. So it was a lot of work to conceive prison law for the [SPIP] program.

* Judicialization.

So for me, after the reform of the SPIP, the main change was the work I've done on the prison law, not only the detailed content of the law, but also what is comprised in Article 1 where the mission of the prison administration is now defined by words that one can find abroad—such as talking about supporting persons who should live a responsible life and not [just] to talk about preventing reoffending.

Q: What would you say about the last 10 years of the prison and probation changes?

A: It is a clear improvement. We moved from weak discussions to a very organized one on this issue, even if it is not linear. You only need to look at Ms. Taubira [the minister of justice] where she clearly spoke about the need to work on the probation sentence and how France is far behind other countries in terms of research. So I think that there is a very positive evolution. We went from a structural reform of the SPIP to now a discussion of the content. We created the SPIP [but did not discuss] what we do there. What do we do to make it meaningful and the same for prison sentences? Prison law is not perfect regarding these issues. It might be repeating, but what we do during the time we have persons in prison or in the community, what we do with this person to make something positive happen for him/her and for society matters. This kind of reflection didn't really take place 15 years ago. Back at that time, we said that the prison administration has a double function of security and reintegration. We said one mission was "to guard," although to guard is not really a mission, it is only something we do. It is not an aim and reintegration [at that time] was a fuzzy concept where one can put everything and its opposite.

Personal Correctional Philosophy

Q: What do you think should be the role of prison, jail, and community supervision officials in society?

A: For me, it is linked with the prevention of reoffending in the way that we shall work with the persons in our charge who are offenders in order to make them more able to live a responsible life by respecting others and the law. Of course, reoffending depends on various factors, and one of them is the way the sentence will be executed and served. This is important since, if we execute sentences, they should be executed with intelligence. Thus, I don't make any distinction between the meaning of prison and the meaning of probation, there are different modalities to reach the same aim. Once you have said that, the main objective is to organize prison and probation in a clever way to reach this output [prevention of reoffending]. It is not enough to consider only the constraint part of prison and the obligation part of probation. We should not be content to just follow the person, to check if the person complies with his/her obligations, to respond to convictions, and to prevent escape from prison. These are just the minimum [things we must do in prison and for probation]. There is more work to do on the content of the sentence. The prevention of reoffending is not simple but is best understood as social reintegration. For example, if the issue causing reoffending is a need to provide housing to somebody deprived of it, then it is not very smart simply to focus on putting him/her into prison. The core of the problem is to work so that sentenced persons reoffend less often.

Q: Which organizational arrangements work and which do not?

A: Actually, there is a lot of improvement to be made because the ideas that I speak of are seldom implemented. Indeed, the improvements made in France over the past 10–20 years are mainly legal ones. Examples include the amelioration and responses regarding inmates' rights. They [prisoners] can appeal. The disciplinary procedure has been reformed and improvements made in detention conditions. So, we have improved the legal and material frame, but what's missing now is to implement some content, programs, intervention modalities for all staff members—especially PO and wardens. There has been work done since the beginning of the 1980s about how to answer inmates' claims, but the more proactive work regarding "what do we do with them," remains a primary question at the moment. There was a start with the programs on reoffending prevention, but these are still limited to discussion groups for certain types of offender, but it [these discussion groups] are better than nothing. There is a lot of work to do on what PO and wardens do with offenders on a daily basis—How do they answer them? What is the relationship between inmates and wardens, POs and offenders? How do you convey a positive meaning, and not only "hi, how are you," but "hi, how are you not?" There is a lot of work to do which is imaginable today but not 10 years ago. So this is the improvement, there is now more and more thinking [that] "yes, maybe we should work in that direction." Some practices have already been initiated, for example, restorative justice is being discussed in a limited way. So there is a need to read about it [restorative justice] and to adapt it to the French context to make it more meaningful.

Q: As a head officer, what are your challenges to bring things forward?

A: Unlike many agencies, the challenges we have are not financial or material resources because we have had significant changes and improvements in that area during the past few years. For example, the service where I currently work in Nouméa, there are 24 staff members. When I came to Nouméa in the 1990s to help create the SPIP unit, there were four—one head officer and three POs. Of course, when evolution happens we forget about the past and we think that something has always been like that [like the improved situation]. As to material resources, we have five cars but for 10 years there was none. It was not even thinkable to have a car [available for use]. But nowadays there are cars in all SPIP units, so there is not really any problem at this level. The problem is more cultural and philosophical, that means succeeding in convincing everyone that there is work to do—how to give any meaning to sentences and how to do it concretely. And in the French system, there is the difficulty of overcoming the almost permanent mistrust of what is done abroad—especially strong mistrust when it deals with Anglo-Saxon countries because culturally we have another story. But the fact is that it is in Anglo-Saxon countries that criminological literature on prison and probation issues is the most developed. There is no comparable literature in France. [France] should not stupidly copy and paste. But since this intellectual resource exists, take it [adapt it to fit France] and overcome cultural mistrust. We know that, fortunately, it is a bit more complicated than that. I have the feeling that this cultural overtaking is being done through practical experiences with aspects taken from other countries. For instance, as we developed the [SPIP offender] support groups to prevent reoffending. It was very concrete and gave a meaning to PO actions.

A second important aspect as to organization and legal frame is to evaluate prison and probation services. We need to know which programs are implemented and to evaluate them. For example, with probation we need to know more than the number of persons who have fulfilled their obligations, or for inmates the number of those who have received disciplinary measures. If we content ourselves with this, we remain at the previous [less-developed] stage.

Theory and Practice

Q: In your view, what should the relationship between theory and practice be? What can practitioners learn from studying and applying theories? What can those who create theories of punishment gain from practitioners?

A: Currently, from necessity, the ENAP is a central element because French universities have not dealt yet with this issue. We have a handicap in France in that we lack a criminology curriculum in the universities. Criminological research at the university is also very disparate and due more to persons than to a common will. I'm convinced that a curriculum in criminology at the university can lead to professional studies.

The ENAP, within a few months—if you take the traineeships apart—must train people for their future job in the prison administration, for instance as a PO. The training should provide them with the rudiments of criminological reflection, a bit of applied criminal procedure, and some [understanding of the] social sciences. Regarding the current situation, ENAP must compensate for this lack of training by orienting its lectures toward foreign knowledge on how to evaluate offenders to better fit them into programs, on how to evaluate programs to measure their efficiency, and based on this notion, training could be developed according to actual knowledge and literature. Since there is a research department at the ENAP, it could be the link between integrating existing foreign research and current training for prison administrators. But no professional school such as the ENAP would be able to replace 5 years of education at a university.

Q: Where do you find theory-based information? Where do you look: journals, professional magazines, books, publications, reports?

A: There are few and not enough things available because the university does not play this role. There are a few scholars who are linked to correctional practitioners such as Martine Herzog-Evans or Robert Cario. But there remains little in France because 90% of the criminological literature remains Anglo-Saxon or from Nordic countries that have much better developed literature than we do. In addition, we have difficulty reading literature [from other countries] because very few of these texts are translated into French, which means that we have to read them in English.

Transnational Relations

Q: How have you been affected by the following in your organization's work by developments outside the country?

A: We have been most impacted by the Canadian example, England and Spain. I am referring more to the federal correctional example and not about provinces where it can be very different from one province to another. In Canada, the majority of knowledge production is Anglo-Saxon, but Québec is a large province with big universities and the Criminology School of Montréal. There are French speakers who produce related texts and translate others which enable us to have a basis. We have also been impacted by the recommendations of the Council of Europe that are based on knowledge since those [recommendations] related to prison and probation mention the need to make good evaluations, to have reintegration programs, and to implement something [programs that are] rational. And there is also the work, maybe less visible, done by the European Organisation for Probation (CEP), which France participates in. The CEP is rightly influenced by criminological ideas. As a result, French practitioners have participated in conferences, trainings, and traineeships organized by the CEP.

General Assessment

Q: What do you think of the relationship between sentencing laws, public opinion, mass media, and politicians as they relate to the functioning of prisons, jails, and community supervision?

A: The first problem is the media, since what we've talked about previously—programs, evaluation, etc.—are apparently too subtle for some media because the media has focused over the last few years on detention conditions. These [concerns] are of course important because if we put people in a negative living environment, there is no point in developing programs because we won't be able to implement them properly.

Q: And if you had to choose two examples—one in prison and one in probation—that could be advertised?

A: I think we should present actions that are linked with offenders' behavior. For instance, what I have implemented here in New Caledonia, a kind of program to prevent reoffending. Since there are a lot of horses here and a culture similar to Westerns and Australia, we have created the roughrider program. We have selected inmates who exhibit very difficult behaviors, those who are always borderline toward violence and end up in prison, to participate. The roughrider brings us wild horses and he works for 2 months with inmates on taming the horses—the aim is to tame horses and for the inmates to learn to control themselves. The main advantage with taming horses is that any mistake in relation with the horse creates a reaction, and thus the inmates learn a lot about control, and it works. It has been instantaneously successful because it is linked with people's lives and the horse. We could reproduce it with other things somewhere else. Moreover, people understand that we are doing something more than seeking jobs for them and that [the program] can really influence offenders' behavior. To advertise that we look for jobs for offenders, everybody [in the public] will think "of course." But I'm not sure that people feel safer. "Ok, he's got a job, but does it mean that he won't reoffend?" So we have to find actions like this [roughrider] that are supporting and that show people that it is possible to do something meaningful during the sentence.

To conclude, what is really interesting nowadays in French prison administration, beyond the SPIP reform in 1999 and the prison law in 2009, is that we face an open field with many perspectives. We are now in a situation where we can make progress on these [probation and prison] issues.

Conclusion

This interview was a great opportunity for both the interviewer and the interviewee to share important thoughts and discuss major issues in the French prison system. Philippe Pottier has been a key leader of the penitentiary reform movement over the last decade and the time has come, beyond his professional achievements, to provide him with an academic platform to present his progressive and qualified views on imprisonment and resettlement. Since he is an expert in offender supervision, the main themes of the interview focused on prisoners and probationers' programs and support. As a matter of fact, his views are strongly in accordance with the known literature. He has been advocating European and international collaborations and exchanges on both practitioner and researcher levels. Indeed, his recent nomination as the head of the National School of Prison Administration makes sense because it is a central institution where prison and probation officers are trained and where penitentiary practice and science are taught together.

Glossary

Badinter: Robert Badinter, former minister of justice (1981–1986). He has contributed to major improvements in prison conditions such as direct contact during family visits and television monitors in cells.

Baumettes: Called "Les Baumettes," it is a prison in Marseille that was the subject of a scandal in December 2012 because of its very poor detention conditions and its overcrowding.

Cario: Robert Cario, professor of criminology at the University of Pau. He (with Martine Herzog-Evans) is one of the few French academics promoting criminology as an independent scientific discipline.

CIRAP: Interdisciplinary Research Center in the prison field (*Centre interdisciplinaire de recherche appliquée au champ pénitentiaire*), as a unit of the ENAP.

CNO: National Center of Observation (*Centre national d'observation*). All long-term prisoners have experienced the former National Center of Orientation, since 2010 called the National Center of Evaluation (CNE). It was established in 1951 and it is located in the remand prison of Fresnes near Paris with two sections; the first section has about 100 cells dedicated to the purpose of evaluation.

criminology in France: There is an ongoing major debate in France about considering criminology as an autonomic scientific discipline or not. French academics are strongly divided and there is a status quo at institutional levels on that issue (including curriculum at university and PhD level).

DAP: Central Prison Administration (*Direction de l'administration pénitentiaire*) based in Paris. It includes all prison facilities and probation services.

ENAP: National School of Prison Administration (*Ecole nationale de l'administration pénitentiaire*). All prison and probation officers receive their initial training in this school (over 2000 per year) and benefit from continuous training along their career (over 3000 traineeships every year). There is also a research unit (CIRAP) attached to the school.

Fleury-Merogis: The biggest prison facility in France, located in the Paris suburbs, with 2800 places. It is a remand prison for adults (male and female) and a detention center for juvenile prisoners.

Foucault: Michel Foucault (1926–1984), French philosopher, published *Discipline and Punish: The Birth of the Prison* in 1975 and founded the prison information group (GIP) in 1971.

French Polynesia: Overseas region with around 300,000 inhabitants.

GIP: The Prison Information Group (*Groupe d´information sur les prisons*, 1971–1972) was founded by Michel Foucault among others and was promoted by newspapers and radio access in prisons. It remains a symbolic and strong example of prison activism.

Harcourt: Between 2006 and 2010, Claude d'Harcourt was the director of the Central Prison Administration.

Herzog-Evans: Martine Herzog-Evans, law and criminology professor at the University of Rheims. She (with Robert Cario) is one of the few French academics promoting criminology as an independent scientific discipline.

PMJ: Offender supervision unit (*Personnes placées sous main de justice*) at the central direction.

PPR: Programs of Reoffending Prevention and their discussion groups (*Programme de prevention de la récidive*).

Prison law: The French prison law was passed in November 2009 and compiles for the first time in France all rules, regulations, and legislation concerning prison.

probation sentence: Beyond the *sursis simple* and the SME, the idea is to introduce in France a probation sentence in the community with obligations, but without a recall meaning imprisonment.

sentence management: (*Aménagement de la peine*) It deals with all types of measures affecting the length and the execution conditions of a prison sentence, such as conditional release, electronic monitoring, or semiliberty.

SME: Community sentence with obligations (*Sursis avec mise àl´épreuve*). Its recall means imprisonment.

SNEPAP: Labor union of prison staff (*Syndicat national de l'ensemble des personnels de l'administration pénitentiaire*).

SPIP: Probation services (*Service pénitentiaire d´*insertion et de probation), affiliated to the Central Prison Administration.

sursis simple: Community sentence without obligations. Its recall means imprisonment.

Taubira: Christiane Taubira, French minister of justice (May 2012–present).

Michael Donnellan, Director General, Irish Prison Service, Republic of Ireland

2

DEIRDRE HEALY

Contents

Overview

The Irish Prison Service is an executive agency within the Department of Justice and Equality. Its mission is to provide "safe and secure custody, dignity of care and rehabilitation to prisoners for safer communities" (Irish Prison Service, 2012a). Its management structure consists of a director general, who reports to the minister for justice and equality, and eight directors who have responsibility for specific areas of prison policy and practice, including operations, health care, and human resources. The Irish Prison Service deals with male prisoners over the age of 16 and female prisoners over the age of 18. In Ireland, prisoners are held in 1 of 14 custodial institutions, 11 of which are classed as "closed" prisons. There are also two "open" prisons and one "semiopen" prison in this jurisdiction. In 2011, there were 17,318 committals to prison and a daily average number of 4,390 prisoners. The vast majority of prisoners that year were Irish, male, and serving sentences of 1 year or less.*

Introduction

Michael Donnellan was appointed director general of the Irish Prison Service (Republic of Ireland) by the minister for justice and equality on December 5, 2011. He has a great deal of experience as a leader of corrections in the country. The interview with Michael Donnellan, director general, was conducted at a Dublin office of the Irish Prison Service. The interview conducted reflects an open and honest exchange between two professionals. Director Donnellan was very willing to share his experience and views on corrections. What follows is a verbatim account (with minor editing) of Director Donnellan's views on the criminal justice system with a particular focus on penal policy and practice.

Career

I started as a psychiatric nurse when I was 18 and qualified when I was 21. After about 6 months of being a staff nurse, I [went] on secondment to do a postgraduate course in Child and Adolescent Psychiatric Nursing. After that, I became charge nurse at the adolescent unit in the Maudsley Hospital, London. Then, in 1983, I went back to university to qualify as a social worker. I worked in a really deprived inner-city area of South London as a social worker. It was a great job, working mostly [in] child protection, families, and mental health. Because I had the mental health [background] I became an approved social worker [and was] called upon regularly to access people for admission to psychiatric hospitals. That job was really interesting [but] very pressurized. I got promoted after a few years to a senior social worker and I moved to a more leafy area of London.

* This summary is based on information published in Irish Prison Service (2012a).

[Next] I [worked] in a South London borough for the Department of Education [as a principal psychiatric social worker] in charge of [the] child guidance unit and we also serviced a number of special schools [for] children with special needs. While I was there, I trained in systemic management [at Kensington Consultation Centre]. I left London in 1994 to come back to Ireland [where I became] director of a detention school. I was asked by the Department of Education about 3 or 4 years later [to] manage the secure unit in Trinity House. Then I felt that I'd done enough in institutions because institutions are very limiting. You think you're so important when you're in there but the reality is you're a small cog in a much wider system because the wider system—the community system—is so large. The director of probation service job came up and I got it. I really loved working there—new organization, new problems, but the same issues. Every organization I've worked in has the same problems, just [on] a different scale. [However] the challenge was gone from me because, after about 5 or 6 years in a job, the system should be working well and my deputies were now as competent as I was. I always think that a good manager is somebody who wants to make the next person down better than them. That's success.

It was time to move on and I applied for the prison service job the year before last. What drives me to any role is that I genuinely feel that I can make a difference. I've been in this job just over a year and it's all that everybody said it was going to be—difficult, stressful, pressurized, but brilliant. It was a natural progression. I had been dealing [with] very specific parts of the human condition—mostly adult/child mental health, child protection, and all that goes with poverty—and people were always on the edge of criminality. I felt that it was an area that [would be] so interesting to work in. Everything I've learned in social work, family therapy, group work, psychotherapy, nursing, psychiatry—everything comes into my job. Good managers need to have a combination of [practical and managerial experience]. You need to intimately understand what it is to work on the ground and then translate that [into strategies for managing and motivating] staff. So that's my career so far. That's the 37 years.

Changes Experienced

I joined the criminal justice system in 1994 and the biggest [change] has been the Children Act of 2001.* It has made a phenomenal difference to the structure in that at last we [have] a piece of legislation to manage people

* The Children Act, 2001, overhauled the Irish youth justice system. It introduced new community sanctions and stated that detention should be used only as a last resort (see http://www.irishstatutebook.ie/2001/en/act/pub/0024/index.html).

at the earliest phase of the spectrum. It replaced the industrial/reformatory thinking and gave a menu of about 13 options for community interventions. It led the change in other areas. In the adult area, I can refer to the logic of that approach—detention as a last resort, community intervention, a stepped approach. It was very innovative. Now it was very long in gestation but it was well worth it. Children previously had been coming into the system [as young as] 9 and now they were coming into the system at 13–15 and the numbers in the detention side have gone down dramatically. Despite ourselves, something quite radical has happened.

Punitiveness

You're competing against this punitive element all the time. Whether we like it or not, a lot of people in middle Ireland have a punitive attitude. They don't read the *Times** where you get a balanced view. They read the redtop papers† and believe that crime is out of control and we're in crisis. The reality is that we are nowhere near it. International evidence from America and England shows that building more [prison] places and locking up more people doesn't really make communities safer. What makes communities safer is engaging with the hearts and minds of people who offend at the earliest possible stage and intervening with them. That is an ongoing challenge. No one ever says how brilliant prison officers are because we are the people who occupy the space with a group of people that, by and large, you wouldn't like to be your neighbor or you wouldn't like to be sitting next to on the bus. What we can try to do is explain to people who we have in Ireland's prisons. I always say to people that they're all brothers, fathers, sons, uncles and grandfathers and sisters and aunts. These are just ordinary people whose life chances have got seriously messed up and now they're in prison.

Public Attitudes

What do we as a society want to do with them? In the 1800s, we transported them to Van Dieman's Land‡; then through the early 1900s, we put them in mental hospitals and gave them drugs. Now in 2013, they are in prison. The radical reform of the Children Act has made a statement for Ireland that we don't need to do that and then you can transpose that into the adult prison system. The Children Act specified custody as the sanction of last resort for children. We need the same principle to apply to adults, in a real way.

* *The Irish Times*, national broadsheet newspaper.

† Tabloid newspapers.

‡ Van Dieman's Land was the name given to Tasmania by nineteenth-century explorers. A penal colony was established on the island to which many Irish convicts were transported.

People see me as a social worker and a nurse and a manager, maybe on the soft side of life, but they don't understand me at all because I've always believed you have to have rules [and] structure because rehabilitation cannot work without that. I've always seen the balance between structure, strength, order, clear messages, and then rehabilitation [and] support. At the end of the day, crime does hurt people and that's why I would never want to be seen on the soft side of the page because you would be completely ignoring the damage of the acts that people commit. But I always feel that, rather than joining [victim] advocacy groups, I can help better from where I am by trying to improve recidivism rates. I never feel a conflict.

I've worked with a whole range of ministers since 1994 and there's no doubt that they bring their influence to the criminal justice system. I firmly believe that we in Ireland are moving into a good space where it is possible to have a debate [about] imprisonment. People say it's because we have no money so therefore we have to change.* That's partly true but also it's about doing things for the right reasons. That's why you need to have strength and structure because you have to give confidence to the public that you're not weak and you're not going to be just blown over. Now some people have to go to institutions. There's no other option. The reality is [that] large proportions of people who come into prison could be dealt with through community intervention if we had those resources. As well as being cheaper and more efficient, community programs like probation and community service are more effective at reducing reoffending and enabling desistance from crime. It's about rebalancing that whole criminal justice response and reinvesting resources from custody to community programs. In the political space that we're in at the moment, it is possible for people like me to have a voice and to actually push some of the boundaries that wouldn't have been—maybe couldn't have been—pushed 4–8 years ago.

I don't mind people who are negative as long as they have some constructive ideas about how we might put it right. In my whole life, I'm always a "glass half full" [person]. I have never seen the dark side or the downside. I want to see the opportunities. I want to see the good even in the bad. Even for somebody who has completely let you down, you can still treat [that person] with respect and give them some quality of life. Criticism for criticism's sake is just a waste of air.

Transparency

The criminal justice system has become more open [and] more transparent. The criminal justice system, particularly the prison and the detention side,

* Reference to the economic collapse in 2008, which caused the Irish government to apply to the European Union, the European Central Bank, and the International Monetary Fund ("the troika") for financial assistance.

was behind closed walls and I see an opening out of that [with] the Inspector of Prisons* [reports]. The opening up of the system is also opening up all the faults of the system. The reality is [that] if you want a true system, you have to open it and that means you have to look at the good parts but also the bad parts of it.

Politics

We have now for the first time outside bodies inspecting us [and] setting standards. We have international legislation, guidance, standards, prison rules. The closed, forgotten nature of prison is transforming. [My job is] easier because [of these developments]. For instance, 20% of our prison [population] at the moment [is] slopping-out, meaning that people don't have toilets in their cells. We've been pilloried for years about this but we can do something about [it] and the political pressure helps my hand to sort this out. [The prison is] a closed culture [and] things get dealt with internally. People are afraid to be open [because] there are dangers that come with it. My job is about changing that. I spend a lot of time walking around the prison floors, talking to prisoners, talking to staff, [and] in organizational terms, sharing information, creating a vision of what we want to do. That's all about challenging [a] culture that can sometimes be leaderless. Huge strides have been made over the years to address that. Things change slowly in prisons. If you look at Finland, they did it 10 or 15 years ago. They reduced the prison population and rebalanced in favor of community sanctions such as probation. They [had] political buy-in, a stable policy environment, [no] auction politics, a media that was sympathetic, [and] legislation. We can do this in Ireland because we're a small country and there's a lot on the right side of the page.

Personal Correctional Philosophy

In my lifetime, I have seen really bad people but very few. They were highly disturbed people who just couldn't be saved because they were so damaged. In everybody else, I've always seen the potential for redemption. You have to try and understand what was going on in that person's mind that made them do what they did. I read a lovely phrase the other week: "people fall out of society and they fall into prison" (Flynn, 2012). Those people are fractured from our society and it seems to be the way of the world that we

* The Office of the Inspector of Prisons is an independent office established by the Prison Act 2007. The inspector inspects prisons and submits regular reports on his activities to the minister for justice and equality (see http://www.inspectorofprisons.gov.ie/).

always have to have people at the bottom; that we can't seem to share our resources with them.

The causes of crime start early, from family, housing, and education. Most offenders will give up offending when they're 22 or 23. They pass on to another phase of the life cycle but it takes others until their forties to get out of it.* Most people do give it up but it's a question of how you intervene in those people's lives. It's a very complex area because it's a problem the world over. It's not unique to Ireland. Our statistics show that about 50% of prisoners will have reoffended within 1 year. Probation has studied a similar cohort of offenders who were on probation or community service orders in 2007 and they found that about 33% offended (Probation Service, 2012). The statistics on the probation side are quite good and the statistics on the prison side are quite bad—but quite similar to other countries.

You're going to be working with the whole desistance agenda and time often has to be part of that journey. At the end of the day, only offenders will stop offending. It's such a powerful message: that people can give up, they can desist. But for some, it's a long journey. What we've completely missed in Ireland is the benefit of having offenders help offenders. That's where we can empower people because we need role models who have made the change. Anybody who thinks we can change people: that's not how it works. The penny drops for some people but the counterbalance is that others say "this is what I've been waiting for all my life" and then they continue the same kinds of crime in prison. It's a way of life. Ex-offenders who have made changes for the better are a hugely positive, but so far largely untapped, resource.†

Rehabilitation and the Role of the Prison

We're asked in prison to do this magic. We get a 38-year-old into prison and they have gone through all these problems of being unloved, uncared for, unmanaged, unstructured, uneducated. It's going to take years to transform. What we can do is begin to create some structure, have some relationship with that person, and start building something back for that

* This view is well supported by criminological research. For example, the findings of the Cambridge Study in Delinquent Development revealed that childhood factors, including criminality in the family, poverty, and low educational attainment, increase the risk of criminal involvement during adolescence and adulthood (see Farrington et al., 2006). Furthermore, studies of desistance from crime confirm that the majority of offenders age out of crime during early adulthood (see Laub and Sampson, 2003).

† There is a growing criminological literature that suggests that offenders and ex-offenders may benefit from such activities. In fact, Maruna (2001) identified engagement in generative activities, such as caring for others, as a crucial step in the journey toward desistance. This idea is also gaining recognition among criminal justice practitioners (see Ronel and Segeve, forthcoming).

person. It should be easier in Ireland because we're smaller. We haven't joined that massive bandwagon of punitiveness. We've learned so much from our history. We've learned of the damage that institutions do. That's why I think the inquiries* into different institutions [have] been so helpful. We are beginning to learn that institutions/incarceration doesn't equal better. Institutionalization, in itself, while necessary for some, is a negative force.

The prison system has to be built on relationships, mutual respect, and the dignity of the person. So when somebody has committed a crime, we can't rerun that in prison. We can only take them from the time they come into prison, and staff are phenomenal in the way they take people where they are and try to move them on. The job is more difficult now because of the complexity of our client base, which I genuinely feel has changed over the last 20 years. We're seeing more damaged people. My son sent me an article from an American newspaper last year and there was a very good phrase, which stuck in my mind, which [said]: "criminals are not primarily wrong-doers to be punished, but broken people to be fixed" (Fisher, 2012) and I completely believe it's our job to fix them. The Americans and the Russians have the highest number of people locked up per any country (Walmsley, 2011). And you think how, as a modern society, could that be? It's clearly driven by philosophy, by an ideology, by public opinion, by a theory that the more you lock up, the safer society is going to be. But that has no basis in fact. Harsh punishments turn out harsher people, brutalized people, who are more at risk of further brutalizing others. People are now beginning to rethink. People who come into prison are broken people and the task is: do you break them further by humiliating them or do you say "our job now is to help fix you back up"? And I completely believe that [it's] our job to fix people back up.

In the olden days, people thought that rehabilitation [was] about having professional people parachuting in, giving some service to the people and then parachuting out. I've always believed that rehabilitation starts on the ground in the interaction between the staff member and the prisoner. For me, it's about building that respectful relationship. Maybe for some, it's the first time they feel a little bit of respect. And on top of that, you can build rehabilitation: education, work and training, psychology, social work, medical interventions. But in my view, they are all worth nothing without the everyday interventions. I know it's not politically correct to say this but 20 prison officers would be worth 40 psychologists to me if those

* Following revelations in the 1990s that there had been widespread emotional, physical, and sexual abuse of minors in the care of state and religious institutions in Ireland, the Irish government established several inquiries to investigate and report on these matters.

20 prison officers were doing their job in the way that it should be done. You don't have to go to a room for an hour and lie on a couch and try and create this false environment where you can talk. If that moment can be captured—what is called the teaching moment—and you can say to people, "you did that really well. Well done." For me, that is the building block of rehabilitation.*

We have a captive audience when it comes to drug and alcohol misuse. Eighty percent of our prisoners have drug or alcohol problems and we are doing some really good things in helping people to desist from taking drugs—methadone maintenance and detoxing from methadone. We should be prepared to look at what works and what doesn't work. [Programs have] to be dynamic, innovative, evolving. People say [we will] give people [in prison] a job and [pay them] for that job—now the job might be sweeping the landing with a brush—but we won't pay somebody to go to school. I would much prefer to pay somebody to go to school because there is the possibility that something might happen out of that whereas pushing that brush around the landing—nothing is going to come out of that. Our kitchens in prisons [are] fantastic places. All the prisoners working there are getting accredited training whereas 10 years ago they were simply kitchen porters. They were just peeling the potatoes but now they are getting accredited training [and] skills that they can use on the outside.

Most prisoners, given the opportunity and the right conditions, are interested [in doing rehabilitation programs but] at the end of the day, you have to motivate people into programs. For instance, we have to get over ourselves and simply say that it is in our interest to motivate high-risk sex offenders into programs so that they can see at the end of their sentence that they are going to get some benefit by having joined in with therapeutic interventions. Why would you ever want to do something [when] there was nothing in it for you? Now unless you are really insightful and you say "this will help me in the long-term." But most of our prison population live for the moment. They don't think 10 years forward so therefore you have to motivate [them].

Structured Release

If you had structured early release under the supervision of the probation service, you would get better management of the transition from prison into

* Research confirms that high-quality working relationships between offenders and criminal justice practitioners may enhance compliance among offenders and ultimately reduce reoffending. On prisons, see Leibling (2005). On probation, see Robinson et al. (2014).

community.[*] Whereas bringing it to the last day and opening the door, it doesn't work. For me, every release from prison should be structured, that is, structured release that gives people the best opportunity to get back into society—even short-sentence people. They have no structure so if we simply give them their black bag and tell them to leave without giving them the supports, without helping them with housing, social welfare, and getting back onto the medical card, it doesn't work. At the moment, the probation service have limited funding so they're only taking the ones who are on court orders, postrelease supervision, or who are high-risk offenders.[†] They give a good service in my view, but we could get so much more from probation. We have developed a "Community Return" scheme where people swap prison time for community time where they're under probation supervision.[‡] That's working really well and the prisoners like it. What we have found is the ones who got on community return from the prison, they are very well behaved because they understand the structure and they see the benefit. But there are still too many people leaving prison without proper structure.

We have an incentivized regime in prison.[§] Everybody comes in at standard level and then you can either go up to an enhanced level or you can drop down to a basic level. This Christmas, we sent out 30% more prisoners on Christmas leave than we did the previous year and we selected those prisoners from the enhanced level. We had 100% return this year. They all knew that it was to their benefit to come back. To get onto the enhanced level, you have to be in education or work and training, your behavior and your whole interaction has to be good [and] respectful. You can't be hitting anybody. You can't be losing the head. Then, for that, you're going to live in a nicer cell with a lot more freedom. You're going to have more visits. You're going to have more telephone calls and you also get more pocket money. So life becomes a better place and

[*] Prisoners may be granted early temporary release from custody under the Criminal Justice Act, 1960, as amended by the Criminal Justice (Temporary Release of Prisoners) Act 2003. This practice differs from parole, which is available only to prisoners serving sentences of 8 years or more. Prisoners serving between 8 and 14 years can apply to the parole board after half their sentence is served, while prisoners serving 14 years to life can apply after 7 years (see http://www.justice.ie/en/JELR/Pages/Parole_Board). Prisoners on parole are subject to supervision by the probation service since there are no parole officers in Ireland. For further information on the parole system, see Griffin and O'Donnell (2012).

[†] The probation service supervises prisoners who are serving suspended prison sentences in the community (Criminal Justice Act 2006, s99), who are on temporary release from custody (Criminal Justice (Temporary Release of Prisoners) Act 2003) and who are on postrelease supervision (Sex Offenders Act, 2001) as well as prisoners on the nonstatutory Community Return scheme.

[‡] Under the Community Return program, prisoners who are serving sentences of between 1 and 8 years and have been assessed as suitable for community work may be offered early temporary release from prison in return for engaging in community service under the supervision of the probation service.

[§] See Incentivized Regimes Policy on www.irishprisons.ie.

you're trying to get people to strive to be in that place. One of the benefits of the enhanced level is that they can be considered for the Community Return program at 50% of their sentence.* In the past, everybody was in the same pot so often people thought "well, what's the point if there's no benefit from trying to do anything." Again, it's trying to incentivize people to come along the journey with you. It's trying to get people, that is, prisoners, to buy into the system rather than just going up against it. The difference has been that people are out of their cells more. Because when there wasn't the enhanced level, what was the point of going to school? What was the point of going to work? What did you get for it? You got the very same as the next guy who didn't. We've had people who are now Red Cross workers or Listeners† within the prison. If you looked at their history 10 years ago, they were the most difficult people ever.

The Prison Environment

Prison is a difficult place because the vast majority of admissions are poor people who come from poor inner-city infrastructures. A lot of them have serious addiction problems. Their life is so difficult and so torturous that they get pain relief from alcohol and drugs and they just lose themselves in that. Also, in Ireland over the last 10–12 years, organized crime has become a lot more sophisticated.‡ On top of that, we have more people coming into prison who have serious mental health problems. Prison is not always a reflection of society because it takes the most deprived elements of society and puts them all together and so you get violence, drugs, and suicides and some people seem to be surprised at that.

I can take the temperature of a prison by simply walking into it and watching how people are with each other. You get a good or a bad feeling when you go into different kinds of prisons because you know that there is a much more open and respectful atmosphere. Prisoners are calling the prison officers by their first name. Prison officers are calling prisoners by their first name. Those prisons, by and large, are safe places to be. Then you go into other places where you can sense the hostility and the standoffishness. You sense that this is not a safe place. The best way to make prisons safe is by

* See press release of June 26, 2012, "Establishment of the New Community Return Unit" on www.irishprisons.ie.

† Reference to the Samaritans Listener Program where prisoners are trained to "listen" to prisoners who are experiencing emotional distress and the Irish Red Cross first-aid prison program.

‡ Organized crime has had a significant impact on the prison population. In his Annual Report 2012, the Inspector of Prisons noted that around a quarter of prisoners were on protection; in many cases as a result of being threatened by gang members. Prisoners on protection spend 23 hours a day in their cells and have only limited access to therapeutic and rehabilitative services (see http://www.inspectorofprisons.gov.ie/en/IOP for further information).

being open, transparent, respectful, and having a clear structure. You also need to give prisoners a voice. Prison officers would say "we don't have much of a voice either!" and they're absolutely right. The voice has been traditionally the managerial, hierarchical voice. Unless you can break that down and give all components in prison—prisoners, prison officers, and managers—a voice, the whole system goes wrong.

If you don't give prisoners a voice, they'll go on the roof, they'll hit you because that's how they get their voice. Giving prisoners a voice cures multitudes—damage is reduced, riots are reduced, hostage taking is reduced, deaths are reduced.* If you give them a voice, an input into their day, they can start policing themselves. They can make the rules for themselves. You would not believe when you give a set of 20 prisoners a job and ask them to come up with a set of rules; sometimes they can be tougher than you would be! That's what keeps prisons safe. But yet, it's been difficult for us to get to it. We put too many resources into security and we haven't put enough into the program end. Last year, just over 17,000 people were committed to prison but 80% of those people came into prison for 1 year or less (Irish Prison Service, 2012a). Do you really need those people on the same level of security as the murderer, the rapist, or the violent offender? The answer is "of course you don't" but we do it and it costs a lot of money.

Problems and Successes Experienced

Because of the economic downturn, we are being forced into more collaborative, joined-up thinking. I've been working for 37 years and I've heard this for 37 years—partnership working, multidisciplinary working, multiagency working—and they will be still talking about it in 37 years time. In order to do it, you need two things: you have to give up power and you usually have to give up money and, unless you are prepared to give up both of those, then people will continue to work within their "silo-ed" areas. But certainly, over the last 12–18 months, huge developments have taken place with the probation service, An Garda Síochána,† and the courts. It's one of the benefits of the downturn. The money is not available any more to keep growing and growing so now, you are going to have to get a better result with less. There [has been] a genuine attempt to join up goals and take the more holistic approach to problem solving. It is hard work because we [haven't] got to the stage yet where it is demanded within the law. Prison doesn't work without the help of all the other agencies before and after it. The challenges to better cooperation are the

* A riot occurred in Mountjoy Prison on October 14, 2010, which was attributed to the problem of overcrowding.

† An Garda Síochána is the Irish police force (see www.garda.ie).

competitiveness that often happens between agencies and especially now with dwindling resources. A lot of people are trying to hold on to what they have. If you really want to work with people, then you have to transfer resources.

I believe we need a strong prison service with reducing numbers and a strong probation service with more staff and more resources to take the balance. We can work side by side but [the probation service] must not be contaminated by the institutional view because the institutional view is always strongest and over time, [the probation service] can get dwarfed by [it]. The real strength and synergy that prisons and probation bring to working together is a result of the very differences between them. Each has something unique to offer, which adds its own value. Now prison will always be required. In any society, you are going to have what I would call the sanction of last resort. I could never imagine a society without prison. There will always be a role for prison but if we are clever, we will try to make that role as minimal as possible and give as much as possible to the community.

You [also] have to have good laws. If you take mandatory sentencing which was flavor of the month 10 years ago, we are now living with the consequences of it. It's not a good outcome for people. It gives them no options. And then follow that by an understanding of what works. The more recidivism studies [we have], the more we are aware of what works for which groups of people. We can now [compare] the outcomes of prison [to] the outcomes of probation, which has about 33% better outcomes. Rehabilitation can and does take place in prison, but prison is a very difficult environment in which to encourage and enable desistance from crime. It is in the community where desistance really takes hold. And it's not just that. Probation is cheaper compared to prison.

General Problems and Successes

On a simple level, the introduction of televisions into prison cells, giving people electric kettles to make a cup of tea—these small things have revolutionized the prison in that the benefit of a television in your cell takes away the loneliness and boredom. Suicide [and self-harm] levels have gone down dramatically because people now have the company and the comfort. They are not big policies. They are shifts in thinking [which] have made a dramatic impact on prisoners' lives. They have their own toilet, washing basin, shower, television, kettle. When the kettle debate started a few years ago—"they'll just scald themselves. They'll throw boiling water into the prison officers' faces." Nothing like that happened and now people can go in, make a cup of tea, settle down, and watch *Coronation Street*,* just like you would at home. It's humanizing, it's normalizing.

* Popular TV program.

[One] thing that has really been regressive is the transference of the gang culture from the community into the prisons and the necessity that now people who come into prison want to go on protection to get away from the gang culture. It has really affected the normalization of prisons. In Mountjoy Prison* at the moment, there are about 14 different factions [and] that has been really regressive because it blights prisons with violence and tension. We have been too accommodating of people who want to have a parallel experience in prison. We have to work much more intensively with people [and] create safer environments for people in prison. In order to keep people safe, we have not taken the risks to start changing the culture. When you talk to people on the incentivized regime and you [ask] them: "what's the best thing about being on this program?" they say "I feel safe. I can walk around the landing. Nobody's going to jump me. Nobody's going to slash my face with a blade. Nobody's going to beat me up in the toilet." The easiest one will be to get prisoner buy-in. Prisoners, I find, are very trusting. They will take a chance. They will take a risk. To get staff buy-in is often more challenging and more difficult—there is a lot more involved.

The biggest problem in prisons today is overcrowding [which] is the biggest [barrier to] rehabilitation. It's the one thing that stops people having the space to develop and move on. If we can reduce overcrowding, we can get prisons working better. Prisoners need to have proper[ly] planned release [and] structured programs but you can't do that if you are working this in-out, in-out system. Our numbers are about 100 [prisoners] per 100,000 [population] whereas England is 153 per 100,000, but in Norway or Finland that could be 65 per 100,000 (Walmsley, 2011). You have to strive downwards and that is why I am so pleased that last year was the first time in 6 years that we have seen a trend down. [In] the previous 5 years, there had been a 42% increase. Now they have dropped very slightly—only by a couple of hundred committals—but it's a green shoot for me, that we can actually reverse this trend (The Irish Prison Service, 2013).

Some countries have waiting lists for prison; others have people serve their sentence at home under curfew as an alternative. Our prison system is plagued with short-term prisoners coming in who get minimal benefit. It's about trying to change that mindset and trying to divert those people a different way. But overcrowding, I think, is the single most difficult challenge because it interferes with everything—rehabilitation, the running of the place. It's crowd control. That's the most difficult challenge and, if you could get that in check, you really could driv[e] on with the resourcing of rehabilitation. Our minister has started talking about

* Mountjoy Prison is the main committal prison in Dublin city and is a closed, medium-security facility.

overcrowding. I've never heard another minister talk about overcrowding. We're on a plane now where we can talk about it and if you can talk about it, you can work on it. There has been a lot of work going on with probation, the courts, the judges, [and] the gardaí to stop this trend upwards. The strategy that we developed last year is built on the whole idea of rebalancing the system because we can't continue where we are (Irish Prison Service, 2012b).

Theory and Practice

The reality is that there isn't the kind of [relationship] that you would want between research and practice. A lot of things have been done in a reactive way but we have made huge improvements in relation to informing ourselves because of better data and research. There isn't a natural fit. Prisons are very good at the practice but when you ask them "where's the theory? where's the evidence?" it's lacking. There is no doubt that we need to do things because we know they work and have good outcomes. Over the years, I have seen prisons used as hotbeds for researchers to come in from the outside to do research and yet, I wonder whether they are answering any of the questions the prison wants answered. Or why the prison isn't designing and developing its own research. We are looking at women offenders at the moment and trying to develop a specific strategy about how to reduce offending by women, but we need research to help us to understand what it is about women offenders, their stories, their experiences that causes them to come into prison.

I have often seen academics driving out their own research agenda for their own needs rather than the need to improve the system. Also the way academic research is written, it's not attractive to practitioners to (a) read and (b) figure out how to implement. It's written with an audience in mind, but I think the recidivism studies are the ones that will actually get you the particular relationship between the theory and the practice. I'm not sure that academics in Ireland have helped us that much in influencing politicians. Often, their views are polarized and it's not a combined effort, therefore people dismiss it. Whereas there could be a very powerful lobby and I think it's a responsibility that the academics should have in universities to think about how to influence the policymakers of the future.*

* Possible strategies for enhancing knowledge exchange between academics, practitioners, and policymakers include: seminars, workshops, and conferences that focus on translating research into practice; state funding for evidence-based research; and open access to academic research publications. Some of these strategies are being implemented; for example, Ireland has introduced an Open Access Policy for publicly funded research (see http://www.research.ie/aboutus/open-access).

Evidence-Based Corrections

Often, the practice overtakes research because the practice is happening in the moment and it's very difficult for research to keep up. The first thing we need to do is get good data. People are going to be shocked but they need to be shocked because they need to see the evidence of how prison works. We will publish recidivism data for 2008 and 2009 this year. In 2007, about 7000 people left prison (we didn't count remands and fines) and the Central Statistics Office* were able to tell us if they ever came back in touch with the criminal justice system [and] what they were in touch for. That's research because it will help us to help the public to understand. The real benefits of the recidivism studies will be 10 years down the road when people can start looking at what happened. Why did we have a 30% increase? Why did we have a decrease?

It has to be information that we use in practice because otherwise there is no point doing it. We need science to tell us what prison interventions work well and what works least well, and how prison does in terms of rehabilitation compared to community programs such as probation—because prison can be damaging for certain groups of people. Then I suppose you are trying to figure out quality of life [issues]. We have never asked the question about the quality of life both for the prisoner and the staff. We are afraid to do it but it's a question we have to ask. It gives you that health check—is this a healthy prison or is this a really damaging place to be? It's a real lack that we do not have a research unit [but] you can start with small beginnings. You can do something modest, answering some important questions.

Transnational Relations

The Council of Europe, the European Union (EU), and the directives†—simple things like the transfer of prisoners‡—are groundbreaking because you are trying to get in standards across the different prison environments. There is also EUROPRIS,§ which is a prison organization of all prison administrators in Europe. It's very interesting to sit with the Nordic countries and hear what they have to say. As an island, we are completely influenced [by international developments] and rightly so but we should be

* The Central Statistics Office is Ireland's national statistics office (see www.cso.ie).

† As a member of the EU, Ireland must transpose EU directives into Irish law.

‡ Reference to the Framework Decision (November 27, 2008) "on the application of the principle of mutual recognition to judgments in criminal matters imposing custodial sentences or measures involving deprivation of liberty for the purpose of their enforcement in the European Union."

§ EUROPRIS is the European Organization of Prison and Correctional Services.

careful that we don't get too much influence from America and England. Traditionally, we look to America [or] England [but] I'm not sure [that] the prison system in either is a system that we should be trying to emulate. There are other models—Finland for instance—that we should be looking to much more.* What we have got to do is look at the best of everything and then design our own.

General Assessments

My proudest achievement is setting out a clear vision of where we want to go within the next 3 years and then communicating that to the people, the governors, directors, the staff, and our prisoners. I see the change in the prison system in three cycles of five [years]. We have had a good start because people want to buy into it. In every organization I've [worked] in, I have always found that people are hungry for change but they are not sure how to get there and, therefore, they are hungry for leadership [and] direction. The rebalancing of prison and the community sector [will] give us dividends for the future. [The current financial crisis is] going to bring about necessary reform [but will also] be challenging in the sense that it [will] make some people more disillusioned. Life is about reform, it's about change [but] nothing will change unless you bring energy to it. I have always believed [that] the future [can't] solve the present. You are better off solving the present and of course always having an eye to where you want to go.

Conclusion

Mr. Donnellan was candid and forthcoming in the interview. He was very well informed about Irish and international developments in the field of criminal justice and was closely acquainted with the academic literature in this area. One of the major themes that emerged during the course of the discussion was the notion of "balance." Mr. Donnellan spoke frequently of the need to rebalance the criminal justice system toward a greater focus on community-based sanctions. He also emphasized the importance of achieving balance within the prison environment, stressing in particular the need to find a middle ground between maintaining discipline and providing appropriate levels of care to prisoners. Finally, he suggested that the pathway to desistance is characterized by balance, arguing that prisoners must accept

* Finland is regarded as a model of best practice in Europe since Finnish prisons have a strong rehabilitative ethos and are designed to "normalize" prison life. See Pratt and Eriksson (2011).

personal responsibility for changing their lives, but must also be supported by others along that journey. The second significant theme in the interview was "cooperation, accountability, and transparency." Mr. Donnellan emphasized the benefits for the Irish prison system of external oversight by international and Irish agencies. He also expressed a willingness to learn from the experiences of prisoners and prison staff and was open to working in partnership with other agencies to bring about the best outcomes for people who come into contact with the prison system. "Rights-based policy and practice" was another important theme, evident in his compassion toward people in prison and his view that the human rights discourse should be central to penal policy and practice. The final major theme was "transformation." This was clear in his acceptance that people are capable of desisting from crime but also in his ambitious but realistic vision for change within the prison system.

Glossary

An Garda Síochána: Irish police force.

Children Act: The Children Act, 2001, overhauled the Irish youth justice system. It introduced new community sanctions and states that detention should be used only as a last resort.

community return program: Prisoners who are serving sentences of between 1 and 8 years and have been assessed as suitable for community work may be offered early temporary release from prison in return for engaging in community service under the supervision of the probation service.

***Coronation Street*:** Popular TV program.

EUROPRIS: European Organization of Prison and Correctional Services.

incentivized regime: Under this regime, prisoners' access to privileges is differentiated into three levels (basic, standard, and enhanced) according to their quality of engagement with rehabilitation services and their behavior.

***Irish Times*:** National broadsheet newspaper.

Mountjoy Prison: The main committal prison in Dublin city, Mountjoy is a closed, medium-security facility.

Van Dieman's Land: The name given to Tasmania by nineteenth-century explorers. A penal colony was established on the island to which many Irish convicts were transported.

3

Jaroslav Jánoš, Prison Governor, Corps of Prison and Court Guard, Slovak Republic

PAVOL KOPINEC

Contents

Overview

The Slovak Republic (also known as Slovakia) is in the geographic center of Europe. It has a population of 5.5 million. The Slovak Republic was established on January 1, 1993, following the division of Czechoslovakia into two countries—the Slovak Republic, with Bratislava as its capital, and the Czech Republic. The Slovak Republic is a member of the European Union (EU), NATO, and the eurozone. The Slovak Republic has 18 correctional institutions capable of holding 9500 inmates. Of these, five institutions hold only pretrial detainees, nine hold sentenced prisoners, and four house a combination of sentenced prisoners and pretrial detainees. All correctional institutions are operated by the state.

The correction system is administered by the Slovak General Directorate of the Prison and Court Guard Corps under the Ministry of the Interior of the Slovak Republic. The prison system is divided into three security levels, which is referred to as "the external differentiation" of prisons. Prisoners serve their sentences in differentiated groups "A," "B," or "C," or in specialized units. Those sentenced to lifelong imprisonment are categorized as "D1" and "D2." D1 consists of one cell and a room that is intended for individual interviews, which allows the regime officer to monitor the situation if necessary. D2 consists of a cell with a capacity for up to four people, a room for educational activities, a room for hobbies or sports activities, and a room intended for individual interviews.*

The internal differentiation of prisons by the Ministry of Justice Decree 368/2008 on regulations of imprisonment sentence, places prisoners of the same security level into similar sections and groups to increase the effectiveness of the treatment of prisoners. Prisoners placed in sections or groups stay together and usually also work together to assist in meeting targets for treatment (93/2008 Coll. of Law amending and supplementing Law No. 475/2005 Coll. of Law on serving of prison sentence and on amendments to certain laws). The purpose of prison is defined as being to maintain the health and dignity of prisoners for the duration of their sentence, and to develop their sense of responsibility and equip them with skills that will help them to reintegrate into society, to live and to respect the law after leaving prison (Council of Europe, 2006).

The term *external differentiation* refers to the degree of imposed penalties and surveillance, governed by the principle that the higher the degree of surveillance, the greater the scope of restrictions, just as it is regulated differently and the performance rights and forms of treatment (93/2008 Coll. of Law). The categorization of the individual is based on the conclusions and recommendations of a psychological evaluation, the prisoner's behavior during previous sentences, an understanding of the emotional and social problems of the prisoner, and the prisoner's attitudes to following a rehabilitation program. The categorization of a prisoner does not change if he or she is relocated between institutions of the same security level (Decree No. 368/2008).

Introduction

The Slovak General Directorate of the Prison and Court Guard Corps responded positively to the request of the Institute of Social Studies and Curative Education of Comenius University in Bratislava to authorize an interview with a senior correctional leader. The prison director requested that the theoretical questions be asked first. The interviewer asked additional questions to elicit examples and fuller details relating to the written text. All answers were directly incorporated in the chapter based on the interview.

* General Directorate Collection Orders of the Prison and Court Guard, Order No. 86 on the treatment of inmates, 2009.

Career

Q: Tell us a little bit about your career: length, organizations worked in, movements, specializations, trajectories in your career that might differ from those expected.

A: I started to work in prison without any previous experience or information about that line of work. I was hired through a recruitment program conducted in 1987 by the Correctional Educational Institute for convicted women in Bratislava—*Mlynska dolina*. At that time, the Corps of Correctional Education offered attractive benefits particularly as regards housing, contributions to retirement, and a slightly better salary than in the civil service.

Q: What was your first position and how did your career develop?

A: I started as a regime officer in the prison for women and continued as an educational specialist in cultural awareness. After 11 years in front-line service, I was offered policy work at the Directorate General. After 12 years in this position, I returned to work in a prison.

Q: Did the way your career developed surprise you?

A: After induction, I worked systematically to progress through my career, through continuous self-education and by undertaking activities beyond the call of my duties. For instance, I worked as a methodologist (person responsible for the development of working methods) through regular contacts with the third sector, through socio-psychological training for educators, social workers, and health professionals, work with alcohol abusers, a 3 years training cycle working with specific clients (people with aggressive tendencies, drug users) led by colleagues from the United States in Warsaw for Russian-speaking countries. A number of other external circumstances helped my career development such as changes in the political situation in the country and the opportunity to associate with a wider range of professionals etc.

Q: Did your work prove as interesting or rewarding as you thought it would?

A: The work of prison staff in direct contact with convicted prisoners is very dynamic and requires a lot of personal invention (I worked with these prison staff for over 10 years). In this respect, the work is really interesting. With a minimum amount of optimism and a positive approach to life it could certainly also be considered useful from a society-wide perspective. The work of the higher and senior prison management is also similar, if this work is related to the specific clientele—prisoners with their specific problems of all kinds, whose needs will never be met by a civil service clerk. Personally, I was fortunate enough to be able to have a direct impact on the formation of the national policy on the treatment of prisoners, as well as on the legislation dealing with pretrial detention and imprisonment.

I was fortunate enough to contribute to national policy when I authored about two-thirds of the Act No. 475/2005 on serving of prison sentence. In 2003, I was accredited to help outline the new directions of the prison system. The regulations and law were later on adopted. Methods were my work. In this respect, my career certainly exceeded the expectations that I had when I started working in this profession.

Q: Do you have any regrets about any opportunity you pursued or chose not to pursue during the course of your career?

A: Every working opportunity in my career has enriched me. Over time, and particularly in relation to my academic activities carried out concurrently, I regret perhaps only my benevolent approach to professional publishing activities, when I didn't claim authorship of documents produced and I retrospectively accepted others' claims to authorship, both coauthors and merely formal collaborators.

Changes Experienced

Q: What do you see as the most important changes that have occurred in the field of corrections over the course of your career (philosophies, organizational arrangements, specializations, policies and programs, equipment or technologies, methods of rehabilitation, methods of community supervision, intermediate sanctions, personnel, and diversity)?

A: By 1965, Czechoslovakia was one of the few countries that had incorporated conditions of imprisonment into law to comply with most of the Standard Minimum Rules for the Treatment of Prisoners. During the changes to the political system in Czechoslovakia (1989), the prison system was exposed to a number of interventions by people other than prison professionals built on a fictive premise (related to the changes in the political system) of the total elimination of crime. Due to the massacre in Leopoldov Prison in November 1991, Slovak prisons decided to address the chaotic situation of uncontrolled access to prisoners. The Leopoldov massacre itself, during which prisoners brutally murdered five members of the prison staff and a cellmate, was only the culmination of an emotional and humanistic influence on the security situation in prisons that was reflected in endless concessions to the requirements of inmates and by the change in the role of prison staff to figurants and providers of comprehensive services to detained persons. As a result, this legislation was changed.

Q: Please, could you specify how the legislation was changed?

A: The main changes included a new definition of performance (standards for) custodial sentences, treatment, and treatment programs. They were defined before, but now they have been incorporated directly into the law. For example the law specifies how many sentenced prisoners a single educator will work with (30) and how many in specialized sections (20). New types of departments were created, dealing with the management of special groups of sentenced prisoners, coordination with security, and a special treatment section. Their purpose was clearly defined and the way in which they deal with clients and the procedures to be used were specified.

Following the incorporation of the EU rules into the law, these items had already been included in the previous legislation 59/1965. It was important to define precisely the activities connected with the rights of the convicted and the security categories. The terminology was changed to "treatment," which is used in the EU rules. We are limiting as well the impact of the security category on the scope of the prisoner's contacts with his neighborhood. These rights are equal for all. Before this change, for example, the number of visits was determined by the security category. Maximum-security prisoners were allowed one visit every 6 months. Now all convicted prisoners have the same entitlement to contact with their neighborhood. They have the opportunity to make phone calls under certain conditions. We work mainly with those convicted for the first time, because we believe that there is a greater opportunity to change the person. In times past, we focused more on those with longer sentences, more time, or repeat offenders. Rehabilitative methods are now applied mainly at lower security levels. The higher security category prisoners were overwhelmed by activities, for example, for those with lifelong sentences who were focused on activities to support their release. For 5 years, we experimented to see what worked and then we translated it into rules and regulations for implementation. In addition, we started new, more effective forms of staff training. The material conditions of prisoners and prison staff were materially improved, despite several years of problems due to insufficient accommodation capacities and inadequate funding.

Q: Please, could you explain why the financing is not sufficient?

A: Well, the state has problems in financing education and health and the prisons are relegated to being a side concern. The increased number of prisoners has not been recognized. In the last 5–6 years, the number has increased more than 100%. Capacity and staff numbers remain the same. Until last year, it was not reflected in the state budget at all. And of course the prices of goods and energy costs are growing and it's very visible in the prisons. We are pursuing funding as best we can. We also have problems with public tenders, which do not reflect and respond to the market. Despite occasional inappropriate attacks on the Slovak prison system as well as on legislation dealing with pretrial detention and imprisonment, today's prison philosophy in Slovakia may be described as balanced from the point of view of the purpose of imprisonment, as well as in terms of meeting the basic minimum standards for the treatment of prisoners.

Q: Overall, has the quality of prisons, jails, and community supervision in your country/community improved or declined over the past 10 years? (Such as the number of personnel per inmate ratio, amount and type of training offered, programs offered to inmates, rehabilitation strategies, and the amount of money available to implement these programs; what percentage of inmates are able to have access to programs?; how recidivism of both technical violations and new criminal activity has been affected, interagency cooperation, the effectiveness of top management providing quality control and directing managing and line personnel, inmate and staff safety, and inmate suicide rates.)

A: The significant development of prisons can be dated to somewhere between 1992 and 2008 after a change in political regimes, when new accommodation capacity was built and there was an improvement in the material conditions in prisons, new conceptions and implementation of legislation, standards, and norms. In 2005, new legislation based on a very good concept of prisons was adopted, but this concept has still not been fully implemented today, because there was inadequate funding for the changes were not financially covered, for example, for the construction of new specialized departments. Because of the onset of the global economic crisis, prisons are now even more unfunded. The increasing numbers of prisoners has not been taken into account and prison staff are demotivated by the constant attacks on their social security (benefits), as well as by initiatives that reduce their actual wages.

What is positive is that prison staff have been able to continue with the quality programs with sentenced prisoners, which were in place before 1989, and they have developed treatment programs with more meaningful activities. Every sentenced prisoner may enroll in any of the programs, if he meets the requirements for the program.

Unfortunately, I can't provide you with information about the impact of the implemented programs on prisoners and their recidivism, because it is not currently possible to give you a quantified answer. This area has not been measured in any relevant way and only partial information can be gleaned from the statistics which are kept. (For example, if we consider the number of released prisoners repeatedly returned to prison in a set period of time, such as 10 years, the statistics do not take into account other penalties or prosecutions and offenses which do not result in imprisonment.) In the prison which I govern the average number of prisoners repeatedly being imprisoned ranges up to 16%, various authors give figures for the average recidivism rate among such persons ranging from 26% to 35%. In extreme circumstances, the authors of the studies, who are also trying to get some financial support for their activities in resocialization, indicate that up to 80% of prisoners relapse. For your reference, please see the Statistical Yearbooks of the Slovak Corps and Prison Court Guard.*

Q: What are your recommendations?

A: It is difficult to collect data on recidivism for prisons. A prisoner who reoffends need not be returned to prison, but could receive an alternative sentence, such as a conditional sentence, which the prisons are not aware of. Data are collected from different sources and should be completed by one institution—courts or jurisdiction and evaluated by the criminal record offices. So, for example, if I look at the statistics I see XY people reentering prison. Prosecutors started to collate statistics 5 years ago, so we don't know what the situation was previously. Different statistics should be combined. We don't have information on those who were sentenced and did not return to prison after their release, therefore we don't know what our success rate was.

Q: In general, is it more or less difficult to be a correctional officer (or supervisor, warden, regional management) now than in the past?

A: Given the complexity of the current economic, human, social, and legislative aspects of this issue, the current position of the director of the Institute for Imprisonment is more difficult in all respects. In the past, there was not such great pressure on the directors, for example, within the public procurement process which is, in the interests of transparency, so complicated that it leads to the situation where it is impossible to comply with the law and provide prisoners with the required quality and variety of food and so on.

* http://www.zvjs.sk/?rocenky.

Increasingly more damaging are the inadequate personal qualities and physical fitness of the staff who are joining the prison service. That brings many personnel challenges in ensuring the proper and safe performance of prison services. Furthermore, the strong influence of the human rights organizations "supervising" the rights of sentenced prisoners creates an atmosphere leading to speculative placement of the prisoners' requirements, where it is obvious that they cannot be subject to the conditions of the sentence. This is creating pressure on the prison staff through repeated complaints based on a variety of requirements. For example, more and more prisoners are "having fun" by increasing the strain on the staff and their activities by taking advantage of the law on free access to information. They require a huge amount of different, often absurd information. (For example, prisoners requested information on food menus and their content for the past 10 years.) This is just a basic overview of problems that managers did not have to wrestle with in the past.

Q: What would ideal cooperation with human rights organizations look like?

A: First of all, they should define the area in which they would like to operate. They are not aware of many security risks. Many times, they are more damaging than helpful. What is ideal are educational activities, such as follow-up educational activities provided by other organizations, which are good, but prison staff don't have enough time to do. The prison staff can then tackle a broader range of issues.

Personal Correctional Philosophy

Q: What do you think should be the role of prison, jail, and community supervision officials in society?

A: It is important to significantly differentiate between the functions and roles of the prison staff. The role of prison staff is based on teamwork. The position and role of a guard on the tower is different. He comes into contact with the prisoners usually only in case of emergency and his role is strongly oriented to security. The role of the officer in direct contact with prisoners is a different one, where the rehabilitative and protective functions are properly balanced. Educators and social workers have other roles, which are primarily rehabilitative. Then there are specialized staff—psychologists, psychiatrists, doctors, medical staff, all of whom have precisely defined roles and perform their usual tasks in addition to specific educational tasks, rehabilitation, and therapeutics. The common task for all is to ensure that the purpose of custody and the respective purpose of imprisonment are in accordance with current legislation.

Cooperating organizations should primarily focus their activities on helping sentenced prisoners make a smooth transition to civil life, that is, creating social networks with close links to the resocialization and reintegration efforts of the prison staff. Prison staff are tired of the range of activities intruding into so-called community supervision. Visits by representatives of these organizations are usually conveyed by negative messages about unprofessional ignorance about issues and are often followed by aggressive, arrogant stands against prison staff and triggering of tensions between the prisoners and so on… It is obvious that often the main motivation in these organizations is an easy source of funding, when such activities and projects are earmarked significant sums from various donors as well as government organizations or committees of the Council of Europe.

Another point is that these organizations' reports indicate only issues and shortcomings, which prison administrators know and publish in various internal documents. Unfortunately, we can't solve them due to lack of appropriate funding. Therefore, it would be more effective if the agencies and organizations sponsoring the "control" were prepared to react to the prisons' requirements and needs and used the funds directly to eliminate known deficiencies that are notoriously presented. Even better, it would be helpful if they used those funds to improve conditions in general, rather than simply bring negative criticism. We consider as sufficient the internal controls, state surveillance, and control exercised by the committees, boards, and authorities established by supranational organizations such as the United Nations and the Council of Europe to ensure compliance with the law and respect for human rights. The number of official, established control procedures will allow, for example, a full calendar year of continuous inspections in prison facilities. Educational activities, lectures, and cultural activities are very useful and are well received by prison staff.

Q: What organizational arrangements work and which do not?

A: In general, the organizational measures for prisons are established and formulated in collaboration with the prison administration. Such measures usually work and are useful. From time to time, we perceive as "tampering" interventions and policies based on politicians' emotions, which are difficult to implement in practice or cannot be applied at all. In the recent past, for example it was decreed that all prisoners with the potential for self-harming or suicide should be identified to prevent them from self-harming in prison. All this resulted from one case of suicide by an imprisoned regional politician of the ruling party. This order is not in force anymore.

Q: What policies does your country have in regard to relations with the community, political groups, and other criminal justice organizations? Do these policies work well? What hampers cooperation with other agencies and groups?

A: I think that broad communication of criminal policy in the Slovak Republic is good. Legislative and organizational measures are publicly discussed before adoption and rational and effective changes can be made to proposals. Personally, I consider that criminal policy in European states underrates the importance of the restorative aspect of the sentence—actively remedying the damage caused to the victim and addressing the future relationship with the victim. The orthodox "humane" theory that punishment for the offender begins and ends with imprisonment and does not require further satisfaction to the victim has serious flaws in this respect.

The terms and conditions of prison administration collaboration with other bodies and organizations are transparently governed by the relevant legislation. If an organization meets the conditions and has a legitimate interest, there is nothing to prevent mutual cooperation. For example, we are running a program called "Everyday Law" in cooperation with Trnava University. Students help prisoners with things like filling forms, making appeals, and resolving accommodation problems.

Q: How should corrections institutions be run? What programs should be provided and how would you prefer sentencing laws to be modified so as to have prisons and jails include the individuals most deserving of incarceration? What are the best correctional strategies to ensure the safety and security of the inmates, staff, and community? What services should prisons and jails provide that are currently not offered? What services are provided that you believe should be cut?

A: Correctional institutions should be separate legal and budget entities—a state organization dedicated to the management of sentences. This would eliminate political influence and ensure the independence of external audits conducted by, for example, the Ministry of Justice. In prisons, there should be meaningful programs to help offenders to understand the seriousness of their actions, to recognize the damage caused, and to lead them to actively remedy the damage to the victims and the relationship with the victims. The ideal goal of treatment should be active efforts by the prisoner to integrate into society and live in accordance with the law and accepted social norms.

The introduction of segregated specialized sections helps us to separate aggressive prisoners from others and to reduce the number of fights. As regards victims, we have managed to introduce a new system of shopping for selected goods, which enables the prisoner to buy goods when he pays some compensation to the victim. For example, if a prisoner buys 20 euros worth of cigarettes, he will also pay 20 euros compensation to the victim. In the past, when the offender had debts, he didn't pay them and the victim received nothing. There was the moral satisfaction that the offender was sitting in prison, but practical compensation was missing.

Criminal sanctions are regulated enough. What is problematic is law enforcement, complicated procedures, questionable "protective" mechanisms, which often bring the law into disrepute, allowing criminals to go unpunished in cases where guilt is clear, due to procedural error.

Q: What changes would you suggest?

A: I would appreciate it if we had the same retraining funds as the Ministry of Labour, Social Affairs and Family offices do to help long-term unemployed prisoners to enter the labor market. The best strategy for ensuring internal and external security is consistent application and implementation of the categorization of prisoners and category-based differences in the approach to contact with the external world. Prisons should legally be required only to provide services necessary for the provision of the basic social rights of sentenced prisoners and services which are directly related to the delivery of individual treatment programs. All other services should be considered as above standard. It should be clear to the prisoner that the provision of these services has been earned by the prisoner's exemplary behavior and achieving the goals of an established treatment program or because the prisoner is socially deprived or economically insecure. This should be an essential part of the philosophy of the treatment of prisoners in accordance with the purpose of the sentence. Offering the current range of services often conflicts with the prison's responsibilities in regard to ensuring the necessary security measures are in place, ensuring good order and discipline and is counterproductive to the efforts of prison staff to encourage the cooperation of prisoners with social reintegration activities.

If it is possible, the service should reconsider the arrangements for the delivery of food packages. This is currently the most pressing issue of prison facilities and the policy should be abolished and replaced by wider choices for the purchase of food items and personal items in internal stores. Packages are perceived as risky in terms of internal security (penetration of drugs, explosive devices, and other health- and life-threatening objects) as well as from the epidemiological point of view (distribution of contaminated or unhealthy foods). Nowadays, synthetic drugs are almost impossible to detect within food articles, cosmetics, and other personal things. From a review of the recorded contents of packages, it can be seen that these are not intended for the supply of goods for domestic agricultural production and fruit production, as argued by the advocates of packages. The commonest commodities are coffee, tea, and meat products. Coffee and tea in particular, are often blended with synthetic drugs or other addictive substances. Meat and other foods requiring careful transport and storage are served in uncontrolled conditions with epidemiological risks and prisons are anxious and have to take all the actions that are necessary to ensure the health, hygiene, and safety of food items, so the thousands of euros which have been invested in the Hazard Analysis and Critical Control Points (HACCP) system for kitchen equipment are being wasted.

Q: How should supervision postprison or postjail (or in lieu of prison or jail) be dealt with? Is the procedure used in your country working, or do you see an increased recidivism rate due to issues those supervised in the community experience? How would you improve this problem or why is this process working in your country?

A: First of all, supervision after release is important only in specific cases, usually for conditional release, with released prisoners convicted of crimes caused by psychiatrically diagnosed abnormalities or addictions and for repeated offenders. Supervision should be based on individual programs with specified, dated goals agreed between the released person and the workers monitoring him. As well as probation workers and assigned social workers, relevant experts, for example, psychiatrists and doctors should be part of the supervision system. In the Slovak Republic, the system of probation is makeshift and is far from meeting the real requirements of such services. This, of course, has an impact on recidivism. Formal conditions have been created for the probation services, but as yet the desirable personnel, material, and economic structures, without which no program or service can operate, have not been put in place.

Q: Do you feel that your country uses appropriate intermediate sanctions when needed or is there a lack of such sanctions? Are intermediate sanctions such as treatment programs, intensive supervision, or electronic monitoring utilized, and do they reduce recidivism while keeping those in the community safe? If not, what do you feel is the problem?

A: Officially, since amended criminal codes came into effect in 2006, there have been plenty of alternative sentences to prison (intermediate sanctions) in the Slovak Republic, but no implementing regulations have been implemented to support these. There are no stated competencies for their application and there is no cushion, no means for their creation. To date, no detention facility for the isolation and treatment of deviants exists. Only rarely is house arrest given as a sentence as this power is not covered in the regulations and no center of the control of electronic monitoring and so on has been established. The problem is that the resolution of any issues in the state is rigidly dependent on allocations from the state budget and state budget officials (economists) decide which are important. Addressing crime and dealing with the social circumstances of criminals are not unrelated things.

Problems and Successes Experienced

Q: In your experience, what policies or programs have worked well, and which have not? Can you speculate for what reasons?

A: In principle, all policies and programs that are preceded by detailed, complex preparation are good (legislative, methodological, personal, material, and economic). They are accepted by sentenced prisoners to the extent that they accept their implementation and participate fully if they are generally perceived as meaningful and useful.

Q: What would you consider to be the greatest problem facing the correctional system at this time?

A: Long-term underfunding of basic needs, the lack of application of alternative sanctions, and the consequent overcrowding of accommodation.

Q: What problems in corrections do you find are the most difficult to deal with? What would be easy to change?

A: Internal problems (culture of the organization, managerial deficiencies, allegations of corruption, or gender-related problems) or externally generated problems (resources, community support, parole or probation procedures, or lack thereof).

The most difficult problems to deal with, which the prison administration cannot influence as their solutions do not depend on their actions, concern funding of some of the basic needs of prisons. This is very frustrating for the prison staff, especially when facing criticism from inspecting bodies who ask why various tasks are not being performed. Moreover, in accordance with the Law on Control, the superior of the service office allocates blame within his own ranks for the shortcomings and takes appropriate sanctions against him or her. In practice, I know of no manager who would not attempt to tackle the deficiencies that occur continuously or occasionally in his prison, whether or not detained people or control authorities point them out. It would be done if he had sufficient funds, either from the state budget, or if we could invest at least part of the profits generated by employment of prisoners or production within prisons. Underfunded state organizations should be exempt from the law that prevents state budgetary organizations using loans, leases, or similar forms of financing for restoration and care of state property. There are many financial products whose relatively favorable conditions would allow the enhancement of existing assets and improve the material conditions for ensuring the enforcement of penalties without increasing the budget.

The prison system continually faces problems due to unsuitable appointments to management job positions, which usually create a number of problems, both in practical terms and internal relationships. The position of the prison administration in the public is being weakened through publicity about the excesses of some executives, especially where the appointment to the office is a purely political one.

Q: What is the most successful program you have worked with in corrections? What is the most successful policy in regard to the positive improvements that have been made to prisons, jails, or community supervision?

A: From my position, I consider to be most successful the series of prosocial programs that were prepared and published with input from prison staff. Then the training cycles put into practice during my tenure on the governing body. From that period of time, I consider one of the most successful measures the annual professional monothematic interactive workshops designed for professionals and specialists in prison services, the adopted conclusions of which were put into practice and in many cases incorporated into the relevant legislation.

Theory and Practice

Q: In your view, what should be the relationship between theory and practice? What can practitioners learn from studying and applying theories; and what can those who create theories of punishment gain from practitioners?

A: For a long time, there has been a vacuum in the area of theory and research in penology and penitentiary treatment in the Slovak Republic, with the exception of work by university students. Until 2005, a penological research department formed part of the governing body of the prison administration and later began to establish itself at the Ministry of Justice as a criminological research department, but the research department no longer operates. In practice, we use the theoretical knowledge of Czechoslovak penitentiary schools, summarized in the past and contained in the penological booklets issued by the prison administration and to a lesser extent in the present ministerial magazine of the Prison and Court Guard. Thanks to the functional system of lifelong education of prison staff, theory and practice are quite closely linked.

Q: What kind of research, in what form, and on which questions would you find most useful for practice? If not very useful, what could or should creators of theory do to make their ideas more useful to you?

A: Today, we could surely benefit from research which evaluated the effectiveness of the measures implemented in the so-called humanization of prisons, comparing the effectiveness of resocialization efforts by prison staff at various stages of the sentence and identify the real demands of society and of the victims of crime for imprisonment in order to determine the optimal threshold of humanization, which would accommodate these demands in a balanced way. It seems to me that this research should be based on the premise that if the sole criterion for the humanization of imprisonment is to prevent cruel, inhuman, and degrading treatment and punishment, and this has been achieved in principle and in practice, we should begin to address the question of how further to apply penal policy and penalties. It is essential to note that if a society wants to use imprisonment as a punishment, it is not possible in those circumstances to eliminate its essential features, because eventually the prison staff will have no room for practical convenience, implementation of the prison regime, and application of restrictions on the movement of prisoners. The sentence itself will lose sense.

Q: Where do you find theory-based information? Where do you look: journals, professional magazines, books, publications, reports?

A: I am continuously monitoring published reports and articles related to crime and prison. Thanks to my academic activities, I have an overview of publications and research reports from the field of penology and penitentiary treatment.

Q: Are there any specific publications that influenced you in your work?

A: Research is not currently being carried out because of funding restrictions. If you are looking for recent publications, you read work from Czech or Russia, where they publish enough on this topic. From time to time, I attend conferences. At the pedagogical university

(Novosibirsk), they have a dedicated section dealing with the prison system. They also translate many books from English, and carry out their own research. In some ways, prisons in Russia are significantly better than in the rest of Europe, even if they have a problem in that they have 800,000 prisoners and it will take time to rebuild all the accommodation capacities (which have large-capacity rooms). They are far ahead of us as regards treatment. In the past, monothematic meetings were held every September. As regards the West, material conditions are better but the eastern countries have more sophisticated programs and access to treatment. Qualified staff has been working in our country for over 50 years.

Q: Does the department of corrections you work for conduct research on its own? On what types of issues or questions?

A: No systematically organized research is being conducted. Screenings are continuously performed for monothematic reports and tasks deductions. At irregular intervals, university students carry out surveys as part of their theses.

Evidence-Based Corrections

Q: Do you feel that it is best to use evidence-based practices (or "what works") or that this focus is not important?

A: It is definitely important to measure all useful practices that are functional and meet the minimum requirements on the treatment of prisoners, especially if positive results are targets imposed on prisons.

Q: Do you read information on evidence-based practices? Where do you get this information? If you do not have this information, would you be interested in having access to these practices? What programs have been proven to work best in your country?

A: Although previously tabooed, prisons are gradually opening up to the public. The news media and publications are not concerned with the presentation of positive practice and the public are more often presented with negative news. Therefore, it is almost only possible to familiarize oneself with positive practice in departmental publications and journals.

Transnational Relations

Q: How have you been affected by the following in your organization's work by developments outside the country (human rights demands, universal codes of ethics, practical interactions with corrections officials from other countries, personal experiences outside the country, programs developed by other countries, new sentencing laws, political strife or war in your or neighboring countries)?

A: After the change of the political system in Czechoslovakia, there was a boom in invitations to experts from other countries and to a lesser extent, in travel to gain experience from other countries. There was mutual surprise at the fact that, as I mentioned earlier, Czechoslovakia was one of the few countries which had, since 1965, adopted statutory conditions of imprisonment, which incorporated into the national legislation most of the Standard Minimum Rules for the Treatment of Prisoners 1957, which many of the experts from abroad only theorized about in their countries. Also, experts who travelled from Czechoslovakia were often surprised that in some countries the prisons focused more on material security and imposing penalties, or there was a complete absence of meaningful treatment programs for prisoners. This does not mean that there is nothing to learn. On the contrary, each national strategy for the enforcement of penalties has its positive aspects, which it is possible to change and modify to improve conditions in one's own country. In this respect, the international seminars which were organized later were also useful. At the present time, it is more based on individual contacts with no real impact on the further development of the prison system.

Q: Have those interactions been beneficial or harmful? What kind of external international influences are beneficial and which ones less so?

A: The interactions which took place cannot be clearly evaluated. In reality, only a few elements of our well-functioning system were adopted or modified (for example, the drug-free zones). Some have been shown to be insignificant in our country or unhelpful (e.g., the so-called scoring system, which limits the amount of things that a person in jail can keep together). The usefulness and the actual impacts of certain practices are under discussion (e.g., imprisonment of mothers with children). International pressures, which do not fully take account of regional customs and mentality, have been less beneficial. For example, the pressure to introduce single cells for convicts. It is clear that such a measure would be perceived in our region as a deterioration in their status and prisoners are desperately fighting against the measure themselves. They are currently facing the problem of separate accommodation in countries where they have one-bed cells and imprisoned people from the eastern regions are asking to be accommodated together (e.g., German North Rhine—Westphalia).

Q: How have international relationships with other countries or other political influences had an impact on correctional policy or practice in your country?

A: International relations help to optimize prison legislation in the country and to improve treatment, but also to learn from errors and inefficient practices in other countries.

General Assessments

Q: Are you basically satisfied or dissatisfied with developments in the field of corrections?

A: Currently, I cannot express full satisfaction with the development of the prison system, which has been stagnating for several years. Proposed development and training events have not taken place. There are no research activities and every activity in the prison system is limited by the amount of funds allocated. From a long-term perspective, there is significant underfunding and we are only able to maintain things on a temporary basis... Despite the long-term overcrowding of accommodation, no new capacity has been built and other measures to reduce the numbers of prisoners are still only good intentions. In addition to material and economic security, there is the problem with experienced staff leaving because of the constant threats to social security and a reduction of real wages.

Government contracts are not working, the state is not taking produced articles from us, which is a paradox. For example, in Russia, prison retraining programs have all government contracts for army uniforms and sewn blankets and clothes for orphanages. The state thus makes a saving and prison labor pays part of the costs of the prisoner's stay in prison. For example, our activity was in furniture production, but it is not a success and in fact the state does not take anything. It is better if the prisoner does something (works) in the prison because it's good for his mental health.

Q: What do you think of the relationship between sentencing laws and public opinion to the functioning of prisons, jails, and community supervision?

A: In particular, thanks to the influence of media, the public thinks that prisoners have a much better life than most lower- or middle-class people. The media do not report positive results from the work of prison staff. Prisons are mentioned only when there is an incident (escape, death, revelations about the penetration of drugs, etc.) or in connection with the conditions of a prisoner who is interesting to the public (member of a criminal group, well-known personality, etc.). I personally often encounter the view that prison conditions should be much tougher.

Q: How do you view the release procedures in your country and do they contribute to or inhibit recidivism?

A: Relevant statistics, with which I am not currently familiar, would answer this question. Logically, I assume that conditional release has a positive influence on reducing recidivism. This provides controls over the released prisoner for a limited time and motivates the released person not to commit further crimes.

Q: What rehabilitative programs could be offered either in or out of prison or jail that could decrease recidivism?

A: I think that there are currently enough meaningful and useful programs in prison to reduce recidivism. Many programs require to be continued after release to achieve the desired effect. This, however, doesn't currently happen.

Q: How are intermediate sanctions (such as house arrest, ankle bracelets, rehabilitative programs in the community, or intensive supervision, among others) in your country used and how are they working or failing to work?

A: Legislation recognizes and allows the use of alternative sentences, but suitable conditions for their implementation do not yet exist and that's why only the minimum (house arrest) has been applied. Electronic monitoring—that is, ankle bracelets—has not been introduced at all. The civic associations declaring the penitentiary and post-penitentiary work, except for one or two exceptions are trying to work toward a prisoner rather than a protectionist position. This position is for them a fairly good source of income without effort and without any liability for what might have resulted from their activities. By contrast, the operations of prison staff often require great inventiveness and professionalism to eliminate the potential damage caused by the disruption of order and discipline established in places of imprisonment, after the civic associations have carried out visits and incorrectly interpreted the determination and motivation of resentenced offenders to participate in resocialization activities. Intensive supervision can work well only under optimal conditions. These have not yet been created.

Q: Which intermediate sanctions would you increase or create, and why?

A: House arrest and probation with the use of electronic monitoring seem to be very efficient, economical, and humane alternative punishments. These alternatives reduce the economic burden of the sentence on public resources and reduce the pressure on prison capacity. There is a human dimension in eliminating the negative effects of imprisonment, such as job loss, disruption of social ties, and so on. Proper implementation of alternative sentences can accelerate the process of reconciliation with the victim and compensation for damage and this is an area which current criminal policy seems wrongly to regard as secondary.

Q: How could changing the balance between intermediate sanctions affect prison and jail environments? Would that be an improvement?

A: As I mentioned in the previous question, alternative punishments reduce pressure on the accommodation capacity of detention facilities. They also can help prison staff as a possible incentive to the imprisoned person for his cooperation in social reintegration activities.

Q: What are the developments you see as most likely to happen in the next few years, and which developments would you prefer to see happening?

A: The period when tumultuous changes in European prison systems occurred has passed and prisons have generally stabilized. In fact, for decades, no major changes have appeared in prison systems and innovative practices are recorded only sporadically. It is a shame that even sporadic innovations are generally directed only to the so-called humanization of prison in the form of prisoners' rights and improvement of their material conditions and not to activities that could lead to more effective social reintegration in order to reduce recidivism.

It seems to me that the so-called humanization of prison must be limited so that it does not challenge the characteristic features of imprisonment with the legislative governed by specific constraints. It is essential to realize that if a society wants to use prison as a form of punishment, it is not possible to change prison essence, since procedures leave no room for the prison staff to comply with the provisions' recovery mode (as the basis for the application of any social reintegration activities with prisoners). Internal security and the penalties themselves would be meaningless.

Q: What is most needed now to improve prisons, jails, community supervision, and the overall punishment process in your country?

A: As I have mentioned several times in the interview, the concept is given but its implementation is linked to economic and material resources and the satisfaction of personnel. If we manage to reach the point where prison systems are supported in this, nothing will preclude prisons from fully fulfilling their roles and meeting public expectations. The same applies also to the application of alternative sentences, but these should first be established and implemented.

Conclusion

The interview with Jaroslav Jánõs provides an open and honest look at the correctional system in The Slovak Republic. The interview connects changes in correctional practices with changes in the political regime within the state. At the same time he indentified some of the major challenges facing the system. For example, the lack of adequate data to inform decisions remains a problem. Thus, evidence-based practices have yet to be fully implemented in the country. As is the case in many countries, he identifies fiscal challenges as a main theme during the interview. Budgetary problems have prevented the system from fully evolving by hampering the ability of corrections to train staff and implement new programs.

Glossary

external differentiation: Refers to the degree of imposed penalties and surveillance, governed by the principle that the higher the degree of surveillance, the greater the scope of restrictions.

internal differentiation: Places prisoners of the same security level into similar sections and groups to increase the effectiveness of the treatment of prisoners. Prisoners placed in sections or groups stay together and usually also work together to assist in meeting targets for treatment.

Ministry of Justice of the Slovak Republic: General directorate of the prison service manages and controls the prison institutions.

prison governor: The prison institution is headed by the prison governor who is appointed to the function.

Slovak General Directorate of the Prison and Court Guard Corps under the Ministry of the Interior of the Slovak Republic: Armed corps that fulfill the tasks regarding pretrial detention, serving a sentence of imprisonment, security and guarding of prison facilities, and protection of order and security in court and prosecution facilities.

Standard Minimum Rules for the Treatment of Prisoners 1957: Voted into action by the United Nations in 1957. This established the principles and rules for the treatment of prisoners.

Dušan Valentinčič, Director General of the Slovenian Prison Administration, Republic of Slovenia

4

GORAZD MEŠKO

Contents

Overview

After the collapse of Yugoslavia in 1991, Slovenia became an independent country and applied for membership in European and international organizations. In 1992, the Republic of Slovenia became a member of the United Nations (UN) and accepted international standards for the protection of prisoners' rights. According to the most important nonbinding UN instrument, Standard Minimum Rules for the Treatment of Prisoners, adopted by the First United Nations Congress on the Prevention of Crime and the Treatment of Offenders, held in Geneva in 1955, and approved by the Economic and Social Council on July 31, 1957 and May 13, 1977, Slovenia has strived to reach the minimum conditions in Slovenian prisons, as defined by the UN. Therefore, one of the minimum UN standards for the treatment of prisoners, which the Prison Administration of the Republic of Slovenia should pursue, is defined in Article 9, Paragraph 1 and Article 10 (Standard Minimum Rules for the Treatment of Prisoners, 1955).*

In 1993, Slovenia ratified the UN Convention against torture and other cruel, inhuman, or degrading treatment or punishment, which was upgraded by ratification of the Optional Protocol in 2006. The Committee against Torture monitors the implementation of the convention, and is mandated to evaluate states' periodic reports, while the protocol establishes inspection mechanisms at national and UN levels.

Slovenia became a member of the Council of Europe in 1993 and began implementing declarations, recommendations, and rules as well as all the ratified conventions and protocols of the Council of Europe.† In 1994, Brinc (1994) conducted the first in-depth study of the capacity and standards of Slovene penal institutions. Regarding international conventions and the practices of other east European countries, the study proposed the minimum capacity for one prisoner, which was later adopted as standard in national legislation. Thus, according to Article 42 of the Enforcement of Penal Sanctions Act, cells have to meet the requirements of health and hygiene, and enable the realization of psychological treatment (Zakon o izvrševanju kazenskih sankcij, ZIKS-1-UPB1, 2006). Prisoners could also be accommodated in individual cells according to the capacity of the institution. The rules on the implementation of the sentence of imprisonment require a minimum 9 m^2 per prisoner in an individual cell, and at least 7 m^2 per prisoner in a dormitory (Pravilnik o izvrševanju kazni zapora, 2000). Moreover, Slovenia also received recommendations on the capacity standards from the European Committee for the Prevention of Torture in

* "Where sleeping accommodation is in individual cells or rooms, each prisoner shall occupy by night a cell or room by himself. If for special reasons, such as temporary overcrowding, it becomes necessary for the central prison administration to make an exception to this rule, it is not desirable to have two prisoners in a cell or room.

All accommodation provided for the use of prisoners and in particular all sleeping accommodation shall meet all requirements of health, due regard being paid to climatic conditions and particularly to cubic content of air, minimum floor space, lighting, heating and ventilation."

† The European Prison Rules, adopted in 1987 and upgraded in 2006, appealed to members of the Council of Europe to implement the following minimum criteria into their prison services (European Prison Rules, 2006):

"Prisoners shall normally be accommodated during the night in individual cells except where it is preferable for them to share sleeping accommodation.

Accommodation shall only be shared if it is suitable for this purpose and shall be occupied by prisoners suitable to associate with each other.

The accommodation provided for prisoners, and in particular all sleeping accommodation, shall respect human dignity and, as far as possible, privacy, and meet the requirements of health and hygiene, due regard being paid to climatic conditions and especially to floor space, cubic content of air, lighting, heating and ventilation."

its report on a visit of Slovene penal institutions, which proposed only one prisoner in 8 m^2 sized cells (Council of Europe, 1996). In addition, in the majority of the Council of Europe member states, the average capacity of individual cells is between 7 and 12 m^2 (Smole, 2009). Despite signed international documents and all the proposed standards that should be implemented in practice, the increase in the prison population in Slovenia in the last 13 years has resulted in overcrowding. This trend was noticed for the first time in the history of Slovenian prisons in 2000 and it is still growing. The average prison population of 1416 in 2009 exceeded the design capacity of 1098 by almost 29%, according to the Prison Administration of the Republic of Slovenia (Uprava za izvrševanje kazenskih sankcij, 2010). The growth in the prison population began in 1996 and it has continued into the second part of the 2000s. One of the problems related to prison overcrowding is that there are no parole or probation services in Slovenia (Smole, 2009).

The largest prison is in Dob, near Ljubljana, where male prisoners serve sentences ranging from 18 months up to 20 or 30 years. The central women's prison is in Ig, also just outside Ljubljana; the juvenile prison is in Celje and there are regional prisons where sentenced prisoners serve up to 18 months in Koper, Maribor, and Ljubljana. Each prison has an open, semiopen, and closed unit, which differ by the degree of security applied and the restrictions placed on the freedom of movement of their inmates. The correctional facility is in Radeče (Slovenian Prison Administration, n.d.).

Introduction

The Faculty of Criminal Justice and Security (FCJS), University of Maribor, Slovenia, cooperates with criminal justice practitioners to provide students with up-to-date information on the practice of different criminal justice institutions. Mr. Dušan Valentinčič has cooperated with the FCJS since the mid-1990s and has contributed significantly to the development of criminal justice studies, especially penology. We decided to conduct an interview with him due to his knowledge and expertise in penology and his management of prisons and the Slovenian Prison Administration for many years as well as his endeavors to improve the quality of work and life in Slovenian prisons.

An interview with Mr. Valentinčič, director general of the Slovenian Prison Administration, was conducted in spring 2011 by Gorazd Meško, professor of criminology at the Faculty of Criminal Justice and Security, University of Maribor. The interview took place at the Slovenian Prison Administration headquarters.

Career

Q: Tell us a little bit about your career: length, organizations worked in, movements, specializations, trajectories in your career that might differ from those expected.

A: After secondary school, I enrolled at the Faculty of Sociology, Political Science and Journalism. I finished my studies in due time in 1981 and became a professor of sociology. After the first 2 years of joint study, I had to further my studies, and since I believed that I liked to work with young people, I chose the pedagogical course of sociology. This decision was also influenced by the possibility of getting a national scholarship, which was, in this case, provided to me by the end of the study.

At that time, I met my current wife, with whom I had already started living with in the student dormitories. We got married the same year as we graduated, started a family, and in the beginning moved to her parents in Koper, on the Slovenian coast. At that time, we were not anxious about where we would get a job and an apartment; we just had a great time and were full of optimism, confident that we would make it somehow.

We were soon aware that real life is not as friendly as the life in student dormitories. After a few months of unemployment, in the autumn of 1981, I first got a part-time job in a secondary school, and then a full-time, fixed-term job at the secondary metalworking and traffic school in Koper. A very nice school year was over and when other teachers went for a well-deserved vacation, I was called for compulsory military service in the Yugoslav People's Army. Because I had a family, I asked if they could send me somewhere near my home, so I was kindly sent to Bosnia and Herzegovina.

When I returned, I was once again unemployed and because our second child was on its way, I searched intensively for any kind of job. In the secondary schools on the coast, all jobs that would suit me were already taken. Since I had very good experience in teaching, I was at the time convinced I should continue searching for a job in this field.

I came to the prison system completely by accident. A colleague from the university and a friend who worked for a year in the Koper prison informed me that they needed a teacher/therapist, so I immediately signed up. As I completed all the interviews and tests, the governor of the Koper prison informed me that for an indefinite time period, the ministry restricted all new employment, and that I could be first employed as a guard and then later on, when possible, transferred to the position of a teacher. Even though I have never imagined myself working in prisons, especially not as a guard, I accepted the offer, firmly convinced that it was only a temporary solution which would make it easier to support my family. Ultimately, this turned out to be a false presumption. I began my career in prisons in 1983, the first 8 months as a guard, and then I continued to work for several years as a teacher. Later on, I became the head of the education service and also the head of economic units and in early 1992 the prison governor. Apart from working, I received constant educational and training opportunities. I acquired various skills to work with prisoners, especially knowledge in communication, social learning, solving conflicts, teamwork, addiction treatments, management, leadership, and so on. Soon thereafter, the prison system was reorganized and the head office of the Prison Administration of the Republic of Slovenia was established. The then minister of justice invited me to oversee the entire prison system. The experience and knowledge that I gained in various positions in the prison helped me to understand what is happening in prisons, solve issues associated with offenders, collaborate with employees, and govern the entire system. Given that the prison system is a very specific and extremely sensitive social organism, I cannot imagine that it could be successfully led by someone who comes from the outside, without prison experience, since it would be very difficult to comprehend the depth and complexity of operations. I was the director general from 1997 to 2006, and during this time I worked with five different ministers. Everything went well until the fifth came, since he appointed a new director general, and I was redeployed back to the position of the governor of the Koper prison. The return to the "base" and the deviation from the center of decision making and politics was very positive for me, and although the work with prisoners is extremely difficult, it was often easier to communicate with them than with politicians. As the director general resigned, at the end of 2009, the current minister of justice invited me to once again take over the governance as a director general and in April the government extended my mandate. In July this year, I will have had 27 years of experience in the prison system, and if my beginnings were full of frustration and personal uncertainty, I am now proud of my career and have a lot of motives for continuing, since I now love what I do.

Changes Experienced

Q: What do you see as the most important changes that have occurred in the field of corrections over the course of your career (philosophies, organizational arrangements, specializations, policies and programs, equipment or technologies, methods of rehabilitation, methods of community supervision, intermediate sanctions, personnel, diversity)?

A: There have been several significant changes. The most important change is definitely associated with the first years of my work in the prison system. The 1980s were a period of boom for sociotherapeutic programming in the prison system. The sociotherapeutic model, which was based on a democratic, horizontal mode of management, teamwork, social learning, direct communication, and creating appropriate relationships at all levels—between offenders and employees, as well as between participants of each of these two groups— was gradually replaced by the classical, predominantly supervisory management model, with a strong hierarchical, pyramidal structure of management. A system of strong supervisory emphasis gradually changed to a role which gave more importance to treatment and resocialization. A lot of effort has been invested in creating a good social climate in prisons. Prisons as traditionally closed institutions have begun to open outwards and inwards. The emphasis on sentence fulfillment was getting more relaxed, new open departments were created, and the number of external benefits for offenders increased. The cooperation with centers for social work, employment services, housing communities, educational institutions, and businesses that were employing prisoners was getting better and more efficient. The growing sense of freedom and a growing spirit of democracy and liberalism in society were also reflected in the prisons.

The sociotherapeutic orientation of prisons was popular and often mentioned, and even verified by the assembly of the then Socialist Republic of Slovenia. In that period, the number of professional staff in prisons increased—there were many new and mostly young psychologists, educationalists, sociologists, social workers, therapists, and so on. I was also among them, and we were all representatives of these changes. Although the sociotherapeutic direction, at least theoretically speaking, had no competition and found favor among academics, professionals, and even politicians, its enforcement turned out to be much more complex and complicated. This was not only about introducing new forms of work, but a lot more; it was about changing the mindset, entrenched behavior patterns, treatment of prisoners, and also the redistribution of power. The employees, especially the guards, who were gradually losing their power, found it difficult to adapt to new developments, were negative toward new forms of work and new staff at least in the beginning, warned that order and discipline were being "destroyed" and the security of prisons was being threatened, which all proved to be unfounded. Real changes in practice occurred gradually, as generations of staff were slowly replaced.

Another major change occurred after the change of the political regime and the independence of Slovenia. Overnight, all forms of "comanagement" of employees (workers' councils, workers' meetings, various committees) were abolished, and prison governors could decide on the position of employees, without having first to obtain their opinions. This turned out to be interesting, because at that time, many experienced this as a relief rather than a deprivation of rights.

Due to the breakup of Yugoslavia and democratic changes in eastern Europe, in some prisons the structure of offenders changed significantly. In particular, the number of immigrants from eastern Europe, who for economic or political reasons tried to escape to the West and create a better life there, decreased. Although Slovenia was among the countries that had fewer offenders in terms of population even before its independence, after independence this number declined even further. In 1996, only 682 persons on average or 31 persons per 100,000 inhabitants were detained, "which meant that Slovenia had the lowest number of offenders compared to other Member States of the Council of Europe" (SPACE I, n.d.). The decrease in the number of offenders was certainly greatly influenced by milder penal policy, which occurred in the context of major sociopolitical changes. Although nobody made a serious analysis of the reasons for the decline in the number of offenders, the Ministry of Justice and certain experts believed that the reduced number of offenders was expected and "was largely a reflection of the multi-annual trend, which could be called civilized engagement in crime," that Slovenia was an exception in this area, and that in the coming years it is unlikely to expect significant changes.

What happened was just the opposite. Just as quickly as the number of offenders decreased, it also rapidly increased in the following years, and in recent years even exceeded the situation before independence. Based on the comparison with other member states of the Council of Europe (SPACE I), one can establish that in the period from 1996 to 2000, Slovenia actually had the largest increase in the number of offenders. Later, the upward trend was slower. It should be kept in mind that a large number of offenders is not a reflection of higher crime rates, but rather the tightening of the penal policy in recent years, since courts usually imposed longer sentences for the same offenses. Politicians contributed importantly to this with their frequent discussions of punishments, which as a consequence led to the change in the penal code and increased criminal penalties for certain crimes. The maximum prison sentence has risen from 20 to 30 years of imprisonment, and 2 years ago, life imprisonment was introduced. Nevertheless, there is no reason for excessive concern since Slovenia, with its 67 offenders per 100,000 inhabitants, is still one of the countries with the least offenders and has fewer offenders than all of its neighboring countries and less than one-twelfth of those in the United States.

During this time, another major change happened. In connection with the reform of the entire government administration, the Office of the Prison Administration of the Republic of Slovenia was established in 1995. The organization of the prison system thus became similar to that of other European countries. Formerly independent prisons, which had been directly linked to the Ministry of Justice as independent constituent bodies, became internal organizational units of the newly established prison administration overnight. Certain powers, and thus the decision making, transferred from the minister (ministry) and governors of prisons to the director general of the new administration. This change, which was quickly adopted on paper, needed quite some time until it had its real effect in practice. During this time, we were forced to focus on ourselves and our own organization, which was often more difficult than working with offenders.

Among the changes in the last decade, it is necessary to mention the position of employees. If the position of offenders, at least in the formal sense, was constantly improving and the protection of their rights was more systematically taken care of after independence, the position of employees, on the other hand, gradually began to deteriorate. The employees lost many rights, such as accelerated pension benefits, early retirement under more favorable conditions, allowance for empowerment, and so on, and thus their status was becoming more and more aligned with the status of regular officers, which definitely does not have a positive influence on the social climate in prisons.

I personally believe that the quality of prisons in the past 10 years has improved in some ways and declined in others. Today, the position of offenders and the protection of their rights is addressed in a much more systematic manner, and they have more programs and opportunities for a better use of time, while on the other hand, individuals receive less attention and there is greater potential for conflict due to a worsening in the overcrowded living conditions. Although the number of offenders increased, the number of extraordinary events (such as the number of suicides) did not significantly increase. There are more options for alternative custodial sentences. There are fewer opportunities to work while serving the sentence. Compared to the period from 20 or more years ago, which dates back to former Yugoslavia, the possibilities to regulate postpenal issues has worsened, because at that time it was easier for the offenders to get work and housing after serving their sentences. Overcrowding on the one hand and the lack of human resources on the other, hamper the possibilities for good management, which also raises a number of problems in the administration.

Personal Correctional Philosophy

Q: What do you think should be the role of prison, jail, and community supervision officials in society?

A: My entire professional career in the prison system is accompanied by the eternal dilemma: should prisons be punitive or treatment institutions? Although it appears that both in theory and in practice this dilemma was resolved long ago, since nowadays, at least on the outside, we all support the treatment role of the prison, the actual situation is not so clear. Prison is punishment by nature, so we must never forget this aspect. The prison withdraws or limits what is most precious, freedom. For a limited time, people are excluded from society, separated from their family and friends, have the freedom of movement and some other rights limited. For what purpose? To punish them for something they did which was not in accordance with the accepted social norms, or to prevent them continuing with their socially unacceptable behavior, or to "improve" them, educate them, teach them to work, heal their addictions, and return them to society "better" than they were before the sentence—so that they will be willing and able to live in accordance with social norms? I believe the question is not whether we should focus on one or the other, but rather consider what a prison can offer apart from punishment. It is a way of enforcing a custodial sentence.

The basic mission of prisons is certainly to provide safety for society, offenders, and staff, as well as being treatment oriented, ensuring the respect of human rights for offenders, and the possibility of successful reintegration into society after serving their sentences. It is an implementation of various roles that a prison has, which are at first sight even contradictory, since the classical approach to provide increased security means taking action, which on the other hand restricts the rights of offenders, thus exacerbating the regime and stressing the supervisory role of the prison, and vice versa. The loosening of the regime, enabling contact with the environment (more visits, free exits, unlimited communication options, etc.), and the reduction of control, increase the potential for abuse (of drugs) and (increase) other items that can be used for attack and escape, thus reducing the security of the prison. It is quite clear that the prison, which is strongly oriented toward supervisory concerns, cannot at the same time implement effective treatments and reintegration programs. The opposite is possible—the more the basic role of the prison is to treat, the safer it is. This demands the fulfillment of certain conditions. In particular, a prison must not be too large, so that direct communication at all levels is enabled, both with offenders as well as between the offenders and employees themselves. I'm talking about a prison where everyone knows each other and communicates directly, where the prison governor (management) daily walks through the whole prison and talks with both offenders and employees, provides fresh information, advice, detailed instructions, answers to questions, and also exercises control. I'm talking about a prison which has less than 100 offenders, since an increased number of offenders generally decreases these options. Most Slovenian prisons are such, and therefore they offer real possibilities for the implementation of treatments and achieving security in a different and much more effective way.

Of course, the size of the prison is only one of the conditions. How each prison carries out its mission depends especially upon its leadership, especially its governor (a prison director), who is by law authorized to make decisions on most matters relating to the offenders. We must not ignore the role of other staff, especially professionals who are responsible for treatments, and guards who are constantly present in prison, even when there is nobody from the administration present and they are alone with the offenders. It is very important that the prison governor provides a good example and that they communicate in the right way. If the governor is respectful, fair, shakes hands with offenders, and listens to their requests, sets clear rules that apply to all, encourages all sorts of useful activities, and places only such limitations that are necessary for the enforcement of the sentence or the operation of the prison, it is more likely to be followed by others, and vice versa.

It is important that between employees and offenders a "fair" relationship is created in which we all operate first and foremost as people whose communication is based on mutual respect and fairness. In doing so, we must be aware of one important difference. We cannot choose the offenders who are as they are, while we can choose the employees, so it is extremely important who and on the basis of which criteria chooses new employees. I have had excellent experiences with my coworkers, who came here more or less by accident, because they needed a job and have been or are personally mature, mentally stable, with enough sympathy for others, and who are able to see the offender above all as a person and not a criminal. I am most careful choosing those who regard their work in a prison as their life goal. In such cases, they always get detailed questions about the reasons why this is so.

Working with people is difficult and demanding, and when it comes to offenders it is especially sensitive, since a wrong approach and communication can very easily lead to conflict situations, including those that are caused by the employees and could have been avoided. Such conflict situations, to which employees contribute more than offenders, are most difficult to solve, also because they constantly repeat (The same conflicts occur over and over again.) Therefore, it is very important to choose the right employees. The other extreme type of employees are those who never have any conflicts, prefer to turn away, do not hear or see anything, and come more or less just to work, while they do not bring any benefits to the job.

I am personally convinced that the most secure prisons are those which are the most treatment oriented. This is based on my experience, since I worked in the prison in various positions for more than 17 years. When our communication was effective at all levels, we focused more on the treatment, and we all felt that the social atmosphere was better, we had better work results, and this ultimately contributed to the greater safety in the institution. During periods when the treatment role stood in the background and the supervisory role of the prison gained importance, the communication was worse, there were more conflicts, and the social atmosphere and the prison safety deteriorated. If we illustrate this more simply, we could say that what some were building, the others simultaneously destroyed. Usually, but not necessarily, the first group contained professional staff, while the other was made up of guards led by executives who did not have a clear direction. There was a big gap between words and actions, and the offenders were well aware of that and some even took advantage, mostly in a negative sense. In such an environment, there were more possibilities for the functioning of the prison underworld. Of course, normally these situations are not black and white, but the nuances are sometimes difficult to recognize. Nevertheless, it is certain that individual prisons are differently oriented; some give more and some less emphasis on the treatment. This orientation, viewed over a longer period, changes also within a certain prison. It is important to constantly maintain the right balance between the supervisory role and the treatment role of the prison. This is the "art" of our work.

It is also very important what programs and opportunities the prison offers for the offenders serving their sentence. Given the fact that most people in prison are young, and that many are without a profession, the prison has to offer opportunities for education, and for getting a profession, since this will help offenders after they finish serving their sentences. All other forms of education are also very important. The offenders must have the opportunity to use computers. The use of the Internet is by itself not controversial, but for security reasons it is necessary to prevent the possibility of misuse. The prison should also offer the possibility of work and employment while serving the sentence, and thus the preservation and acquisition of work habits. Other programs that deal with drug addiction and alcohol abuse, suicide prevention, and the perpetrators of sexual violence are also important. The prison should offer opportunities for sports and recreation, leisure activities, and also provide spiritual care. There must be as many opportunities as possible for a beneficial use of time in prison, since this eliminates the time and space for nonsense and the operation of the prison underworld.

Because of the power of the staff over the offenders and the associated potential for abuse, it is necessary to have good and constant supervision, both internally and externally. The internal control starts with those who manage the prison. They must know what is going on in the prison at the time when they are not present in the institution; they must be able to check the information given to them from all sides and solve conflict situations appropriately. In this case, it is best to have direct and open communication. A special role in the implementation of internal control is awarded to the General Office, which is the holder of the operation and development of the entire prison system and, ultimately, the Ministry of Justice. One can gain real insight through external control mechanisms, which has to be implemented by politically independent institutions, such as the human rights ombudsman, various nongovernmental organizations, and the Committee for the Prevention of Torture of the Council of Europe (CPT).

A very important part of serving a prison sentence is the preparation for release, which may not be limited only to the time immediately before the release, but must begin much earlier. The preparation for release should be an integral part of a personal plan for each offender, which is prepared approximately a month after admission, and is specified during the serving of the sentence regardless of its length and individual problems. Such personal plans can be a good and feasible method only if its preparation actively involves the offender.

Preparing for release and successful integration into society after serving a sentence is a very complex task beyond the capabilities of a prison. The coordinated participation of the wider social community is essential, especially between the prison and social work centers, employment services, residential communities, educational institutions, healthcare institutions, individual companies, and so on, which can, depending on the issue, help the offender to reintegrate into society. The realization of a personal plan should continue even after serving the sentence, since at that time some other forms of assistance are much needed (housing, employment, addiction treatment, counseling). The more this system is regulated, the fewer chances there are of recidivism. But at the same time, we have to be aware that for some offenders crime is a way of life in which they can function, earn more money, and feel relatively good in what they are doing, so they do not want to replace it (yet). Others, which represent the majority, would like to change something and live in a different manner, but are unable to do that themselves and need help. The third group of people consists of such offenders, who have simply served their sentence and do not need a lot of help afterwards, because their basic conditions are in order (employment, housing). Such people need support especially while serving their sentence.

In our country, there is no supervision of offenders after they serve their prison sentence. There is also no probation or parole services in the country. When an offender is released from prison, there is no authority that would systematically implement the probation. This function is partly performed by social work centers. Offenders, including those that are released on parole or dismissed early (approximately 65% in 2009), have no responsibilities during this time. The revocation of parole is possible only if during this time they commit a new criminal offense for which the envisaged penalty is more than 1 year. The amended Enforcement of Criminal Sanctions Act of 2008 introduced the possibility of parole release combined with supervision, although in practice this has not yet been implemented (two cases). It is interesting that our country has never had problems with this, so it would be quite unnecessary to start supervising them widely. Examples of good practice from past decades confirm that the majority of offenders who were dismissed early do not need special control. However, for certain offenses and offenders, such control is required, and with the increased use of this solution the number of conditionally dismissed people would increase and thus the overcrowding in prisons would be reduced.

In my opinion, probation, which is implemented by various authorities today, inevitably needs its own organization, which would cover the whole field. This is also due to the more effective implementation of alternative forms of prison and detention, which are highly underutilized. Between the suspended prison sentence on the one hand and imprisonment on the other, there is a broad, unutilized space for various alternatives, which are rarely enforced, also because the system of implementing alternative sanctions is unfinished, not established enough, and many offenders are not even aware of this option, so the courts apparently prefer to opt for one of the two extremes. Among the newly admitted offenders in the last year, there were more than 80% with a penalty of up to 2 years, which is the upper limit for the replacement of imprisonment with work for the benefit of the community. One-third of them served their sentences alone, which means that they were unproblematic persons in terms of security and could all be candidates for replacing their imprisonment with work for the benefit of the community. Electronic control is not used in any of these options, and is not yet seriously considered.

Problems and Successes Experienced

Q: In your experience, what policies or programs have worked well, and which have not? Can you speculate for what reasons?

A: Despite major changes in the prison system after Slovenia's independence, and the fact that the number of offenders in the last 15 years doubled and in the past 10 years we witnessed the state of absolute prison overcrowding, with all the negative consequences that overcrowding brings, we nevertheless managed to successfully carry out our core mission. We have provided a stable security situation. There were no revolts or other major excesses. We assured the respect for human rights, gave the offenders options for various programs, and offered them help to reintegrate back into society. Given the limited spatial, personnel, and material resources this is certainly a success. I would like to point out some other successes as well:

- The construction of a new, alternative prison in Koper (the first after 50 years and the second after World War II)
- The opening of two new open sections
- The renovation of more than 40% of all spatial capacities
- The regulation of technical security systems at most locations
- The purchase of new equipment, vehicles, and uniforms
- The improvement of the training system and education of employees
- The introduction of new programs to deal with drug addiction, the adoption of the suicide prevention strategy and a strategy to address sex offenders, the introduction of new education programs
- The inclusion of health care of offenders in the public healthcare system

Currently, the biggest problems of the prison system include:

- Prison overcrowding
- Lack of staff in prisons
- Lack of funding for new programs, equipment, renovation, and development
- Poor social atmosphere
- Inadequate organization of probation activities
- Underutilized opportunities for the implementation of alternative forms of punishment

I have to emphasize that the last two points are not within the ability of the prison administration or the Ministry of Justice, but of the Ministry of Labour, Family and Social Affairs. Alternative penalties are implemented directly by social work centers and there are no serious debates in either of both ministries regarding the establishment of an independent probation service.

In my opinion, the biggest challenge is to find out how to improve the social atmosphere, especially in those areas of the correctional system that we can influence. The fact remains that spatial, personnel, and material problems cannot be solved overnight, because these are systemic problems beyond the capacity of the prison administration, and can be, according to the real situation in the country, only gradually improved. I believe that the construction of new, additional prisons is not necessary and that it would be possible to eliminate the problem of prison overcrowding with the increased use of alternative and cheaper forms of punishment and with the increased use of probation (Šugman Stubbs and Ambrož, 2012).

Theory and Practice

Q: In your view, what should be the relationship between theory and practice? What can practitioners learn from studying and applying theories; and what can those who create theories of punishment gain from practitioners?

A: To ensure quality development, it is necessary to achieve a good mix between theory and practice, which is not yet present in Slovenia, where the situation is even worse than in the past years. It is difficult to say what the reasons are for this. On one hand, there are very few theorists, who would be interested in prisons, and on the other hand, the needs of the prison system are very different from the topics of theorists, so it is difficult to find a common language. One of the best applicable research studies was carried out by Brinc (1994), which closely examined the spatial possibilities of the prison system and recommended the use of standards in our system while taking into account international recommendations and standards. Based on his findings and recommendations, new spatial standards and the calculated capacity of prisons have been adopted and are still in use today.

This year, we will repeat the study on the social atmosphere in prisons, which has been carried out every 5 years since the 1980s using the Moos social climate scale (http://srmo.sagepub.com/view/encyclopedia-of-measurement-and-statistics/n418.xml). In my opinion, each bit of research is a good basis for straightforward discussions on relationships, problems, and general conditions in individual prisons and in the system as a whole; so as the prison governor I intend to make even better use of it than in the past, when certain directors did not even show it to their colleagues, which actually makes sense, since some findings pointed out that the management was not the most appropriate.

I see a benefit in the collaboration with various faculties, enabling researchers and especially graduate students to carry out research in prisons. Slovenian penological research has a long tradition as researchers from the Institute of Criminology at the Faculty of Law, University of Ljubljana and the Faculty of Criminal Justice and Security, University of Maribor have conducted numerous research projects on prisons, prisoners, and prison staff. A good example of such collaboration is a special issue of *The Prison Journal* on the Slovenian prison system and execution of penal sanctions (Meško et al., 2011) where the reader can learn about the state of affairs of prisons and punishment in Slovenia. The main characteristic of this publication is a variety of joint papers of researchers and prison professionals.

Evidence-Based Corrections

Q: Do you feel that it is best to use evidence-based practices (or "what works") or that this focus is not important?

A: I can say that Slovenian authorities mainly use those programs that are prepared on the basis of past experience and in collaboration with external experts. I believe that it is good to operate on the basis of past experience and implement programs that prove effective. One such example is our communication model, which is unique and has not been observed in any other country. The interesting part is that it is not normatively defined and binding, nor has it ever been, but nevertheless, it survived for decades and we do not intend to replace it. It is about group work and the functioning of small groups and the prison (department) community. Each has their own group, some even two, which they meet every week. Meetings are usually not on the agenda, they are intended for various issues, and the focus is on direct communication, social learning, and information transmission. From once a week to once a month, depending on individual prisons, prison communities, and in major institutions also department communities, meet separately in small groups, where in addition to employees who work directly with prisoners the management is also present. These forms of work are very good, because many misunderstandings and conflicts can be solved there, the circulation of misinformation can be prevented, and, in particular, appropriate relationships and trust can be achieved in this way.

Transnational Relations

Q: How have you been affected by the following in your organization's work by developments outside the country (human rights demands, universal codes of ethics, practical interactions with corrections officials from other countries, personal experiences outside the country, programs developed by other countries, new sentencing laws, political strife or war in your or neighboring countries)?

A: The growing links between European countries, greater openness in cooperation, and the transfer of effective practices all contribute to the development of the prison system. We can learn a lot from each other, provided that we can take into account and respect each other's differences and uniqueness. In the absence of scientific, theoretical research in Slovenia, we intensively monitor such research in other European countries. We also monitor other developments, the implementation of programs, good and bad experience in other prison systems, and compare and study what to imitate, which mistakes should not be repeated, and so on. Having such information means that we are aware of where we are and in which direction we should proceed. Past experience has shown that international cooperation can be very useful but in the present time characterized with austerity measures of the Slovenian government brought to discontinuation of international cooperation of practitioners in the field execution of penal sanctions.

General Assessments

Q: Are you basically satisfied or dissatisfied with developments in the field of corrections?

A: Most attention is given to prisons when certain excesses happen, such as escapes, fights, drug intakes, or suicides, where relatives attribute the reasons for this to the prison management and report it to the media. When such events occur, we are always on the front pages of newspapers and daily news, explaining that prisons do not have magic wands which would resolve recidivism, heal drug addictions, and remove all those personal and relational imperfections that individuals acquire through family and school education on the way to adulthood. On the other hand, the public understands positive developments within prisons as self-evident and does not pay special attention to this topic.

Furthermore, a large part of the public believes that only those who steal a little are imprisoned, while those who steal a lot never come to prison at all. Preparing for release is worse than it was a few years ago. In order to improve the situation, we will need closer and more coordinated cooperation with various external institutions. An offender is on their own after release, both in terms of providing material support and in terms of psychological support and counseling, which inevitably means that many people quickly return back to prison. To improve this situation, we would have to clarify the role of individual institutions and establish a link between them, already at the time when the offender is in prison. Every offender would have to get an external consultant, if they needed and wanted one. The Center for Social Work should continue the activities that have been jointly agreed on at the time of serving the sentence. We would have to improve the possibilities of obtaining employment and housing.

The alternative forms of punishment are seldom carried out and there are many opportunities for improvement. If I had the power and the opportunity, I would mainly increase the work for the benefit of the community, which can replace a prison sentence of up to 2 years. I am sure that in doing that, we could reduce the number of offenders by at least one-third without consequences, reduce the costs, and do something useful. I would rather send all drug addicts who got into crime due to their addiction, and have the motivation to change, to a treatment program in an appropriate external institution than to prison. Imprisonment should actually be the last choice. I would introduce the possibility of electronic surveillance, not in the areas where it has not been used until now, but rather as an alternative to detention and shorter prison sentences. I am also a supporter of various programs for rehabilitation (for example, for the perpetrators of crimes in traffic, etc.).

Today, there is practically no one to control the offenders at the time of parole. Nobody is responsible for violations of previously set arrangements and obligations at the time of parole, which were written in the personal plan of an offender, and nobody can prevent them. I would change this in a way that would offer the offender more opportunities for parole release and create mechanisms to require them back to serve their sentences if they breach their agreed upon requirements. I think this would be better for everyone, including the offenders.

I believe that the development of the prison system in the next few years will change in the direction I have indicated. Extending prison sentences for individual offenses and the tightening of penal policy are not the right solutions and perspectives. I believe that at this moment it would be necessary to provide funds for the replacement construction of the prison in Ljubljana, where overcrowding is the greatest, provide at least 50 new vacancies, and increase the funding to ensure the smooth functioning of the prison system. There is another, faster and cheaper way to improve the situation in prisons. We should opt for a partial amnesty, and reduce the number of offenders and the overburdening of employees, which would certainly contribute to a better social climate. Prison conditions would improve, and the security in the country would certainly not worsen. However, since amnesty is a political and not a professional measure, I will leave it to the politicians to ponder this.

Conclusion

The Slovenian prison system found itself in times of change. After 1991, when Slovenia became an independent country, new challenges appeared. From 1996, the prison population increased significantly. Slovenia adopted international recommendations regarding the quality of treatment and life in prisons and implemented them as much as possible. Changes in legislation also incorporated international and especially European requirements regarding the treatment of prisoners. The economic crisis in Europe and consequently in Slovenia brought new challenges in the public sector, and especially in crime control institutions, including problems with staffing, increased prison population, and recently overcrowded prisons. Slovenia is also known for not having a parole/probation service, which needs to be established in the near future. Nevertheless, Slovenia still has one of the smallest prison populations in the world. A special issue on the penology and execution of penal sanctions has recently been published in *The Prison Journal* (issue 2011/4; http://tpj.sagepub.com/content/91/4.toc), where readers can learn about the developments in this field in the last two decades.

Glossary

Faculty of Criminal Justice and Security, University of Maribor, Slovenia: www.fvv.uni-mb.si/en.

Institute of Criminology at the Faculty of Law in Ljubljana, Slovenia: http://www.inst-krim.si/index.php?id=1&L=1).

SPACE 1, Prisons and Community Sanctions and Measures: http://www.coe.int/t/dghl/standardsetting/prisons/space_1_en.asp.

Ramon Parés, Former Director of the Catalan Prison System, Spain

5

JOSÉ CID AND MARÍA CONTRERAS

Contents

Overview

In order to describe the Spanish correctional system, we will focus on five aspects: the constitutional rights of people who are accused of having committed a criminal offense, the main features of the criminal code, the use of noncustodial sanctions, the characteristics of the prison system, and the trends in incarceration rates.

Regarding constitutional rights, it should be underlined that Spain is a constitutional state where citizens are protected against violations of their rights. The power of the police to arrest is restricted to citizens who are suspected of having committed a criminal offense. Once a citizen is arrested, a maximum time of 72 hours is permitted before he or she must appear before a judge. If the judge believes that there is enough evidence to accuse the person, bail or pretrial detention will be decided based on the risk of absconding, committing a new offense, or altering the evidence of the offense. From the moment that the police arrest the person, he or she has the right to legal assistance. The principle of the presumption of innocence prevails during the procedure and, except when the accused person admits to the offense and agrees on the sentence, the sentence should be preceded by a trial. Convictions are only accepted when the judge reaches the conclusion that the offense has been proved beyond any reasonable doubt. Once the sentence has been served, criminal records can be sealed after a period of time has passed with no new convictions. The right to vote is not affected by a conviction or by being sentenced to prison.

With respect to the main features of the Spanish Criminal Code, it should be mentioned that although the regions of Spain are autonomous, there is a single criminal code for the entire country. The main rationale of the criminal code is proportionality. Consequently, penalties are legally established according to the seriousness of the offenses. For misdemeanors, the usual penalty is a fine. Less serious crimes can result in imprisonment, but this is more prevalent for serious crimes where imprisonment is the rule. For every offense, a minimum and a maximum sentence are established. Within these boundaries or margins, the judge or the court has discretionary power to choose the penalty. The sentences for the most serious crimes are 15–20 years (murder) or 20–30 years (terrorism) imprisonment. The criminal code establishes that prison sentences of up to 2 years may be discretionally suspended or replaced by a noncustodial sanction.

In relation to noncustodial sanctions, it is worth highlighting that approximately 75% of offenders are sentenced to a noncustodial sentence: fines, community service, suspended sentence, and suspended sentence with probation. Some of these noncustodial sentences are mandatory by judges, but most of them are discretionary. The relevant factors impacting whether judges decide on prison or a noncustodial sanction are the seriousness of the crime and the criminal record of the offender. Some penologists argue that a larger number of offenders who are sentenced to prison could be dealt with using intermediate sentences if Spain had an effective system of community supervision (Cid and Larrauri, 2002).

Regarding the prison system, the main point is that the Spanish Constitution (passed in 1978) lays down the principle that "prison sentences should be devoted to rehabilitation and reintegration." According to this principle, the Prison Law (passed in 1979) is based on a progressive system that allows inmates to progress from an ordinary regime to an open regime and finally to parole. In order to progress, inmates receive an assessment of their criminogenic needs and an individual rehabilitation program is arranged. Some authors have criticized such a discretionary system as too selective. As a consequence, most inmates fail to progress and they finish their sentence without an early release measure (Cid and Tebar, 2010). It should be noted that although the penitentiary legislation is common for the whole country, the Catalan government deals with Catalan prisons.

Spanish democracy is now 35 years old (1978–2013). Surprisingly, democracy has not been coupled with a reduction in the incarceration rates. In 1978, the incarcerated population was 10,463 inmates (a proportion of 28 inmates per 100,000 inhabitants). In January 2013, there were 68,597 inmates in Spain (a proportion of 149 inmates per 1,000,000 inhabitants). In 35 years, the prison rates per inhabitants have increased more than fivefold and by now Spain is one of the countries in the European Union with the highest rates of imprisonment. The reasons to explain this growth are controversial but probably the increase in crime rates in the 1980s and the new criminal code established in 1995 that abolished good time credits are key factors (Cid, 2005; Cid and Larrauri, 2009).

Introduction

Over the last two decades, Director Parés has had a prominent career in the Catalan justice system. For this reason, we believe that in the Spanish context, he was a very good candidate to provide an inside view of the correctional system. He accepted our proposal to be interviewed when he was the general director of the prison system. However, this meeting had to be postponed because some days before the appointment, Director Parés was dismissed as a result of the change in government that followed the elections held in Catalonia on November 25, 2012. Eventually, the interview was held at the Center for Legal Studies and Specialized Training (CEJFE), where Parés was temporarily located as advisor to the Catalan minister of justice while awaiting the decision on his new position. What follows is a review of Director Parés' responses given during the interview conducted for the Trends in Corrections: Interviews with Corrections Leaders Across the Globe series. The interview has been edited, but we have faithfully respected the ideas of our interviewee.

Career

Ramon Parés (1955) studied law at the University of Barcelona. After finishing his degree, he was involved with Catholic Church–related organizations that helped disadvantaged groups, and he worked in community prevention in relation to gangs. He moved to work as a private criminal lawyer and once Spain had recovered its democracy and Catalonia its self-government, he joined the correctional system. He contributed to the creation in Catalonia of a new juvenile system based on community control by juvenile probation officers. In the early 1990s, he moved to the prison system, starting as a prison inspector, where he developed a tough regime that was not always well understood by the prison staff. After spending some years as a director of the CEJFE, a training and research center of the Catalan Justice Department, he became the director of the Catalan correctional system (2001–2003) and the director of the Catalan prison system (2010–2012). Between these two periods, he worked as a rehabilitation officer in a women's prison and lectured on prison law at the University of Barcelona.

Changes Experienced

Ramon Parés has extensive experience in the correctional system. He started as a street worker in the second half of the 1970s, just as the transition to democracy in Spain was beginning, and during this time he held different positions in the correctional system. We ask his opinion of the principal changes that have occurred in the Spanish correctional system over the last 35 years of democracy.

Today, many people who work for the correctional system have not fully experienced change, but for those who have been fortunate enough to live through the entire shift to democracy, the changes have been spectacular: in terms of the rights of inmates and prison workers, and the quality of the work done by prison personnel and in resources.

First, in relation to the inmates' rights, it is clear that the Spanish Constitution and the Prison Law were a turning point. Before the constitution, there were no rights for free citizens and of course none for inmates. Given the lack of prisoners' rights, there was impunity, abuse, and uncertainty. Inmates were serving their sentences without knowing when they would be released or which activities they could do in prison. After the constitution, not only were the rights of inmates guaranteed by law but also the rights of prison staff.

Second, in terms of quality, a new professional model was created in the prison service. It was based on the division of two functions: on the one hand, we have prison guards, who are responsible of keeping order, but who must also be aware of the personal circumstances of inmates; on the other hand, we have rehabilitation officers, including different bodies: psychologists, teachers, lawyers, educators, and social workers. It is true that maybe it was a mistake to create too many specialties and it would have been better to have a single rehabilitation body.

Finally, economic resources are a key issue. The last budget of the Catalan prison system was over 300 million euros. It should be noticed that Catalonia devotes an important part of its resources to prison. However, in recent years there have been small reductions in the budget.

After having lived through these 35 years, we ask Mr. Parés to talk about the most positive aspects of the system.

One of the positive aspects of our correctional system is the treatment programs available for offenders with specific needs, like sex offenders (SAC) and violent offenders (DEVI), but I would not make an assessment because I don't have enough data on effectiveness. One problem with these programs is that although in theory they are voluntary, in practice inmates can only get leave and early release if they complete the program. We should ask whether doing the program is a guarantee of rehabilitation. Even the most psychopathic prisoner will try to convince rehabilitation officers that he has changed, but he possibly will relapse after release. Another positive aspect is education programs.

Probably the most relevant strength of our system is our prison staff. Most of our personnel are really good and this is very important because it is essential to have highly trained and motivated employees. Nevertheless, we should have trained prison staff in a more proper way.

We ask Mr. Parés what aspects of prison do inmates value as the best ones or see as most improved?

Besides conjugal visits, young inmates especially value the opportunities for physical activity and sport. Poor inmates appreciate the opportunity to work in prison because they can earn about 200 euros per month. This amount may seem small, but it is crucial for inmates in order to buy goods not covered by the state, like tobacco, coffee, or coke, and prevent them from begging or stealing. Food is also highly appreciated. Finally, programs addressing addiction issues, particularly the therapeutic communities inside prisons, are well regarded by inmates.

In relation to the weakest points of the correctional system, we ask our interviewee to discuss the aspects that have declined and should be reformed.

First of all, we need a model of professional career. A prison officer who starts from the bottom should know that time in the service, positive assessment by their supervisors, and training should allow for promotion to senior positions, such as head of unit, prison director, and, why not, general director of the prison system. Currently, we have trouble because lots of prison staff are not permanent, so they cannot access command positions.

The second problem I foresee is related to inmates with specific needs: inmates with psychiatric disorders and the elderly population. There are an increasing number of people coming into prison with psychiatric disorders, especially those with drugs addictions, and the number of psychiatric units is scarce. On the other hand, the elderly population will grow. For these inmates, work or treatment programs are not real options, and what should be promoted, according to international standards, is an open regime and parole. It should be underlined that the recidivism risk of the elderly population is very low.

Correctional Philosophy

Since Catalonia manages its prisons within a legal framework common to all Spain, we ask Ramon Parés about the Catalan prison system and the aim of prison.

Probably the main difference between the two systems (Catalonia compared with the larger Spanish system) is that Catalonia has more rehabilitation officers than the rest of Spain. This is important because the more rehabilitation officers you have, the more time you may devote to prepare the early release of inmates. That's why the ratio of inmates serving their sentence in an open regime is higher in Catalonia than in the rest of Spain. Probably in Catalonia we take more risks than in the whole of Spain.

According to the rehabilitative aim of the correctional system, inmates should be reintegrated into society in a gradual way, starting with leave. But this is a risk because the techniques we apply to assess inmates are not mathematics and you can make mistakes. One inmate may "shit" the rehabilitation officers, the reports may be inaccurate, or simply one released inmate may be involved in an unforeseen situation that triggers his violent behavior. But if you don't risk, you can't give leave.

Of course we take very much into account the risk posed by the inmate before deciding on his release. In the case of female inmates, we tend to grant a higher percentage of leave and early release because women are not normally convicted of violent offenses and their risk of reoffending is smaller than that of males. But with some kind of offenders, we do not assume risks and they serve the entire sentence inside prison. For example, in cases of recidivist sexual or violent offenders, I have to admit that I support a tough position. Except in the case when I have a unanimously positive report from the rehabilitation board of the prison, I am not going to start the process of early release and the person will be imprisoned until the expiration of the sentence, even if I feel a lot of pressure from the loving families of the inmates.

Problems and Successes Experienced: Noncustodial Sanction Issues

So far, we have talked about prisons, but the Spanish correctional system has other sentences for those who commit a crime. These sanctions include fines, community service, and suspended prison sentences. We ask Mr. Parés for his assessment of these noncustodial sentences.

The whole system of noncustodial sanctions is very badly organized in Spain. In 1995, when the current penal code was approved, it was the right time to have it done well, but the government of the day, the Socialist Party, was very frightened and didn't do much when it came to noncustodial sanctions. Community service orders didn't help to reduce the incarceration rate because they were only available for misdemeanors. Weekend arrest was very badly implemented and the government decided to eliminate this sentence a few years later. One of the novelties of the new criminal code was the possibility to sentence the offender to probation (suspended prison sentence with probation), but judges have been reluctant to use this new sanction because they don't benefit from a probation officer who would write a presentence report. The 1995 Criminal Code was supposed to be a criminal code of a new democratic era, in which noncustodial sanctions play an important role, but it was not.

I am of the opinion that lacking a good system of noncustodial sanctions, the real alternative to incarceration is an open regime in prison. Currently, the law requires that before a prisoner is allocated to an open institution, he should serve some time in prison. But before I left the prison system, I was working on a project aimed at allowing persons who are convicted of short prison sentences to be sent directly to an open institution. I think this is a good idea because you save money and prevent the person from losing his job as a consequence of going to prison.

But I wish to insist that the real place for imposing front-end alternatives to incarceration is not the prison system but the judiciary. What we should have is a good system of probation that deals with suspended prison sentences of up to 3 or 4 years.

Problems and Successes: The Economic Crisis

Since 2008, Spain has suffered the consequences of the economic crisis. The building industry has collapsed, the unemployment rate has reached 25% of the labor force, the state has been forced to make a major fiscal adjustment to reduce the deficit, and all budgets, including the correctional system, have been reduced. The crisis issue is very present in the dialogue that we have with Mr. Parés.

Before the economic crisis, we probably spent too much, especially with the construction of new prisons; maybe we have built more than necessary. In Catalonia, the prison system has a debt of 2258 million euros that must be paid before 2042. This is the debt for five prisons we have built in previous years. Two of these prisons, with a capacity for 1000 inmates each, are empty and may not be able to open due to the lack of resources.

A second dimension refers to the need to make cuts in the budget of the correctional system. Mr. Parés discusses the budget cuts below.

In 2011, the budget of the Catalan prison system was about 300 million euros. In 2012, we were forced to save 20 million. In order to achieve this reduction in the budget, we had to eliminate some snacks for inmates, abolish newspapers in prisons, and negotiate prices with private companies hired by the prison system. We have also reduced the expenses in personnel because substitutions are not covered and fewer people are using medical leave to keep wage supplements.

The economic crisis also seems to have had an impact on the establishment of new policies to reduce the prison population. The prison population in Spain has decreased by approximately 10% between 2010 and 2012. This reduction, although not as significant, has also been observed in Catalonia and we ask Mr. Parés about the causes.

In Catalonia, about 40%–50% of the prison population is composed of foreign citizens. We thought that we needed new policies to confront this reality and we passed a new penitentiary rule (Rule 1/2011 on Foreigners in Catalan Prisons).

We considered that if our correctional system states that we must work toward rehabilitation, and these people cannot be reintegrated because they are not legal citizens and don't have a family in the country, then we have to look for a different policy. The new policy consists of informing those inmates that they can replace part of their sentence by being deported to their own countries.

Thanks to the new rule, in 2 years we have reduced the prison population by nearly 500 inmates, and voluntarily.* The project I had before leaving the

* The prison population in Catalonia at the time of this interview was about 10,000 inmates.

prison system was to establish mandatory deportation, not conditioned on the consent of the prisoner.

Finally, Ramon Parés talks about other dimensions of the economic crisis such as the impact on recidivism rates.

These days, we are in the midst of an economic debate, and the main theme is now about efficiency, and therefore, recidivism. We need to justify to society that the cost of the system is justifiable in terms of recidivism. As I said before, in Catalonia we have invested a lot in rehabilitation (with good provision of rehabilitation officers) and the rates of recidivism are good. According to the latest study from the CEJFE,* the reincarceration rate is 40%, below the European mean in similar 5-year longitudinal studies.

However, I think if you do a new study now, the recidivism rate would be higher. The current social situation has a particular impact on the reentry process of inmates. We are experiencing new situations like people resigning from an open regime because they can't find a job, people returning prematurely to the open centers to have dinner. Furthermore, resources to NGOs who deal with the aftercare of released inmates have been reduced. I think all of this will have a negative impact on the rate of recidivism.

Theory and Practice

We ask our interviewee to assess the relationship between theory and practice. We start by asking if the research done by universities is of use to the correctional system.

I think that universities are not interested in the subject of prisons; at least I am not aware if they are. But I think that in the past there was more interest in the topic of prisons: you were called to participate in debates about many relevant topics, like the age of criminal responsibility or about noncustodial sanctions, even students' unions were organizing debates on prisons, and I don't see this anymore.

Now the only thing that interests the media about prisons is cases of violence or riots. Maybe universities continue to be concerned with relevant issues but I'm not aware of it. In any case, we are fortunate in Catalonia to have the CEJFE, which is the institution that transfers the relevant knowledge to the correctional system.

* Parés is referring to Capdevila and Ferrer (2009).

Evidence-Based Practice

We ask our interviewee about evidence-based practice, the idea of applying models of rehabilitation that work and whether this principle inspires current practice.

No, evidence-based practice has not arrived here. The principle that inspires practice is that of costs. For example, now the correctional system is very interested in alternatives to incarceration because the costs of imprisoning offenders are too high. I think that in Europe there will be a move in favor of less-expensive alternatives because the cost of prisons is unaffordable.

What are the grounds for the new policies of the correctional system?

We have the program *Compartim* (sharing knowledge) developed by the CEJFE, which consists of working groups formed by professionals from the same discipline. Although they are open to everyone, only few people are involved.

When I was working as a rehabilitation officer in prison, we wrote a document about classification. The Prison Law states that to classify a prisoner in an ordinary or an open regime, you must consider items such as the personal trajectory, the criminal career, and the duration of the sentence, but it doesn't give you specific indications. In this document, we established that some factors—like voluntary admission to prison, good conduct inside prison, or taking responsibility for the offense—should be valued when recommending that the person be assigned to an open institution. These criteria for classification were based on our experience. Surely the document should have been done by the director of the prison system, but it was done by us.

Transnational Relations

Regarding transnational relations and Catalan prisons, the interviewee makes a positive statement and tells us about the European Committee for the Prevention of Torture (CPT), leading us to ask about the fulfillment of the standards of humanity laid down by legislation, case law of the European Court of Human Rights, and the recommendations of the Council of Europe and the European Union.

Evidence of good practice comes from the European CPT. After their visits, they report a positive atmosphere in Spanish prisons, because there is always a lot of activity, sports, and a lot of female staff. In fact, the conditions have to be good because inmates from other states of the European Union don't want to return to their countries to serve their sentence. The reasons I think they prefer to stay here are the personal attention, the quality of the food, the conjugal visits, and the activities. I would say that prisons in other European countries are in general harsher or the environment is not as good.

The European CPT only criticizes the restraint system we apply to an individual in temporary solitary confinement who is out of control. Before we used handcuffs, but we realized that they hurt so now we use psychiatric retaining straps. They say the inmate must be in a room adapted for individuals with psychiatric conditions. However, Spanish law and the judges allow it, and I don't think you need to change a model that works.

One problematic situation we face is related to some old prisons. In these places, some dreadful situations occur at nighttime when inmates must enter their cells. In the male prison of Barcelona, the cells are too small for the five inmates usually allocated and the prison of Tarragona has cells with bunk beds four high. In any case, the cells are only for sleeping.

Apart from that, human rights are well respected in Catalan prisons. Use of violence by prison guards is rare and is only used for security reasons. Because the Catalan prison system is very open to visitors, like volunteers and lawyers, any abuse done by prison guards will be noticed and the general director of the prison system will be immediately aware of it. Nor would the prison staff tolerate the commission of abuses.

Continuing with human rights compliance, we ask whether internal or international controls may be relevant to explain the changes experienced by the correctional system in Spain and particularly in Catalonia.

We consider the recommendations of the CPT, the ombudsman, and the prison judge, but we only take into account those that are feasible and don't put security at risk. For example, the ombudsman used to complain about the price of goods, criticizing that they are more expensive in prisons than in supermarkets, but we can't compete with large stores because they buy much more product than we do.

General Assessment

In the last part of the interview, we want to know the personal view and assessment of Parés about reforms that may improve the Spanish correctional system.

On the one hand, in order to promote the use of alternatives to incarceration, I would like the sentencing judge to decide on the sentence with the help of a presentence report. The judge needs some advice to decide, among several options, which is the appropriate sentence for an offender.

The preliminary report should inform whether this person has a problem with alcoholism, whether he has a job, and his financial situation. All this information would be useful, for example, to avoid imposing a fine on an offender with no financial means.

Secondly, we should emphasize policies aimed at reducing the prison population. Spain cannot afford to have a prison population that is the second largest in the European Union (Figure 5.1). We know that the big increase in the prison population is due not only because our system is harsh—in fact, the average length of sentences is above the European ones—but also because of the increasing number of foreigners entering prison. The immigration issue has not been managed properly, neither in general nor inside the correctional system. Policies to reduce the prison population adopted by the prison system would allow us to redirect some rehabilitation officers to advise judges and promote front-end alternatives to incarceration.

Then, I would say it is important to continue working in a progressive system. We must try to increase the rate of sentenced inmates placed in an open institution, which is currently around 25%. I know it is difficult now, because many inmates are foreigners and we cannot place them in an open institution, others are drug abusers, others have very long sentences. Moreover, parole should be promoted. It seems ridiculous that in Catalonia, adding inmates and parolees, only 8% are on parole. An open regime and parole should be extended not only because it is the policy recommended by the Council of Europe but also for the reason that we save a lot of money: one person in an open institution costs less than in a closed institution, and one person on parole costs less than in an open institution.

Finally, I would back reform to include a good system of probation for adults. Now, the real alternative to incarceration is the open regime, but if we had a fair system of probation, judges could sentence some offenders to community control without the need to have had a previous stay in the prison system.

Conclusions

We consider that the following four themes are the most relevant in the interview.

Good and Not Only Bad Practices

In Spain, scholars who have written about prison have paid more attention to bad practices than to good practices (Cid, 2005; González, 2012). The interview, without disregarding bad practices (such as cases of prisons with overcrowded cells), is probably more focused on underlining good practices. There are a lot of examples in the interview: the good environment of Spanish prisons, the good qualities of the prison officers, the work in prison that allows a poor prisoner to provide for some goods, visits by volunteers to prison who operate as a control over the system, and the use of open prisons as an intermediate sanction for persons who do not need to be incarcerated.

Of course, some of the claims of the interviewee may be controversial and any disagreement is very much based on the lack of good research in some areas, for example, the conditions of imprisonment from the viewpoint of inmates. But we think it merits highlighting that knowledge of the correctional system may not only come from emphasizing the bad things but also remarking on good practices, as theorists of appreciative practices have proposed (Liebling et al., 2011).

Crisis, Cost of Corrections, and Decarceration

Some Spanish scholars have remarked on an important difference between Spain and some Anglo-Saxon countries in the debate on alternatives to prison. The rationale of reducing the cost of prison, which seems to explain the emergence of new alternatives to prison in the last century in some European countries such as England and Wales (Young, 1979), has rarely been used in Spain.

The interview with Parés shows that things have changed. It seems very clear that the economic crisis of 2008 has made the theme of cost central in the field of corrections too. Most of the policies backed by the interviewee, such as the increase in the use of alternative sanctions, the greater use of open prisons and parole, and the use of deportation for irregular migrants are overtly linked to the idea of saving money. Also, the criticism of the interviewee to the big expenditure in building new prisons in the past years has only emerged in the context of the economic crisis.

Although we hope that this economic crisis may be overcome in the medium term, we suggest that the cultural change of considering cost as a relevant point in the discussions between prisons and alternatives to prison will last. Of course, cost is only one aspect to be considered when discussing corrections, but we believe that it should not be disregarded.

Rehabilitation as a Rationale

According to some scholars, Spain has also suffered the evolution described by Garland (2001) from welfarist penal policies to incapacitative ones (Diez Ripollés, 2004). Although this thesis may be sustained, it seems from the interview that inside the correctional system rehabilitation continues to be the main rationale of action.

We think our interviewee has made a solid defense for rehabilitation as a rationale for punishment. When discussing the prediction of recidivism, Parés claims that in every case of early release a risk is taken and in some cases persons will fail, but this failure is highly compensated for by the number of people that succeed in their rehabilitation.

Critics of the discretionary models of early release state that these models tend to select the best candidates for release and max out the most risky offenders who will be released with no supervision in the community. Although the interviewee does not directly confront this point, he seems to be aware of the problem when he favors a policy of increasing the number of inmates who get parole.

Theory and Practice

As academics, we remain highly surprised and a little disappointed by the opinion of the interviewee on the relation of theory and practice. Basically, our interviewee considered that the research that universities may do on corrections was irrelevant for persons working in the correctional system.

Of course, many of the programs that the interviewee considered good practice—such as the cognitive programs for sexual and violent offenders—have been included in the correctional service after being evaluated as effective in other countries and in Spain. But, beyond that, the opinion of the interviewee is that university research and correctional practices are very distantly related and that the new policies of the correctional system (like the criteria for classification) are decided without taking research into consideration.

Belonging to a research group that has been doing research on the correctional system for the past 15 years, there are two critical reflections

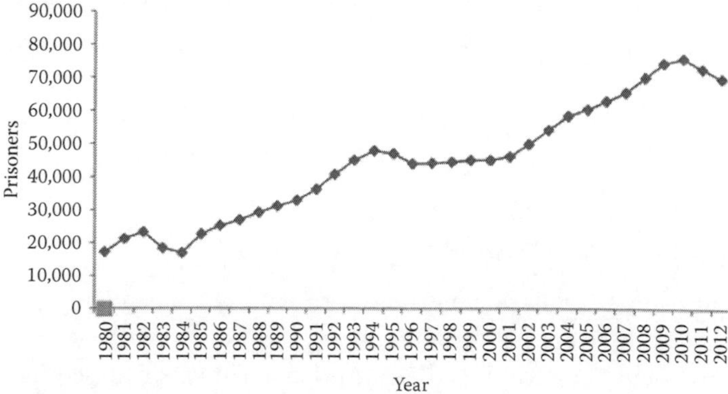

Figure 5.1 Number of inmates held in prison.

to be made: on the one hand, probably the research done by university scholars has not always had direct relevance for correctional authorities and, on the other hand, perhaps researchers do not always pay enough attention to the aim of transferring knowledge to correctional leaders.

Acknowledgments

For the task of editing, we wish to thank Aina Ibañez (who made a revision of the Catalan version of the interview with Mr. Parés) and Eugenia Albani (who made a first version in English of the interview). Beatriz Tébar has made useful comments to the introduction and conclusion. The project has benefited from funds provided by the Catalan government (AGAUR) to the research group: Grup de Recerca Criminologia Aplicada a la Penologia, 2009-SGR-01117.

Glossary

Center for Specialized Studies and Training (CEJFE): An autonomous organization from the Catalan Department of Justice, established in 1990 to develop specialized training and research in criminology, penology, the judiciary, and Catalan civil law.

***Compartim* (sharing knowledge):** A program of the Catalan Department of Justice managed by the CEJFE that promotes learning through the exchange of experiences and best practices. Since it was launched, more than 800 people have participated. The knowledge that is produced is collected and issued in papers, protocols, manuals, templates, working papers, and procedures. More information about the program can be found on the official website of the Catalan Department of Justice: http://web.gencat.cat/ca/inici/.

European Committee for the Prevention of Torture and Inhuman or Degrading Treatment or Punishment (CPT): An institution that belongs to the Council of Europe and has the aim of preventing ill-treatment of persons deprived of their liberty in Europe. The CPT organizes visits to places of detention to assess how persons deprived of their liberty are treated. After each visit, the CPT sends a detailed report to the state concerned, including findings, recommendations, and comments, and also requests a detailed response to the issues raised in its report. http://www.cpt.coe.int/en/about.htm.

penitentiary degrees: According to the Prison Law, the regime of life in prison is determined by a classification system based on four grades (first, second, third, and fourth). The initial classification can be done at any level, except the fourth, which is parole. Progression or regression depends on the individual's development during the period of his or her sentence. The first degree is exceptional, and safety control measures are more restrictive (closed regime). The second degree is for those who attend normal living circumstances (ordinary regime). The third degree is applied to inmates who are qualified to work outside prison (open regime).

Prison Law (Ley Orgánica 1/1979, de 26 de septiembre, General Penitenciaria): Approved in 1979, the Prison Law establishes the rights and duties of inmates, the inmate's classification system, and the competent authorities. The law can be accessed at http://www.boe.es/buscar/act.php?id=BOE-A-1979-23708 (accessed November 11, 2013).

prison judge: A special judge who has the duty to control the prison administration. This judge decides on complaints from inmates and appeals on disciplinary sanctions and on classification. He/she also has the power to approve leave and parole.

Rule 1/2011 on Foreigners in the Catalan Correctional System: The rule's objective is to optimize the social integration of the foreign prison population. It offers two possibilities: integration in Catalonia or return to the country of origin. This second option mainly affects those who have no possibility of obtaining permission to legally reside and work in Spain. http://www.derechopenitenciario.com/comun/fichero.asp?id=2212 (accessed November 11, 2013).

Spanish Constitution: The constitution was ratified by referendum on December 6, 1978. It led to the culmination of the so-called Spanish transition that took place after the death of Dictator Franco (1975). It established a democratic state under a parliamentary monarchy.

Walter Troxler, Head of the Unit for the Execution of Sentences and Measures, Federal Office of Justice, Switzerland

6

NATALIA DELGRANDE AND
CLAUDIA CAMPISTOL

Contents

Overview

Switzerland is a federal state that includes 26 cantons. Each canton has its own constitution, executive, parliament, and courts. This federal organization allows the cantons a large degree of independency. Switzerland has four national languages: German, French, Italian, and Romansh. The linguistic diversity, the complexity of legal traditions, and the large prerogatives that are managed at the cantonal level represent significant peculiarities of the Swiss federal system.

In order to emphasize the unity of the criminal justice system in the described state diversity, it should be highlighted that since 1942, Switzerland has had a unified criminal code. With small adjustments, this criminal code lasted until the early 2000s. A new revised criminal code (SCC-CH) was adopted in 2002 and entered into force on January 1, 2007. Compared with the previous criminal code, the new criminal code provides two main categories of sanctions: sentences and measures. The category of penal measures is an important element in the general development of the Swiss system of sentencing. Measures differ from sentences in their duration, as they are not based on the gravity of the offense, but on their intended effect. Therefore, measures are intended to last as long as necessary to avert the risk of reoffending and are only used when the prospects for success are good (art. 56 SCC-CH).

Article 123 of the federal constitution (FC) states that the legislation in the field of criminal law and the law of criminal procedure falls within the competence and responsibility of the federal government. However, the execution of sentences is the responsibility of the cantons unless the law provides otherwise. Thus, cantons perform the duties of organizing and managing institutions that supervise persons sentenced to penal sanctions or measures. Each of the 26 cantons decides on the orientation to be adopted in the execution of custodial and noncustodial sentences as well.

The federal legal background leads the frames of the cantonal competencies. Accordingly, the cantons are competent in the following matters: the assessment of the dangerousness of prisoners, the categorization of prisoners, programs of rehabilitation and social reintegration, and any other activity related to practical aspects of sentences. However, three concordats supervise and evaluate the competences of the local practices. Moreover, local politicians and practitioners look for the best practices in the field of assessment and the management of dangerous offenders. As a consequence, in 2013, the National Conference of Directors of Cantonal Departments of Justice and Police led to an initiative to create a National Center of Competences. All these activities tend to equilibrate the balance between the federal legal framework and the cantonal diversity and specificity in the field of corrections and noncustodial forms of punishment.

In the same perspective, the federal body that seeks the common view in the field of penal policies is the unit that implements the Federal Contributions to the Execution of Sentences and Measures Act (*Bundesgesetz über die Leistungen des Bundes für Straf- und Massnahmenvollzug*). The head of the Unit of Execution of Sentences and Measures (UESM) at the Federal Department of Justice and Police is Mr. Walter Troxler. His office provides the grants and subsidies for the construction, renovation, and expansion of facilities in which adults, young adults, children, and juveniles can serve their sanctions. The UESM defines the quality standards in educational programs and training for juvenile and adult offenders.

Furthermore, the unit supports the Swiss Prison Staff Training Center, which is the main vocational training center for the whole of Switzerland that certifies law enforcement officers. All members (junior and senior) of staff working in custodial and noncustodial bodies across Switzerland are required to be certified by this center.

Finally, this office publishes a regular bulletin containing information on its particular field of operation. This newsletter represents a platform of exchange for practitioners from different parts of the criminal justice system as well as for researchers from each linguistic part of the country.

Introduction

Walter Troxler graduated in education sciences from the University of Fribourg, Switzerland. During his studies between 1970 and 1976, he was part of a discussion group on the criminal justice system and—more particularly—on corrections. During that time, Switzerland was going through an important change, promoting the separation of the sentences applied to juvenile offenders and reforms inside correctional institutions. An important event that had an influence on Mr. Troxler's decision to pursue a new career was a visit he made to the *Henri van der Hoeven Kliniek* in Utrecht, the Netherlands, which was at that time one of the most advanced forensic psychiatric institutes for high-risk criminals. It was then that he decided to merge his two main focuses of interest and to make a career of educational work inside the correctional field.

Career

His first working experience in corrections was as an educator in a low-security penitentiary center. He remembers that—at that time—the facilities were rather old-fashioned, wooden constructions with small-sized cells (4 m^2). It was a fruitful experience because he was appointed to lead a project to integrate the therapy treatments for inmates with special needs. Additionally, he was also involved in the construction of a new building for this prison. He considers that at that period a really valuable network started to form with other colleagues from the psychology and social work fields throughout Switzerland. Together with this group of colleagues, he created an association that included experts from different prisons from the cantons of Zurich, Neuchatel, Geneva, and Ticino. They organized meetings where different experts were invited and interesting outcomes were discussed. Despite Mr. Troxler's belief that he would work in the corrections for no longer than 5 years, he ended up with 12 years field experience.

Later, he had the determination to move into a more educational role and he became the director of a detention center for juvenile offenders in the canton of Lucerne. The center hosted about 40–48 youths, who were sentenced by both criminal and civil justice courts. These two forms of sentences are still usual practices in Switzerland.

During the same period, he completed specialized studies in systemic family therapy, and started to implement this model of intervention in the juvenile institution. The systemic-oriented model was used during sessions and meetings organized with juveniles and their families. At this time, the systemic technical methodology (specially arranged room, observation window, video-recorded sessions, etc.) started to be used inside correctional facilities. Staff members were trained in the systemic approach and they were involved in the interventions. Mr. Troxler remembers that the institution conceived all the interventions and activities from a group-oriented model. Recalling his experience, he describes himself as a director who tried to look for the best conditions for his staff members and to have constant and direct contact with educators and other staff while keeping the right distance with inmates.

Mr. Troxler was involved in several focus groups that worked on different topics related to juvenile delinquency at the national level. This engagement allowed him to participate in a network of directors from many institutions for juvenile offenders throughout Switzerland. He also set up links with different actors across the whole Swiss correctional system and headed a sociopedagogic association for educational staff. After 12 years directing the institution, he quit the position stating, "It may have been difficult to take a position as the gap between your own nature and the one of these youngsters is getting bigger and bigger."

The next step in Mr. Troxler's career was to completely change his position, moving to a managerial position in federal administration. Regarding his wide experience in youth and adult correctional systems and considering his great knowledge on the existing differences between both systems, he considered this new position as a good opportunity to bring together the experience he had gained in the two correctional systems. Therefore, he became the head of the UESM, a position that he still holds today. He admits that this was a big step as he was mainly used to working side by side with inmates and being in contact with a lot of people, while his new administrative position was "far away from a lot of emotions, surrounded by papers, folders, and computers." This new professional challenge required "a good knowledge of the entire administrative engine." He overcame the initial difficulties and was facilitated by his extensive knowledge of the Swiss correctional system as well as by the contacts he had previously made all over the country.

Nowadays, Mr. Troxler's task is to grant subsidies so that both adult and youth institutions can offer the best conditions to professionals who work inside the criminal justice system. Even though his work is office based, he still maintains a link with the correctional institutions and visits them around 30–40 times per year.

Indeed, his job requires a close working relationship with the institutions, as one of his objectives is to provide the institutions with the support and advice they may need while developing their projects, as well as to help them to overcome crises or difficult situations. Despite the fact that the subsidies that are granted to the institutions are fixed by law, Mr. Troxler tries to have a direct and fluid communication with each institution so that he is aware in advance of their real needs. Otherwise, it may happen that "the slow Swiss bureaucracy means the problems are solved later than the reality requires." In this context, he gives the example of the time required for building or renovation works in the institutions, which are carried out every 10–20 years. Instead of waiting a long time, he maintains contact with the institutions and—if necessary—he helps them to fulfill the requirements to receive the subventions. Moreover, together with the staff of the institution, he can foresee the real necessities and help them to take the appropriate steps needed to improve the good running of their institution. This close contact also allows Mr. Troxler to be present from the beginning of new projects "to provide them with new information and ideas that can help the institution to open their eyes towards new approaches."

Changes Experienced

Since 2004, Mr. Troxler has held the position of head of the UESM and he continues the policies of evolution and development. Yet, he changed his view on how the work should be done.

> When you work inside the system, for example in a prison, you have a kind of view from bottom-up let's say. And for me it is important to have an overview, to see how each institution is doing in relation to the other institutions, and this has changed my focus.

Such global viewing is not an easy task because of the federal organization of the whole system. Each canton keeps its own direction and manages to follow it by its own means.

From a structural point of view, Mr. Troxler suggests two complementary directions that should be followed. On the one hand, he pays considerable attention to the issue of intercantonal cooperation and the way that the local penal institutions organize their joint work. On the other hand, Switzerland should remain a part of the European and international networks and therefore the Swiss authorities should correctly apply international standards and rules. "And concerning that I'm not always happy about how it works" says Troxler. He argues that the federal system is a good organization, "but sometimes if we need for example new programs or new facilities for specific groups of inmates, it is difficult to know who takes care of that. Normally, each canton is waiting to see how the problem is solved elsewhere. Moreover, once the solutions seem to be found, a discussion on local features starts. This takes a very long time." Such situations are not exceptional. At the local level, before implementing a new standard, every canton must first discuss it at the local governmental level. The cantonal parliament takes a decision on the scope of the project. Larger-scale projects require popular approval or a referendum. "There have been referendums for some projects. For example, one project in Zurich foresaw the creation of a center for Police and Justice, and this center was also to be a prison for 300 inmates. As far as I know this project is now about twelve years old and the last referendum was in 2012," explains Troxler.

In 2007, the new criminal code entered into force. In 2011, the unified criminal proceedings code replaced the 26 cantonal codes and led to the national application of the criminal justice principles. This new code contains many principles on the functioning of the whole penal system and, in particular, issues such as the length of prison stays and the contact between pretrial detainees and their lawyer. Yet, Troxler remains skeptical about the visible changes in the practice. The formal part of the organization has changed, but the decisions on the implementation of these activities are still regulated at a cantonal level and

> for the penal system it is not a big change because it is only the procedure that has changed. Each canton is still responsible to build, to reconstruct and to run each prison. So the competences are still the same, you have the legal basis on the Confederation level but the execution is up to each canton.

Certainly, there are now national standards, but there are still differences between cultures and linguistic parts of Switzerland. The same types of institutions will not operate in exactly the same way in the German- and French-speaking parts of the country. Given such intercantonal and interregional peculiarities, a unique Swiss law on the execution of sentences does not exist. The arrangement procedures and conventions between cantons (concordats) are being applied. As of today, three main concordats exist in the field of the execution of prison sentences: the concordat of central and northwestern Switzerland, the concordat of eastern Switzerland, and the concordat of Latin Switzerland (including the Italian canton of Ticino). These concordats constitute the basis for collaboration between cantons and regulate the rules applicable on transfers, conditions of detention, and activities for inmates with special needs. These conventions are regularly updated and constitute the main source of the prospective evolution of each of the three regions. Troxler is positive about the opportunities to develop these intercantonal networks but warns that, if a unique law of the execution of sentences were passed, there is the possibility of it being misused.

> I don't know in which direction the federal Parliament would go. There are too many questions about security and risks, and only risk oriented procedures cannot be good for the execution of sentences. Such a restrictive law would not be a really good law.

Personal Correctional Philosophy

Mr. Troxler states that when comparing the Swiss prison system with other European prison systems, Switzerland is placed in quite a good position. The biggest prison in Switzerland is designed to house 450 inmates; however, there is one facility in the canton of Geneva with an occupancy rate of more than 150% (the average annual rate in 2012 was more than 640 inmates per 376 officially available places). However, this situation is quite exceptional and it is not fully representative of the entire Swiss correctional system. Given this particular situation, Mr. Troxler states that communication in small-sized prisons is much easier and, therefore, he is confident that Swiss prisons should remain small. In terms of overcrowding, Mr. Troxler compares Switzerland with the Scandinavian countries, which have the lowest prison density figures in Europe. "Because we have a crowding rate of about 90–93% over all, which is high but it's not as high as in other countries. Actually many European countries have a much higher rate." Over the last 10 years, the general prison population rates in Switzerland have fluctuated between 70 and 80 prisoners per 100,000 inhabitants.

In Switzerland, inmates are housed in different facilities or units according to the security level that is required for their detention. Mr. Troxler considers that Switzerland does not have enough low security or open prisons: "I am not sure whether all the inmates in closed prisons really need to be there and if there is a real need for such a high level of security." From his point of view, it would be more useful to have some methodological guidelines for the system and decide the level of security that is required on a case by case basis. Still, persons who are required to be held in low security facilities should be detained in other types of institutions rather than high- or medium-security prisons. However, because these decisions are taken at the cantonal levels—and only a few prisons exist per canton—there are few options to hold low-risk inmates in appropriate types of facilities.

Furthermore, Mr. Troxler is also most critical of the lack of specific institutions for inmates with mental disorders. He believes that it is important to make a distinction between inmates with mental disorders and those who do not have mental disorders. Making effective distinctions ensures that those who need mental health services receive them while, at the same time, preventing malingerers and non-mentally disordered offenders from misusing this system of care. It is very likely that some of them would only need to be there for a certain period of time. He insists "that the final goal is to bring everyone back into society. This means that they have to be prepared for that by following a specific path."

Mr. Troxler expresses his concern regarding inmates who must serve long-term sentences or even lifelong detention, as nowadays the regime is the same for them as for any other inmate. He proposes that these inmates should have different conditions for their detention (e.g., in a special house, in special small units of bigger facilities). He claims that they need to be kept under a different security regime because of their high risk of recidivism.

This issue leads him to talk about another controversial topic in Switzerland, which is dealing with inmates with specific needs, such as females and elderly offenders. Traditionally, female inmates are held separately from male inmates, but there is no distinction made for elderly inmates who are held under the same regime as other inmates. Moreover, Mr. Troxler warns against the definitive qualification of dangerous offenders and stresses the need for regular reassessments to avoid the accumulation of aging inmates in standard prison facilities.

Apart from specific topics, Mr. Troxler takes an overall look at the peculiarities of the Swiss criminal justice system as whole. Thus, he points out the status of federal and cantonal judges in Switzerland and highlights that they are politically oriented. One would think that this feature and their affiliation to a political party may have an impact on their decisions, but Mr. Troxler disagrees with this belief. Rather, he thinks that the decisions that judges tend to make in regard to offender sentencing are similar, regardless of their political party affiliation. Nevertheless, the final decision is taken by the parliament. So, for Mr. Troxler this link between politics and a judicial career is not a problem, "as there are many different parties in the Parliament so there is a good balance." However, he states that sometimes it can be more problematic as there is no open access for anyone wanting to become a judge, as the only way is through parties' proposal.

Another general belief expressed by Mr. Troxler is that a positive point in the Swiss correctional system is the high level of training given to the prison staff. "Everybody working in a prison needs to follow the training at the Swiss Prison Staff Training Center in Fribourg." Mr. Troxler highlights that there is no division between the security and the educational staff. So prison officers are trained to deal with security issues as well as to put into practice social and educational skills. From Mr. Troxler's point of view,

> this is very important because it makes their job more varied and challenging as it is not only about bringing someone from one cell to the other. They also like to know how to deal, to listen and to discuss with the inmates and this doesn't exist in every European country.

On the other hand, he adopts a critical position with regard to the role of directors of prison facilities in Switzerland. First, he criticizes that they do not receive specific training to assume their positions. Then, he mentions the very strong role and responsibility assigned to them. In his opinion, it often happens that a change of prison director brings many changes in the general management of the institution. Mr. Troxler says that it is still more of an individual-dominated culture rather than an institutional one. Finally, he also points out the lack of exchanges between directors of different institutions. From Mr. Troxler's point of view, the French system seeks to implement the same correctional system in every prison while in Switzerland the situation is completely different as the size of the prisons is smaller and directors are given a wide scope for decisions and action. As an example, a Swiss director of an institution takes significant decisions such as the way in which the staff interact with the inmates, the acceptability of inmates' behavior, and the rules of intervention of the staff. This peculiarity is more visible in the corrections rather than in the probation system.

Going through the differences that exist between prison and probation, Mr. Troxler underlines the importance of bringing together the staff working in the penitentiary field and the probation staff. In his opinion, the two fields should not be separated and he stands for merged approaches. The main reason is that the probation officers should start the intervention while the inmates are still serving their prison sentence and not after their release. He believes that better results may be reached when both the prisoner and the probation officer are involved in the preparation for the prisoner's release. Additionally, this approach may make a lot of sense if one takes into account that Switzerland has shorter prison stays compared with other European countries.

In Switzerland, correctional institutions and probation agencies are linked to the canton to which they belong. At the same time, prisons and the probation service are independent from each other, but belong to the same cantonal authorities in charge of the execution of sentences.

In the past, probation agencies and prisons were not only structurally independent but they also worked separately. However, in the last 10 years, several cantons have implemented a system of working together by building offices that locate both probation and prison staff within close proximity of one another and measures that integrate all tasks in corrections. The cantons of Zurich, Lucerne, and St. Gallen, for example, already have their probation agencies integrated in their prisons, and these agencies begin their work before the inmates have finished serving their prison sentence.

In another line of ideas, Mr. Troxler stated that medical services also belong to the correctional system of the cantons. Zurich was one of the first cantons to integrate the different services and—after 10 years of successful collaboration—the penitentiary, probation, general medical, special psychiatric, and psychological services continue to work together in the same units. Many cantons in Switzerland, such as the cantons of Lucerne, Neuchatel, Valais, Solothurn, and St. Gallen, are also following the same model. In Mr. Troxler's opinion, "that is a real improvement of the organization as it allows people involved to have a direct link and a formal exchange of experience."

Successes Experienced

The UESM supervises a part of the innovative projects undertaken in Switzerland. Generally, the confederation supports all these projects only at the early stages of testing and implementation. While a pilot project shows positive results, the competence of the project's management and later development in local facilities is transferred to the cantons. The UESM evaluates the project's needs and may support up to 80% of the whole cost of a pilot project.

Mr. Troxler says that he is personally satisfied and proud of one intercantonal project that involved 64 homes for juvenile offenders in all three linguistic parts of Switzerland.

> The goal of this project was to describe the profiles of those children placed in such special homes and their difficulties, i.e. traumas, psychiatric problems, or other special background features. It was a really wide screening of the situations. Different assessment instruments were used for all children and juveniles in these institutions. That allowed a large overview of the situation.

The results of this pilot project were analyzed and compared between institutions and certain educational goals of the homes were adjusted to the relevant needs that were observed during the pilot phase of the exercise. In response to this research, Troxler pointed out that:

> At the end of the pilot-project, the assessment procedures were introduced in all these 64 institutions. These techniques were very successful. Moreover, a large amount of data was collected. Now there are some studies based on collected information in order to gain a better view on the profiles of juvenile offenders. Some of these juveniles will be followed for the next five or ten years. It is quite a unique database for Switzerland.

Troxler pointed out a very positive result at the level of the new interinstitutional collaboration. All the homes that participated in the pilot project decided to continue to develop the network. This collaboration led to the creation of a shared information technology (IT) system that allows professionals to supervise and adapt educational goals to their populations.

> It was a great experience that merged research and practice and allowed the creation and the implementation of a new instrument. I am very happy that this program did not fail and it continues with some concrete actions.

Another pilot project that was supported by the UESM was the risk-oriented execution of sentences, which was tested in the canton of Zurich. Other partners participated in this project as well (the cantons of St-Galen, Thurgau, and Lucerne). Apart from the questions related to the evaluation of the assessment instruments used across the country, the main goal now is to collect and collate the information on the risk of reoffending and the risk of dangerous offenders in the community. The methodology applied to this project is that based on the theories of risks of reoffending and criminogenic needs. At the end of the pilot phase, it is expected that a tool will be created to allow for more harmonized management of certain categories of dangerous offenders. The tool is expected to be used by professionals dealing with similar inmates in different parts of the country and the information on particular cases may be retrieved from the system to ensure fast and accurate support and care for the most problematic situations. Troxler has an optimistic vision of the future use of the tool and expresses the will to extend its use to the probation service. Moreover, the development and exchange on this platform with external partners (i.e., private institutions dealing with drug-addicted offenders) also need to be taken into consideration: "I am confident that its prospects are good. Yet, we should not forget about the limitations of such programs."

Troxler recognizes some less successful projects such as the one that started with really ambitious goals and ended with only a few of its objectives achieved.

> We spent too much money for something which showed to be less interesting than the initial goals. Normally, it works quite well and, therefore, we remain permanently involved in such pilot-projects.

Problems Experienced in Corrections

The recent concern of the majority of neoliberal Western penal systems is the risk-oriented management of dangerous offenders. Swiss correctional leaders must stay in compliance with the principles of the protection of society and those of the offender. These principles require correctional leaders to stay cognizant of the various levels of risk for different offender groups and to also place considerable importance on assessment tools that are utilized in determining offender levels of risk. Yet, the limitations of the system do not always allow the complementary management of offender risk as balanced against an offender's effective reform. In order to make the most appropriate of risk assessment approaches, several projects have led to the creation of special commissions and working groups using a cross-sectional perspective in dealing with dangerous offenders.

In Switzerland, the legislators have chosen to focus most on the dangerousness of the offender as the primary concern when crafting laws related to corrections. There is a consensus on the need to protect society from the gravest crimes, such as sexual and violent offenses. Nevertheless, compared with other countries, the Swiss penal system allows the possibility to reexamine the most problematic cases and offers rehabilitation and socialization opportunities for a large category of offenders. A large range of penal measures complete the already available penal sanctions. These measures include the treatment of mentally ill offenders and drug addicts, education and work for young adults, and special institutional placement for particularly dangerous offenders (in German: *Verwahrung*). In 2000, the new lifelong detention (in German: *Lebenslängliche Verwahrung*) for very dangerous offenders was proposed for inclusion in the penal code by a popular initiative. Following the results of a plebiscite in 2004, this measure became a rule of law. Compared with other measures, this one is the most restrictive and does not allow an offender to be released into society unless there are new discoveries related to the scientific evidence available (i.e., due to DNA or other similar forms of evidence). Further, this law also prevents the reevaluation of offenders who are classified into the most dangerous categories within our system. Troxler also explains that the development of the procedures led to the creation of the federal commission that deals with cases of persons under life sentence measures. The experts on this commission are forensic psychiatrists. "Based on some first results, the main goal of the preparatory work is to provide guidance on what would be the best way to deal with life long-detention offenders." The question of dangerous offenders remains one of the central concerns and new pilot projects are expected to be tested in the very near future.

Troxler considers it really interesting to combine different programs at the same time for one person sentenced. He gives an example of a person who is sentenced to electronic surveillance and who presents with an alcohol addiction should also be treated for his or her addiction. He explains that although only a few cantons in Switzerland are currently using the electronic monitoring system, some are also merging it with other measures and treatments. Unfortunately, no evaluations have been made to date.

Troxler thinks that recidivism is not directly related to the type of sentence applied. Because no matter the type of sentences or measures that are taken into account, the levels of recidivism can be the same. However, he argues that there are other factors that need to be taken into consideration for their impact on recidivism. Troxler stresses that it needs to be considered that prison is the most expensive form of sentencing. Not only this, but imprisonment isolates the person from his or her family and social life as well as having a strong impact on family functioning, and many other implicit consequences that a sentence can carry. "All these elements make the prison sentence questionable if we might finally reach the same rates of recidivism by applying some other forms of sanction." So for Troxler it does not make sense to keep the most expensive sanction, prison, as the main sentence. He says that the easiest and cheapest sentences should be applied more often, especially if the end result is the same. Although this is a delicate subject to discuss in Switzerland, Troxler is convinced that a new way of thinking is needed.

Evidence-Based Corrections

Switzerland was one of the first European countries to start implementing the pilot projects from the scientific criminological outcomes produced by the research teams of the Universities of Lausanne and Basel. The main projects implemented in the 1990s were oriented to community work, electronic monitoring, and home arrests. Later, the UESM supported projects on corrections in order to develop a national perspective in the assessment and supervision of dangerous offenders. A team of psychiatrists and psychologists from the University of Zurich developed a risk assessment tool that it is now widely used in the German cantons of Switzerland. Mr. Troxler explains that this tool—named FOTRES—is very helpful for taking into account the particularities of offenders in Switzerland rather than using fully imported assessment tools.

Nevertheless, he thinks that "given that in Switzerland there are different commissions dealing with the topics of dangerousness and the risk of reoffending, we would need a much more robust background, some instructions for these evaluators and this is mainly available from outside Switzerland."

Another two projects have started to be implemented, one for adult sexual offenders in the canton of Bern and the other for juvenile sexual offenders in the canton of Zurich. Both projects are mainly based on the assessment of sexual offenders but they also cover the special management skills of these types of offenders.

Apart from these two projects, Mr. Troxler does not seem satisfied with the current situation "as today, we do not have enough programs and results to discuss about evidence-based practices." As an example, up to now not all prisons undertake regular assessment of their inmates. Only some institutions are involved in special programs, which use specific instruments or test some new methodologies of assessment. Generally speaking, the implementation of evidence-based practices is still small and belongs to the decision of the local authorities.

Regarding monitoring, Mr. Troxler explains that Swiss facilities are not obliged to use a monitoring system in prisons. Only some of them use it, but there is no general monitoring established or performed in all facilities.

Theory and Practice

As a general belief, Mr. Troxler expresses his satisfaction with the implications of the research in the local practice of Swiss corrections. Moreover, he stresses that it is really helpful that the different actors of the penitentiary field work together in a multidisciplinary way. Taking into account that the concerns and problems of the political leaders are certainly different from those of the practitioners in corrections, it is essential to have a fluent and close exchange between the different parts that play a role in the correctional system. One of these parts playing an important role is the researcher, says Mr. Troxler. Many universities are involved in the work of interdisciplinary commissions at the local and national levels. However, in Switzerland little research is undertaken in corrections. However, this practice has only come into common use since the early 2000s and today those carrying out research are being increasingly attracted by the penitentiary field. On the other hand, Mr. Troxler believes that the staff working in the field are not ready to receive researchers. Even though directors of the prison facilities are able to give the authorization to the researchers, he considers that there is still some reluctance to show others the work that it is being done behind prison walls. He believes that this needs to change in the future because people from inside the field would really benefit from an external glance, no matter if there is positive feedback to keep on in the same way or to modify things to make them work better.

Transnational Relations

The international visibility of the Swiss criminal justice system fluctuates widely depending on the projects of alternatives to custody tested in the cantons since the early 1970s. Community service, electronic monitoring, home arrests, therapeutic measures, and drug substitution programs in custody are only a few of the examples of Swiss "good practices" that have evolved through collaboration between cantons and between Switzerland and other countries.

Today, Switzerland has several bilateral, regional, and international cooperation agreements. These agreements are based on the will of the Swiss authorities to implement the best possible international standards, for example, the European Prison Rules of the Council of Europe (CoE).

Moreover, Switzerland is one of the European countries with the highest percentage of foreigners in its prison population. During the past decade, the overrepresentation of foreign inmates in the Swiss prison population has remained stable at about 70%. In this line of ideas, under specific conventions, Switzerland has the ability to transfer foreign inmates so that they can serve their sentence in their home countries. However, only a few foreign inmates are transferred each year (not more than 10). Mr. Troxler considers this a delicate topic because very specific conditions have to be fulfilled (e.g., serving long-term sentences). In any case, Mr. Troxler believes that "the topic is mostly politically promoted."

At a cantonal level, some specific direct projects are ongoing in collaboration with other countries. As an example, the canton of Aargau is working together with some German Bundesländer (federal states). Some years ago, the canton of Zurich provided a lot of support for the Czech Republic during the reform of their probation system.

More globally, Switzerland has a lot of contact with different international organizations and commissions such as the CoE and the European Organization for Probation (CEP). Switzerland is collaborating closely with German-speaking countries (Austria and Germany) and the outcomes are really fruitful. Mr. Troxler is personally involved in a roundtable called the "Middle Europe Corrections Roundtable," in which prison general directors from 12 different countries meet twice a year. He believes that

> There is a real open exchange. There are no special protocols, so we can really talk about the problems we are facing, our specific difficulties, etc. It is a good platform for exchanges and to learn from each other. And then we visit some facilities in the organizing country.

Moreover, Switzerland has had some dialogue on the question of human rights with other countries, specifically on issues such as the rights of persons held in custody and the execution of sentences. Together with other countries, Switzerland has programs of support and exchange:

> For example, we work with Russia in the field of juvenile justice. They have started now copying the model of a Swiss institution. Since the project started in 2010 there have been 5 juvenile prisons in Russia based on the Swiss model. The project ended in June 2013 and the Russian Government decided to adopt the Swiss model all over the country. This project focuses very much on education and educational programs. This implies a change of thinking.

Another international cooperation project that Mr. Troxler is proud of is the Swiss support for the training of Vietnamese prison staff. Previously in Vietnam, specific training for prison staff did not exist and prison staff consisted of those candidates who had failed after the first stage of training in the police academy. The results are satisfactory as two schools have been constructed and a third is under construction in Vietnam. There is also an exchange of teachers; some of the teachers from the Swiss Prison Staff Training Center are teaching the same topics to Vietnamese students as they do in Switzerland.

General Assessment

Note: Every interview in this volume has a General Assessment section. In this chapter the authors chose to include general assessment comments in the other sections.

Conclusion

To conclude, one of Mr. Troxler's main beliefs—and suggested by much Swiss research in the field of criminal law—is that the new penal code is not bringing as many positive changes as expected. In Switzerland, a real unification of the rules of law remains to be carried out in the penitentiary field. The autonomy of cantons would not be so important today if the rights and duties of the detainees were better defined under a specific law on the execution of sentences. So, probably a general law covering the frame of the execution of sentences will be necessary in the future.

Another key idea that came from the interview is that in the near future the Swiss correctional system will be characterized by a stronger emphasis on security and public safety and less on offender reform. In the same vein, Brägger and Vuille (2012) point out that there is a significant tendency in Switzerland toward toughening the penal law. The authors explain that criminal policies are based on zero tolerance and so the main goal of the Swiss state is to avoid any crime. Furthermore, following this trend, the only goal of the sanctions is to protect the population so criminal policies will mainly be based on removing criminals from society. This trend will also have an impact on the increase in the length of sentences and the execution of security measures, such as lifelong detention.

Mr. Troxler points to the same direction:

> At the moment there are 7,000 prison places in the whole country and there will be 600–700 places more in 2–3 years.

However, he would like to see this trend changing.

> It will be a matter of experience. We will see that it won't work with security only. There are some other aspects we have to look at.

He fully disagrees with the use of prison as the default sentence especially because research shows similar recidivism rates when serving alternatives sentences. Even though he recognizes that this is a delicate question in Switzerland, he holds that a new way of thinking is required. The toughening of the correctional system and the increase in the use of prison and long-term prison sentences as a main consequence can also lead to significant effects on the profile of inmates as the median age will increase, so facilities and services will need to be adapted to them. Long-sentenced inmates without hope of release will lead to an increase in attempts to escape, depression, and probably suicide risk. Additionally, the education of new staff will need to be modified according to this new picture of the future penitentiary reality and they will need to be prepared to assist an older penitentiary population.

Furthermore, Mr. Troxler expresses his concern regarding the question of mentally ill inmates, which is an increasing category of detainees whose needs will become more specific and more difficult to cover. He states that Switzerland lacks specific institutions for this group of inmates. So the main projects to be developed in this field are appropriate training programs for staff working with these prisoners and the development of special education and therapeutic approaches. Moreover, new dimensions to be explored are those related to work on criminogenic needs and protection factors in order to prevent reoffending.

In conclusion, it should be stated that the discussion with Walter Troxler was extremely rich and provided us with a precious look at the Swiss correctional system from an honest, critical, and consistent point of view. Mr. Troxler is a leader who is extremely involved in the development of the Swiss correctional philosophy, with a long and rich experience and knowledge of the criminal justice system.

Glossary

Article 11 paragraph 1: The Federal Act on the Criminal Law Applicable to Juveniles (JCLA): The criminal law applicable to juveniles provides for two forms of sanction: protection measures and sentences. If the young person who has committed an offense has acted with the required criminal intent, the court will impose a sentence in addition to a protection measure. For more information, see: The Federal Act on the Criminal Law Applicable to Juveniles: http://www.admin.ch/opc/de/classified-compilation/20031353/index.html (p. 2).

Article 56 Swiss Criminal Code (SCC): therapeutic measures and indefinite incarceration: (1) A measure is ordered if: (a) a penalty alone is not sufficient to counter the risk of further offending by the offender; (b) the offender requires treatment or treatment is required in the interest of public safety; and (c) the requirements of Articles 59–61, 63, or 64 are fulfilled. For additional information, see Brägger and Vuille (2012) and Kuhn (2005).

Article 123 of the Federal Constitution (FC): Criminal law: (1) The Confederation is responsible for legislation in the field of criminal law and the law of criminal procedure. (2) The cantons are responsible for the organization of the courts, the administration of justice in criminal cases as well as for the execution of penalties and measures, unless the law provides otherwise. (3) The Confederation may issue regulations on the execution of penalties and measures. It may grant subsidies to the cantons for: (a) the construction of penal institutions; (b) improvements in the execution of penalties and measures; (c) institutions that conduct educative measures for the benefit of children, adolescents and young adults. (pp 1, 8).

CEP: CEP aims to promote the social inclusion of offenders through community sanctions and measures such as probation, community service, mediation and conciliation. The organization is committed to enhance the profile of probation and to improve professionalism in this field, on a national and a European level.

lifelong detention (*Lebenslängliche Verwahrung*): on February 8, 2004, the Swiss people and the cantons voted in favor of the popular initiative "Lifelong detention for extremely dangerous, nontreatable violent and sexual offenders." This requires the addition of a new article in the federal constitution specifying that extremely dangerous, nontreatable, violent and sexual offenders are to remain in lifelong detention and may not be released on parole. The release of an offender may only be considered if new scientific evidence shows that the person can be treated and will pose no further risk to the public. OFD: Swiss Federal Office of Justice (pp. 5, 8, 9, 11).

FOTRES: Forensic Operationalized Therapy/Risk Evaluation System is a Swiss tool for the assessment of dangerous offenders. In daily practice, FOTRES is used as a basis for risk assessment and as a quality management tool for the documentation and evaluation of the progress of therapy. Comparisons of the assessments of the potential risks of reoffending or on the progress of therapy at different points in time and by different assessors from different fields (e.g., psychiatric experts, therapists, probation officers, or attorneys) are made using FOTRES. Official website: http://www.fotres.ch.

Swiss prison staff training center (in German: Schweizerisches Ausbildungszentrum für das Strafvollzugspersonal: SAZ): Located in Fribourg, the training center offers basic vocational training for Swiss prison staff and advanced vocational training for employees of the Swiss criminal justice system. Official website: http://www.prison.ch (pp. 1, 6, 11).

UESM: Unit of Execution of Sentences and Measures (official website in English): https://www.bj.admin.ch/content/bj/en/home/themen/sicherheit/straf-_und_massnahmevollzug.html (pp. 1, 3, 7, 9).

7 Sue McAllister, Director General of the Northern Ireland Prison Service, United Kingdom

DOMINIC KELLY

Contents

Overview

Northern Ireland is a country within the United Kingdom in the northeast of the island of Ireland with an approximate population of 1.8 million people. It was formed in 1921 when Ireland was partitioned by the British government under the Government of Ireland Act 1920 into six counties in the North. The remaining 26 counties make up the rest of the island, which would eventually be known as the Republic of Ireland. Historically, Northern Ireland has been characterized by political and societal turmoil, most notably between the late 1960s and the 1990s in a period colloquially referred to as "The Troubles" (Ryder, 2000). During this period, conflict between the two largest communities (nationalist and unionist) erupted into sectarian violence between paramilitary groups, political activists, and the state security forces deployed to control the violence, namely, the British Army and the Royal

Ulster Constabulary (RUC). An estimated 3,722 people were killed during this period and over 40,000 others were injured (McKittrick et al., 2007).

The Northern Ireland Prison Service (NIPS) was a key institution in the conflict, particularly in the Maze Prison, opened in 1971, which contained largely republican remand prisoners who were interned without trial and those sentenced according to paramilitary activities or allegiances or both (McEvoy, 2001). Notable events within the Maze Prison included the death of 10 republican prisoners through hunger strike in protest against prison regimes and the denial of their political status, and the escape of 38 republican prisoners in September 1983 (McKeown, 2009), which also resulted in the death of a prison officer. Prison officers were often subjected to intimidation, threats, murder attempts, and fatalities throughout the period: 29 NIPS staff were murdered and many others were seriously injured by paramilitary groups between 1969 and 1998 (Challis, 1999).

The Belfast or "Good Friday" Agreement in 1998 facilitated a peace process to end the violence. Reconciliation between the communities centered on the declaration of ceasefires by most paramilitary organizations, the decommissioning of paramilitary weapons, the reform of the police, the withdrawal of the British Army from the communities, the establishment of a power-sharing government, and the recognition of civil and cultural rights. The British and Irish governments committed to the early release of prisoners serving sentences in connection with paramilitary activities on condition that they were committed to the ceasefire. However, a number of paramilitary organizations did not recognize the terms of the agreement. Today, political prisoners still constitute approximately 4% of the current prison population (NIPS, 2013). Furthermore, personnel who are seen to be affiliated to the British state are still subjected to intimidation and attacks by dissident paramilitary groups. Recent examples of continuing paramilitary activity include the murder of a police officer in April 2011 (BBC, 2011) and a prison officer in November 2012 by dissident republicans (BBC, 2012).

The reduction in the prison population in accordance with the Belfast Agreement has necessitated reforms in the prison estate structure, particularly the closure of the controversial Maze Prison. Currently, there are three prisons within Northern Ireland. HMP Maghaberry operates as a high-security prison housing adult male long-term sentenced and remand prisoners, in both separated (paramilitary-affiliated prisoners) and integrated conditions. HMP Magilligan is a medium-security facility, which confines short-term sentenced adult males who obtain lower security categories or are nearing the completion of their sentence or both. HMP Hydebank Wood Prison and Young Offenders Center is a medium- to low-security establishment, which caters for young male offenders (ages 17–21) and all female prisoners including youth offenders. The current total prison population is approximately 1859 prisoners, with males representing 97% (for a breakdown of current prisoner demographics, see NIPS, 2013). The female prison population constitutes a relatively small number (60 adult and youth females are currently in prison in Northern Ireland; NIPS, 2013), although numbers have more than doubled in the last 10 years (Prison Reform Trust, 2012). Northern Ireland has the lowest proportional rate of prisoners per 100,000 of the population in the United Kingdom (NI: 101, England and Wales: 148, Scotland: 147; ICPS, 2013). Conversely, the cost per prisoner place in Northern Ireland is significantly the highest in the United Kingdom, quoted between £73,000 and £89,000 per annum (CJINI, 2011). This extra expense has been attributed to the unique costs of maintaining the separation and control of paramilitary prisoners, a high staff-to-prisoner ratio, higher officer incomes than other UK prison systems, and a general security-centric ideology.

Since the Belfast Agreement, the NIPS has been subject to a range of partial reforms, either in response to inadequacies in specific policies such as suicide prevention, or through inspection reports or inquiries into events such as political prisoner protests and deaths in custody. Since 2005, the number of recommendations from over 20 external reports has totaled nearly 1200, with particular emphasis on leadership and management, performance management, estate structure, industrial relations, and staff culture (CJINI, 2010). The Hillsborough Agreement in 2010 facilitated the devolution of policing and justice powers from the British government in Westminster to the Northern Ireland Executive. This established a wide-ranging review into the conditions, management, and oversight of all Northern Ireland prisons. In July 2010, an independent oversight committee, the Prison Review Team (PRT), was formed to undertake a review. They published 2 reports and provided 40 recommendations that aimed to reform Northern Ireland's prisons and their links with other criminal justice agencies (see PRT, 2011).

In response to these recommendations, the NIPS launched the Strategic Efficiency and Effectiveness (SEE) program in June 2011. The SEE program is tasked with delivering end-to-end structural and cultural change. Innovations include new corporate governance frameworks and business operating models, clearer aims and purposes that focus on prisoner care and rehabilitation, a stronger emphasis on performance targets and outputs, new prison officer grades (prison custody officers and offender supervisors) with modernized and clearly defined working practices, and more efficient use of the prison estate. Current developments include a newly implemented target operating model (TOM) for the three prisons, the departure of hundreds of officers through the voluntary early retirement (VER) scheme coupled with the recruitment of new custody officers, and an agreed reconfiguration of the prison estate.

Introduction

The following interview was conducted with Sue McAllister, director general of the NIPS. Mrs. McAllister is responsible for the operation of Northern Ireland's three prisons, the Prison Escort Custody Service (PECS), prison service headquarters, and the prison service training college. She was appointed to this post in July 2012 after taking early retirement from prison management in England and Wales. She responded to my questions with much interest, and I felt she sincerely expressed her personal and professional experiences, which had an evident influence on her perspectives on the various topics that we discussed. Mrs. McAllister's answers to my questions were often framed with reflections on the progress of the NIPS' current change process. The following excerpts from the transcript may be reported out of order for clarity.

Career

Q: Could you provide an outline of how your career has progressed?

A: I have been a public servant for my entire career. I worked for 3 years in another department before joining the prison service in England as an assistant governor trainee when I was 25. I personally joined the prison service because I wanted to work with prisoners and make a difference to society. If I had not become a prison governor, I would almost certainly have become a probation officer. After my initial experiences as an assistant governor, I then sought promotion through a variety of management roles, first attaining governor grade, then working as a deputy governor in three different prisons, and then as an in-charge governor in two different prisons. Between these progressions, I was also employed in prison service headquarters in England in a number of policy-related roles. Subsequently, after my in-charge governor posting, I was promoted to head of Security Group in prison service headquarters. Here, I was responsible for security policy across the service, operational security measures such as incident response as well as collaborations with other security agencies including the police service. After 18 months in this role, I was promoted as area manager for West Midlands [county in west central England], in which I oversaw 12 prisons within the area. Ironically, that was a much bigger job in terms of the number of prisons, the size of the budget, and the number of staff and prisoners than the current job. I was 1 of 12 area managers at that time. After a secondment [temporary role transfer within the organization] to the Home Office as head of the Police Reform Unit, I returned to the Ministry of Justice to take charge of the Public Sector Bid Unit. In this post, I was responsible for prison tenders on behalf of the public sector as part of the "competition strategy" for prisons in England and Wales. I retired in July 2011 and had a year off.

Q: So, what motivated you to come back from retirement?

A: After the first few months of retirement, I realized that I was still motivated to continue working within prison management. When the opportunity arose through the vacation of the director general post, I felt I was really keen to do the job. I had conducted inspectorate work in Northern Ireland as a member of the Pearson Review Team in 2008/2009, so I had good background knowledge about the prison service in Northern Ireland and particularly a good insight into what issues needed to be addressed.

Changes Experienced

Q: What do you see as the most important changes that have occurred in prisons over the course of your career?

A: In my early career in the late 1980s, one of the major changes was the introduction of Fresh Start. This change in management structures, job conditions, and working practices for staff was introduced to solve some of the long-standing structural and organizational issues in the prison service in England and Wales. I think the Northern Ireland Prison Service introduced a similar change program a few years later [it was known as The Way Forward]. One of its most influential changes was the removal of overtime for prison officers [replaced with a substantial pay increase and a consolidated 39-h working week]. As a consequence, the service evolved from being dependent on prison staff overtime, that is, the "goodwill" of staff assisting in maintaining adequate staffing levels to run the prisons, to where there was an established operating model, which ensured prison regimes could run safely. Fresh Start was also a significant change for prison managers. There was not much of a sense of managerialism when I joined the prison service. The introduction of new management structures, clearer lines of accountability, and dissemination of routine, nonpriority tasks (such as visiting the segregation unit and health care and handling prisoner applications) gave us the ability to manage in a way that we had not done before, where we could focus on the management of *prison operations* (budgets, personnel, estate strategies, etc.).

In terms of changes outside the immediate prison environment, there is one vivid incident which I feel has had a significant impact on the evolution of the prison service—the murder of James Bulger in February 1993 and the sentencing of the perpetrators. It was such a unique case and it was a huge watershed moment for penal policy in the United Kingdom. First of all, it changed expectations of how long people (and especially minors) should be locked up for crimes such as murder. Secondly, it identified the influential role of the popular media and public opinion in influencing the punishment of offenders. Thirdly, it made us question our current punishment practices, particularly the use of imprisonment.

I also see the rise of global terrorism as having had a significant impact on UK prisons. Particular events such as the September 11 and July 7 bombings in New York and London, respectively, and the continuing Islamist terrorist threat in English prisons due to increasing numbers of prisoners affiliated to such causes, has become a significant issue. I feel the latter has particularly increased the political scrutiny on prisons in England and Wales, which has a bearing on the management of the prison and the working practices of its staff.

Q: What impact do you think the global economic downturn has had on prisons?

A: Essentially, governments have less money to run prisons. As a result, the privatization agenda, the view that tendering the running of prisons to private companies will drive up performance and reduce spiraling prison costs, has been one of the most significant changes in my career working in prisons in England and Wales. Now, while the reality of privatization has been effective in changing the working relationship between the prison service and the prison unions in England and Wales, I feel there is less clarity on the long-term effects which privatization is having.

Another consequence of the current economy is the grim climate that people face on leaving prison. As a result, prisons have got to be more imaginative in how we are assisting offenders. For instance, there has had to be a real shift in perspective in terms of prisoner employment on release, and our level of ambition. Traditionally, we would focus on providing construction industry skills in prison: bricklaying, plastering, painting, and decorating. We focused on these occupations because they were the sorts of industries in which prisoners could get employment when released. Well, currently there is no construction industry. So, what do you train people for when there are no jobs for those outside of prison? In Northern Ireland, we are doing some imaginative work with some organizations in the community. One example is the retail outlet Timpson. They actively seek to employ ex-offenders on the same basis as nonoffenders. They meet prisoners at the gate and bring them to work on day one. Prisoners do not get the opportunity to immediately fall back into bad habits, and they are provided with consistent and fair employment. They look after their employees well. We actively work with organizations like Timpson, where you can always give people a fair chance at desistance in a difficult economic climate.

Q: Overall, in your opinion has the quality of prisons improved or declined over the past 10 years?

A: From a prison management point of view, prisons have certainly improved. In fact, compared with when I joined the service in 1986, it is unrecognizably better. I remember back to the disturbances in 1990, starting at Strangeways (HM Prison Manchester), but including other prisons such as HM Prison Cardiff [where prisoners destroyed their cells] and HM Prison Dartmoor [where prisoners displayed supportive banners for prisoners at Strangeways during similar roof protests]. I was working at Pucklechurch Remand Center in Bristol when there were disturbances across England and Wales. Our facility also had one disturbance during this period. [Prison staff were overpowered during prisoner association and prison keys were stolen to unlock other prisoners, although control was regained in a short space of time.] The prison disturbances across the country really highlighted the conditions that prisoners were experiencing. Prisons were clearly overcrowded, under-resourced, and in places not fit for purpose. Prisoners were being held in awful conditions. They were also being held far away from their homes, and thus had difficulties in retaining links with their families. To me, the prison service did not articulate any of the sentiments which we now know to be important to prisoners: decency, respect, and safety. So on reflection, I think we have progressed significantly.

However, if you were to ask *prisoners* the same question, they may feel that the quality of prisons has gotten worse. I say this because, as I have mentioned, money and resources are much more constrained. Prisons have had to become much more realistic with what we can do with the resources we have. In Northern Ireland prisons, for example, we are reducing the time we plan to have prisoners unlocked for.

The core reasoning behind this is that with finite resources it is less important how long people are unlocked for than *what you do with them* when they are unlocked. So, having substantial unstructured time when prisoners have the opportunity for free association is less important than a core day that is based around purposeful activity, which genuinely contributes to reducing reoffending. So, prisoners may respond that this reduction in their vocational and free association periods is making prisons worse for them.

Personal Correctional Philosophy

Q: What do you think the function of prisons should be in society?

A: I have stated publicly that if people did not get ill we would not need hospitals. Equally, if people did not commit crime we would not need prisons. We need prisons because they do. The primary function of prisons is to protect the public, as there are some individuals and groups from whom the public needs to be protected. I am referring specifically to two particular types of criminal: (i) serious offenders, who need to be locked up long term, or in some cases indefinitely; and (ii) persistent recidivists, as in those who are constantly victimizing others through persistent burglary, theft, intimidation, and antisocial behavior. So in my opinion, primarily prisons exist to protect the public.

Q: How should prisons be managed?

A: I am an advocate for prisons because it has been my professional life and I believe passionately that they should be as good as they can be. However, there also has to be an element of realism when we assess the cost of prisons. Every pound we spend on prisons is a pound that we are unable to spend toward improving hospitals or schools. Therefore, we should be expected to effectively manage the resources at our disposal. We ask that our prison governors are managers; they manage big budgets and large numbers of staff, and they manage complex regimes. However, it is also important to note that our roles revolve around working with people, often those most vulnerable individuals in our society. It is not enough just to be a manager and a leader, although that is essential. We need people who are flexible and adaptable and can respond to the needs of people, as people are always the confounding variable in prisons.

Q: What should the role of prison officers be? Has their role become more or less difficult?

A: I think we currently ask much more of our prison officers, because we ask much more of our prisons. Prison officers have a very complex role.

Primarily, they are custodians. We expect officers to keep prisoners in a secure and controlled environment, one which ensures they cannot escape. This is one of the core requirements of a safe and effective prison; if we do not succeed in doing this, we cannot expect to operate effectively. Therefore, officers need to effectively manage the security of the prison, with key tasks including searching, intelligence management, and constant vigilance. Equally, we require officers to engage positively with prisoners. Officers are expected to leave their personal views about prisoner sentences and backgrounds at the prison gates, and interact with prisoners in a professional manner to ultimately reduce their offending behaviors. I feel that our prison officers are very proficient at delivering interventions, whether that is through accredited or structured interventions or whether that is simply interacting with prisoners on a daily basis in a residential setting. They are role models and they are agents for change, who strive in changing prisoners' behaviors while having responsibility toward their care. Again, however, there is caution as while prison officers befriend prisoners, and they should be friendly toward prisoners, we have to be clear that this is not an equal relationship, but one centered on power. So, prison work has certainly become a more difficult task; they are constantly balancing important and often conflicting priorities in working with prisoners, being responsible not just for security and order but also care and ensuring safety.

Q: What services do you think should be provided in prisons that are currently not offered?

A: We certainly need to do more in terms of rehabilitation and preparing prisoners for release, for resettlement, or in some cases settlement because they have never been settled before. In essence, we need to provide more practical interventions with prisoners. For example, I have been corresponding with the Prison Reform Trust about research they have been conducting on prisoner financial management. Currently, when offenders are sentenced and brought into prison, restrictions do not allow them to manage their finances, such as having a bank account or making provisions for their dependents outside. The Prison Reform Trust is exploring the benefits of giving prisoners the opportunity to manage their own money and providing assistance for current and ex-prisoners in managing their finances. I feel this is a useful and taken-for-granted skill, which could have significant bearing on successful desistance. Also, ex-offenders need to have stable accommodation and they need a positive friend or role model on release. That friend might be their wife or husband, a social worker, or even their local church; what matters is that prisoners are not on their own on release. Certainly, we know that people who are released back into their families are less likely to reoffend than if they go out to no fixed abode with no one to support them. Therefore, it is our duty to assist in providing support to establish and/or maintain these social links. Furthermore, there are increasingly significant issues around addiction among the prison population; alcohol, as well as prescribed and illegal drugs. So, key to prison and postprison supervision is addressing some of those needs. We need to start the work in prison and continue it outside.

Q: What services are currently provided which should be cut?

A: Well, that is a tricky one, because the more we can invest in prisoners the better the outcome should be—education is never wasted. However, there is no doubt that some of our resources could be better spent. In particular, I think we need to take a long, hard look at our education provision, and whether we are prioritizing basic literacy and numeracy—education which genuinely benefits prisoners on release. In Northern Ireland, our delivery model is so inflexible that we are delivering programs that were designed and delivered by teachers 20 years ago, which may not be as relevant now.

Education in prison needs to evolve over time. For example, if one was to ask me if we should be investing in educating prisoners on topics such as geography over and above basic literacy during a period of constrained resources, I would suggest perhaps not. Another related aspect to education in prison is what is acceptable in terms of media presentation and public confidence. For instance, currently there is media interest in some of the creative writing courses and the art courses that we provide in Magilligan Prison. However, prior to this, I did suggest that we should be careful to present that as part of a rehabilitative package. Now, both you and I understand that the intention is to use these sorts of courses as a vehicle for positive prisoner development, for confidence building, socialization, and other such skill building. But, if it results in a biased headline in a newspaper, how does it look to the public? One could understand a reaction such as, “my kids are writing on scrap paper and you are running creative writing classes for criminals?”

Problems and Successes Experienced

Q: The prison service is currently undergoing historic changes and I have given a brief overview of the SEE program above. Could you give some insight into the objectives of those changes and their current progression?

A: The current change process is really responding to the recommendations for the prison service made in the PRT reports. Ultimately, we need to modernize our service so that it is appropriate for the twenty-first century. This is not to dismiss the unique historical challenges around separated prisoners and the continuing threat to prison staff. But the reality is that this is a different society and there needs to be cultural change. As such, the offender needs to be positioned at the center—having regimes that meet their needs and positively impact reductions in recidivism. We also need to have a proportionate approach to security and not have a "one-size-fits-all" perspective where we treat everyone as high-security prisoners—security should not dictate all prison practice.

In a sense, I feel fortunate to have inherited a healthy reform program that is clear about what needs to be done and what the timescales are. From the outset, the SEE program has been consolidated as a 4-year reform package. However, that does not mean that reforms will cease at the end of these 4 years. Years 1 and 2 were focused on *planning changes*, Year 3 has been about *delivering change*, and Year 4 will be about *embedding change*. Currently, we are beginning to see actual change "on the ground." So, prisoner health care is now delivered externally by the South Eastern Health and Social Care Trust [part of the National Health Service] and we are moving to new delivery models for prisoner education. We are training and introducing new recruits into the prison establishment and most of our staff who opted for early retirement have gone while the rest will be given the opportunity to leave during the course of this year. We also have an agreed prison estate strategy, including the redevelopment of HMP Magilligan and HMP Hydebank Wood, provisions for a new facility for female prisoners, and reconfiguration of HMP Maghaberry into three discrete "miniprisons." So, I feel we are moving forward.

Independent bodies, such as the Committee on the Administration of Justice, contend that Northern Ireland can be a leader in prison reform, given its potential to be innovative in setting out policies and practices within a relatively small jurisdiction that has financial and political backing for change (CAJ, 2010). However, they and other groups voice concerns as to the scope and depth of the change that is necessary, particularly in relation to international human rights standards and continuing "troubles-related" issues such as the containment of politically affiliated prisoners (Wahidin et al., 2012).

Q: What do you find are the major difficulties in conducting this change process?

A: I think we are fortunate to have a formal reform program in Northern Ireland as well as the political commitment to make it happen. I think one difficulty of prison reforms in other jurisdictions is where political views are not necessarily aligned with the practitioners' views. Although, as a consequence of the current arrangements for government in Northern Ireland, there is also much more political scrutiny in what happens in prisons. I feel much more accountable to politicians on a daily basis here than I ever have in any previous role.

The condition of our prison estate is one of our biggest challenges: we need to provide better accommodation. However, sometimes the difficulties of progress relate to getting through the bureaucracy. One example could be the time required to get business cases approved or to go to procurement for different arrangements. Another difficulty associated with prison reforms is the unplanned lockup of prisoners due to perceived staff shortages. Prisoners will normatively conform to changing situations (such as amended daily regimes) as long as you communicate effectively what is happening and the reasons for doing so. However, the occasional dependence on staff overtime due to debates on changing staffing levels and operating models can be difficult. In these situations, the prison officer unions (POA) can resist such changes, resulting in the withdrawal of prison staff's "goodwill" to accept overtime. This means that prisoners do not have predictable regimes. So, this is at times a difficult issue to negotiate.

Theory and Practice

Q: Currently, what do you think of the links between academic writing and practitioners in Northern Ireland?

A: I find it genuinely interesting to read some of the material that comes out of universities. For example, I have been reading doctoral research from 2007 on the implications of "legitimacy" on the order and quality of life within maximum-security prisons [authored by Deborah Drake, Open University, Milton Keynes]. I feel it is particularly useful for some of the issues in our maximum-security prison, HMP Maghaberry. Also, I met an academic recently at a university event who has been conducting research on how the prison environment can impact prisoner behavior. I am a firm believer that the built environment has a powerful influence on the staff–prisoner relationship. Unfortunately, collaboration between academics and practitioners such as this tends to be "hit-and-miss" in Northern Ireland. Often, it depends on chance encounters or individuals taking an interest in exploring a relevant subject.

Q: What do you think is holding back this collaboration?

A: I think there is no established system in place to make it happen. I am sure there are numerous students and academics out there conducting relevant and useful research on prisons. To be honest, we as an organization have not been as open and welcoming as we should be for those with research proposals. However, in conversations with prison governors, the inclusion of researchers into the prison is a balancing act as well. Having previously been a prison governor, I can empathize with the difficulties they espouse in running a prison. Alongside the daily pressures of prison management, there can be the added pressure of dealing with the various requests from outside individuals and agencies to gain access to the prison: charities such as the Prison Reform Trust, politicians, families, academics, and students. At times, there is a temptation to "pull up the drawbridge" and concentrate solely on managing the prison. However, that is neither in our interests to do so nor in the interests of wider society. Here in Northern Ireland there is also an added security dimension. Due to the legacy of The Troubles, particularly the continued targeting of state personnel by dissident paramilitaries, often our prison staff have preconceived concerns about being identified and quoted in research. So we have a long way to go in terms of improving our links with universities and researchers.

Q: In your opinion, how do we improve collaborations between academics and practitioners?

A: The prison service needs to get more involved in influencing the research that is done by universities and other research agencies, so that the research links in with our current agendas. This will also improve the quality and diversity of research projects which people can get involved in. Equally, academic research will be more valuable if it reflects the views and experiences of practitioners. Really, we need to find ways to make research more useful and accessible, make the prison service more welcoming, but also make it less intrusive so it can be done in a way that minimally disrupts the running of the prison.

Transnational Relations

Q: How has the prison system in Northern Ireland been influenced by developments in other countries?

A: As we are quite a small service, we have often reflected on the research and practice in other services, particularly services in Scotland, England, and Wales. In particular, these jurisdictions have influenced the development of offending behavior programs in Northern Ireland. They have also impacted on some of our policies such as safer custody policies and prisoner incentive schemes. Furthermore, in developing our estate strategy, I have been keen to explore the built environment in other areas to see if we can identify some changes that can have a positive influence on prisoners and staff. I have found that there are lessons to be learned from the prison systems in Scandinavian countries, such as Finland and Norway. However, due to our current reforming state, comprehensive exploration into the beneficial qualities of these countries have been relatively sporadic.

General Assessments

Q: Generally, how satisfied are you in relation to developments in prisons here?

A: I have been genuinely pleased with the progress that I have seen during the change process. The new prison staff [prison custody officers] are really impressive: a lot of them are university graduates and they bring experience from a number of different backgrounds. However, we need to find a way to make this new role challenging and interesting in order to retain them. I feel this is a big challenge, as the pay is less than it would have been previously and we are expecting these staff to conduct more complex roles. We also need to make sure that we reap the benefit of the experienced staff. It is really gratifying when I go onto the landings and see the new and the more experienced staff working together effectively. There is also a much more visible presence of women prison officers, which is great. So, there is quite a lot of good news around, even though I am still conscious that there is much more progress to be made.

Q: What developments do you see as most likely to happen in the next few years?

A: As I have said, the structure and purpose of our prison buildings is one of our biggest challenges. Changes in the estate strategy will be the most immediate and tangible change in the next few years. The

> huge changes for our prison staff in the upcoming years, in terms of levels within the prisons (reductions according to new operating models), demographics (increased diversity), and roles (in line with the current performance agendas), will also have a substantial impact on the prison culture and working practices in relation to prisoners in the years to come.

Conclusion

Overall, this discussion with Sue McAllister brought up a number of fascinating insights into the role of practitioners in a prison system undergoing substantive organizational and cultural changes. One recurring theme in the interview was the centrality of financial management in current correctional work. This frugality toward resources requires practitioners to prioritize targets in terms of offender treatment and care, as well as to become more imaginative in operating and evolving prisons within a culture of austerity. There are also increased complexities for prison staff, who need to balance often conflicting goals and priorities, as well as operate within a continually changing work environment.

Related to this point, prison privatization was identified by Sue as a significant change for prison management within the last 30 years. The United Kingdom currently has the most privatized prison system in Europe, managing 16% of the total prison population (Prison Reform Trust, 2013). Meanwhile, public sector prisons have been subject to reforms according to private sector principles; an emphasis on achieving "results," setting explicit targets and performance indicators to enable the auditing of efficiency and effectiveness, the market testing of all activities to ensure "value for money," and the externalization of nonessential responsibilities (see King and McDermott, 1995).

While Northern Ireland has often reflected on the working practices of prison systems in the rest of the United Kingdom, it has been stated that the finance and management of prisons will remain within the public sector in the short term. In setting out the future direction of the prison service, the PRT states that the intention of the comprehensive reforms is to "create a *public sector* [author emphasis] prison system that is a model of excellence" (Prison Review Team, 2011, p. 7). However, they point to "a window of opportunity" that cannot remain open indefinitely. Indeed, they note the role of prison managers, staff, and governmental officials in resisting a potentially strengthened role for the private sector in Northern Ireland's criminal justice agencies.

The interview indicates Sue's caution in relation to the use of private sector initiatives in operating prisons. Such cognitions are echoed within recent scholarly research on the efficacy of private and public prisons in the United Kingdom. Crewe et al. (2011) compared staff and prisoners' quality of life in two matched pairs of public and private prisons. They suggested that while the highest-rated prison in their sample was privately run, the private sector provided the highest variation in quality, with institutions also at the lowest end of the spectrum. Crewe and colleagues are cautious in dismissing the role of public prisons, as they contend that they provide a number of underestimated strengths in security, the use of authority, and experience.

Finally, it is important to note that the prison reform program is at a significant juncture. There have been substantial gains in the 2 years since the PRT report that outlined the future of the NIPS, which Sue has alluded to in the interview: in estate structure, in management, in staffing demographics, and importantly in provisions for prisoners. However, Northern Ireland is a small jurisdiction that still bears the traumas of decades of political turmoil and sectarian violence. Also, findings from a recent prison inspection report (CJINI, 2013) would suggest that there is much progress to be made in improving our prison system in relation to prisoner care and resettlement. Therefore, it is important to further develop transnational relations with prison systems that demonstrate innovative correctional practices as well as more effectively utilize contemporary correctional research to establish a more effective, efficient, and sustainable prison system.

Glossary

Committee on the Administration of Justice (CAJ): The CAJ is an independent organization that lobbies on human rights issues in Northern Ireland and internationally (see: http://www.caj.org.uk/).

competition strategy: The Competition Strategy for Offender Services in England and Wales outlines the UK government's commitment to encouraging greater involvement of the private and voluntary sectors in the rehabilitation of offenders, to cut reoffending and improve outcomes. This is done through tendering services to private and voluntary organizations and local communities to produce savings in costs and improved efficiencies.

Criminal Justice Inspectorate Northern Ireland: The CJINI is responsible for inspecting a range of organizations in Northern Ireland including the five key agencies that deliver criminal justice: the police service, the prison service, the prosecution service, the court service, the probation service, and the Youth Justice Agency (see http://www.cjini.org/Home.aspx).

Fresh Start: This program was introduced in 1987 following criticisms related to escalating prison costs and deteriorating industrial relations. It saw the abolition of paid overtime in exchange for an enhanced basic salary, the abolition of the chief officer rank, and the introduction of group working (deployed within groups according to line managers rather than being centrally detailed). Fresh Start had a significant impact on the prison service, both positively and negatively. Alongside changes such as the VER scheme, there were positive shifts in staff demographics; older, disillusioned staff were given options to retire, the age profile of prison officers lowered, and there was greater female representation within the ranks. Solidarity and continuity of tasks within wings improved, as officers spent sustained periods detailed in one place. Fresh Start was also seen to weaken the power of the prison unions, which was seen as a crucial success from the prison management perspective. However, some older officers struggled to cope with such substantive changes, and while group working improved wing or area performance, it resulted in officers' isolation from the majority of the prison officer group, resulting in an increase in the formation of group rivalries.

"Good Friday" Agreement: This political agreement aimed to create lasting peace in Northern Ireland following three decades of political violence and sectarian conflict. The proposals included plans for a Northern Ireland assembly with a power-sharing executive, new cross-border institutions involving the Republic of Ireland, and a body linking devolved assemblies across the United Kingdom with Westminster and Dublin. The agreement was signed on April 10, 1998, by politicians from Northern Ireland, the Republic of Ireland, and England, and was supported through referendum in May 1998.

Hillsborough Agreement: This was a governmental agreement signed on February 5, 2010, at Hillsborough Castle in Northern Ireland. It allowed for the devolution of policing and justice powers from the British government in Westminster to the Northern Ireland Executive.

HMP: Her Majesty's Prisons.

James Bulger: At the age of two, James Bulger was abducted, tortured, and murdered by two 10-year-old boys, Robert Thompson and Jon Venables. The pair were tried in an adult court and were found guilty of murder, making them the youngest convicted murderers in English history. After being sentenced to a minimum term of 10 years, their tariff was increased by the home secretary in light of petitioning from tabloid newspapers and the general public. The case is seen to have had wide-ranging implications for debates on the age of criminal responsibility, youth sentencing, the efficacy of imprisonment in terms of reducing recidivism, and the role of the popular media in influencing political decisions.

Pearson Review Team 2008/2009: Colin Bell was a prisoner in HMP Maghaberry on suicide watch when he took his own life in July 2008. Following a highly critical Northern Ireland prisoner ombudsman (inspector) report, an independent review team was established to investigate the death and assess the effectiveness of NIPS' response in implementing recommended changes. The final report outlined a number of failings and maintained that the prison service contained an "insidious subculture" of apathetic staff and weak management that was slow to change, with a particularly excessive adhesion toward security at the expense of all other prison operations.

Prison Officer Association (POA): The POA is a trade union for prison, correctional, and secure care workers, established in 1936 in the United Kingdom. It aims to promote the interest of its members through improving employment conditions, advocating for staff in management discussions, and promoting national issues such as staffing levels, equality, diversity, and training and development.

Prison Reform Trust: The PRT is a registered charity in the United Kingdom. It was established in 1981 by prison reform campaigners to promote improvements in prison regimes, equality and human rights in prison, the needs of prisoners' families, and the use of alternatives to custody (see http://www.prisonreformtrust.org.uk/).

Prison Review Oversight Group: This group was established on 2012 by the minister of justice to provide critical analysis of the progress of change within Northern Ireland's prisons and suggest areas of improvement.

Strangeways Prison riots: In April 1990, prisoners orchestrated a 25-day prison riot and rooftop protest in Manchester Prison. The riots resulted from prisoners' grievances about prison conditions, access to families, mistreatment by prison officers, and ignorance of complaints by prison management. One prisoner was killed and scores of prisoners and prison officers were injured. The riots spawned a series of protests in prisons across England, Scotland, and Wales, ranging from orchestrated "sit-downs," destruction of prison wings, and copycat rooftop demonstrations. After a 5-month public inquiry, Lord Woolf and Stephen Tumin published the Woolf Report in February 1991. Based on their findings, they recommended a major reform of the prison service. Recommendations included a more visible leadership, an enhanced role for staff, a national system of accredited standards, and changes to estate structure. The report became known as the "blueprint" for all modern prisons in the United Kingdom.

Strategic Efficiency and Effectiveness (SEE) program: A 4-year change management program tasked with delivering change similar to the reforms of the police service. It aims to produce end-to-end structural and cultural changes. It is currently in its third year of operation.

The "Troubles": A colloquialism used to describe the ethnonationalist and sectarian conflict in Northern Ireland (also spreading into the Republic of Ireland, England, and parts of mainland Europe), beginning with disturbances following civil rights demonstrations on October 5, 1968, and concluding with the "Good Friday Agreement" (see above) on April 10, 1998, which restored self-government to the country.

Timpson: The United Kingdom's largest shoe repairer, key cutter, engraver, and watch-repairing business with over 2400 staff. The company works with prison industries to set up special training workshops for offenders in a number of prisons in the United Kingdom, which prepare them for employment in the company postrelease. Ex-prisoners constitute 4% of the workforce, with the managing director, James Timpson, quoting on the success of the scheme: "I find the staff we've recruited from prisons are among the best colleagues we've got."

North America

II

Eduardo Enrique Gomez García, Head of Independent Office of Social Prevention and Rehabilitation, Mexico

8

BRIAN NORRIS

Contents

Overview

By 2012, the Mexican federal* penitentiary system was at a crossroads in its history. Mexico had been in the midst of a war on organized crime since president Felipe Calderon (PAN, 2006–2012) took office. While Mexican presidents as early as Carlos Salinas de Gortari (PRI, 1988–1994) and Ernesto Zedillo (PRI, 1994–2000) had attempted to fight organized crime, Calderon greatly accelerated the government's efforts. Calderon's hardline policies triggered a backlash that intensified violence in the short run. The homicide rate in the country increased from approximately 10/100,000 citizens in 2006 to 24/100,000 in 2010, the latter about 5 times as high as that of the US.† Calderon's successor Enrique Peña Nieto (PRI, 2012–present) vowed in his presidential campaign to reduce the violence in Mexico.

Federal penitentiary reform began in 2008 as an integral part of the Calderon administration's efforts to weaken drug cartels such as the Sinaloa Cartel, Los Zetas, the Gulf Cartel, the Juárez Cartel, the Beltrán-Leyva Organization, La Familia Michoacana, and the Tijuana Cartel. Centerpieces of penitentiary reform included increasing the inmate capacity of the federal system and professionalizing the recruitment and training of its personnel.

Mexican History and the Origins of Its Penitentiary System

Mexico shares a common Iberian heritage with all Spanish and Portuguese-speaking countries of the Western Hemisphere. The principal features of this tradition in Mexico include the Spanish language, an established Catholic Church, the Catholic religion, the historical experiences of the Re-Conquest and the Conquest, the distinctive nineteenth-century Latin American independence struggle, and Roman and Iberian legal institutions.‡ The Third Wave of democratic expansion—the transition of some 30 countries from non democratic to democratic political systems between 1974 and 2000—affected Mexico just as it did Chile, El Salvador, Peru, Argentina, Brazil and other Latin American countries.§

* "Federal" in this context means "national."

† Data from Fernando Escalante Gonzalbo, Colegio de Mexico, 7/8/13. The Mexican murder rate is still only half that of Venezuela.

‡ See Morse (1964).

§ Huntington (1991).

But Mexico is also unique in North America. Early on, Mexico developed a strong national identity through war experiences, including its loss in the Mexican-American War of 1846–1847 and its expulsion of Maximilian I, the French Emperor of Mexico from 1864 to 1867 (Bushnell and Macaulay, 1994). The Mexican Revolution of 1910–1920, in which 3% of the population perished, reinforced Mexico's national identity and also founded its modern civilian authoritarian single-party regime dominated by the PRI. While undemocratic, the 1929–2000 PRI regime gave Mexico a level of political and economic stability unrivaled among other Latin American countries. This stability arguably facilitated Mexico's transition to democracy, marked by Vicente Fox's (PAN, 2000–2006) unseating of the PRI in unprecedented free and fair elections in 2000, and its transition to a free-market economy in roughly the same period (Huntington, 2006; Gonzalez, 2008).

Modern Mexico is a middle income country with a per capita GDP of $14,800 (PPP, 2011 est., 86th of 227 countries) and a population of 115 million (2012 est., 11th of 239 countries). Mexico's government today is a federal republic comprising 32 states with substantial autonomy. The president is elected by popular vote for a single 6-year term. Suffrage is universal for those over 18. Congress is bicameral with a mixture of geographic and corporate representation. Written as "the world's first socialist constitution,"* its current constitution dates to 1917. In fact, the Mexican legal system is characterized by a combination of Roman civil law and the influence of the US constitution. Its criminal courts employ a written inquisitorial form of trial, though initiatives to adopt oral adversarial trials are increasingly influential. Mexico accepts the jurisdiction of the International Court of Justice with reservations and accepts the jurisdiction of the International Criminal Court.

The modern Mexican penitentiary system dates to 1900, when Porfirio Diaz, president and dictator of Mexico from 1876 to 1910, built in Mexico City the Lecumberri Prison, a grandiose penitentiary based on Jeremy Bentham's Panopticon design. Bentham's ideas had long been influential in the region. In neighboring Colombia, Francisco de Paula Santander mandated that schools teach Bentham in 1824. In Mexico, the *cientificos*—scientifically-informed bureaucrats—of the modernizing Diaz dictatorship carried the Benthamite torch in the late nineteenth and early twentieth centuries. Lecumberri Prison opened in Mexico City in 1900 with 996 spaces and wards for women and juveniles. During the course of the twentieth century, Ramon Mercader, the assassin of Leon Trotsky, Pancho Villa, the famous Mexican revolutionary, and Goyo Cardenas, a serial killer, passed time within its walls.†

* See Articles 3, 27, 123, and 130.

† On Santander, see Bushnell (2011a).

The first federal prison was Islas Marias, built in 1905 and still in operation today. Until 1991, when Almoloya de Juarez penitentiary was built, Islas Marias was the only federal prison and federal prisoners other than those in Islas Marias were placed in state prisons (García Andrade, 2004).

Throughout the twentieth century, state-run prisons in Mexico's 32 states imitated Lecumberri's modern ethos by building, staffing and filling permanent prisons with inmates. But the administration in these state prisons was never professionalized, and corrections theory was lacking. Today, state prisons are sometimes incapable of resisting external assaults and corruption from drug cartels. Between May 2009 and December 2012, 446 inmates escaped and 84 people died in 6 separate mass jailbreaks in state prisons in Zacatecas, Tamaulipas, Nuevo Leon, Coahuila, and Durango.*

Mexican public opinion has traditionally been deeply divided on the penitentiary system. On the one hand, human rights advocates decried the conditions of Lecumberri, which was designed for only about 1,000 inmates, but by 1971 housed 3,800. Organized groups were successful in getting Lecumberri closed in 1976 and converting the facility into a museum and national archives (Bushnell, 2011a,b). On the other hand, critics of that movement argued that actions like this left the Mexican penitentiary sector under-resourced. By 2005 the entire federal system in Mexico had capacity for only about 3,500 inmates, despite the fact that the Mexican judiciary had convicted about 45,000 individuals of federal crimes.

In 2013 Mexico had a national inmate population of about 242,000 and an incarceration rate of about 211 inmates per 100,000 population. For comparison, the US had an incarceration rate of about 500 per 100,000 (2013), or about 2.4 times that of Mexico. Over the last decade, Mexico's national incarceration rate has increased from about 183 per 100,000 in 2003. In 2013, about 25,000 (10%) prisoners were in federal prisons and 217,000 were in state penitentiaries. Mexico has 15 federal facilities and 405 state facilities. About 95% of the prison population was male in 2013 (Segob, 2013). Since approximately 99% of Mexico's population speaks Spanish, there are no significant ethno-linguistic gang problems in its penitentiaries (INEGI, 2013).

The Context for Penitentiary Reform under Calderon

The Calderon penitentiary reform should be understood as the latest chapter in a long series of efforts by the Mexican government to address an

* Town, state, approximate date and number of prisoners escaped/slain: Zacatecas, Zacatecas, 5/17/2009, 53/0; Gomez Palacio, Durango, 2010, 0/17*; Nuevo Laredo, Tamaulipas, 12/17/2010, 190/0; Matamoros, Tamaulipas, 3/25/2011, 41/0; Apodaca, Nuevo Leon, 2/21/2012, 30/44; Piedras Negras, Coahuila, 9/17/12, 132/0; and Gomez Palacio, Durango, 12/20/12, 0/23. *Seventeen killed were citizens outside penitentiary after corrupt guards allowed prisoners to escape.

increasingly complex security situation. Though violence did increase during the Calderon administration, Mexico has had long-standing elevated levels of violence. The Mexican per capita murder rate averaged about 2.2 times that of the US for the period of 1990–2010. This was so even though Mexico has only about 1/6 the firearms per capita of the United States (Norris, 2013).

Elevated violence is a complex social phenomenon with many causes, but in Mexico it undoubtedly has important links to organized crime. Organized crime began in the 1950s as smuggling operations sought to evade the Mexican government's protectionist economic policies, but by the 1990s these organizations had become increasingly complex and dangerous transnational drug organizations (García Luna, 2011).

The early stages of the war on drug cartels began under presidents Salinas in 1988 and Zedillo in 1994, both of whom relied on the Mexican military instead of police forces. The military was especially important because it was the only security organization that the executive could consistently rely on to follow orders at the national level (Grayson, 2010). As a federal body with a national mission and vertical social integration, the military is generally more stable, less prone to corruption, and more meritocratic than other security forces such as the state police.

By 2006, the Mexican police and penitentiary systems were ready for advanced public administration reforms. The existing federal system was too small, not fully professionalized, and had an inconsistent institutional culture. Calderon appointed Genaro García Luna to head the Secretariat of Public Security (SSP),* the national-level agency overseeing the federal police force and the federal penitentiary system. Under García Luna the SSP expanded the federal police force from about 10,000 to 35,000 men during 2006–2011 through a security sector reform called *Plataforma Mexico*. The SSP also increased the inmate capacity of its federal penitentiaries more than 200% from 2009 to 2011. In 2009 the SSP founded the National Academy of Penitentiary Administration (ANAP), which selects trainees through an unprecedented merit-based civil service process.†

Some reforms were significant for unintuitive reasons. For instance, though it is only a fraction of the size of the Mexico City police force, the newly constituted federal police was still important because it offered reformers the opportunity to build a more professionalized force instead of trying to reform an existing corrupt one.

* In January 2013, the Peña Nieto administration abolished the SSP, and the SEGOB absorbed the SSP's institutions.

† García Luna, national police 95; prison sector 105-11; merit-based criteria 66-7 and 112-5.

Introduction

The principal interviewee in this chapter is General Eduardo Enrique Gomez García, who served 32 years with the Mexican army. Since 2008, General Gomez has led the Independent Office of Social Prevention and Rehabilitation (OADPRS), the operational arm of the Mexican federal prison system. Observations from a tour of Altiplano, a maximum-security federal prison outside Mexico City and comments from other OADPRS employees are also included. Interviews took place in August 2012, and subsequent trips to Mexico were made in March and June 2013. The following interview took place at SSP headquarters in Mexico City. Interviews were not recorded, per SSP regulations.

General Gomez is a portly man with a staid demeanor and tightly-cropped silver hair. During the interview he was dressed in a well-tailored business suit. The SSP headquarters is located in a modern 8-storey office building in the heart of Mexico City. Previously the headquarters of an electric company, the building has a corporate feel and our interview took place in a conference room with modern art, a skylight and leather chairs. At the time of our meeting, the building was undergoing major remodeling. The sound of hammers and power tools filtered through the walls, and SSP employees and construction workers buzzed about. The building exuded an atmosphere of activity.

Career

Gomez comes from an upper middle-class background and studied in the military educational system (*castrense*) from an early age. As a young man in the 1960s he attended Mexico City's University of Anahuac, a Catholic university founded in 1964 that offers classes in business administration, public administration, psychology, law, architecture and the humanities. Early in his college career Gomez wanted to study the public administration of penitentiaries, but such specialized programs did not exist. He studied for a general degree in public administration, eventually receiving a PhD. Gomez served 32 years in the Mexican military and retired with the rank of General.

His reinsertion into public service came in 2000 with the election of Vicente Fox. The alternation in power that the unprecedented 2000 election entailed allowed new political leaders to make appointments to key government ministries. These leaders drew on a new pool of talent. Fox appointed General Rafael Macedo de la Concha as attorney general. Macedo de la Concha in turn brought three trusted colleagues into government, one of whom was Gomez.

Beginning in 2000, Gomez led initiatives in the Mexican Attorney General's Office (PGR) to improve coordination across different ministries within the executive branch and also helped create Metropol, a unified municipal police force in northern Mexico.

Once the Calderon administration began to focus on penitentiary reform, substantive appointments were needed to oversee the major expansion of the federal system. García Luna appointed José Patricio Patiño Arias to be the sub secretary of the Federal Prisons System, the highest prison official within the SSP. Patiño's primary function was external, managing political relations. In 2008, General Gomez was appointed to head OADRPS, the unit responsible for operational policy in federal prisons, including corrections policy, staffing, training, and infrastructure expansion.*

Changes Experienced

There were profound changes in the federal penitentiary system under Calderon. Sweeping reforms manifested themselves in four categories: increase in the size of the sector, merit-based recruiting, enhanced management practices, and the promotion of organizational identity and pride among prison personnel.

Impetus to Change

In the early part of the twenty-first century, the capacity of the penitentiary system needed to be expanded because of decades of neglect by the government. Gomez explained that in the 1960s, the legislature passed new laws creating federal offenses, but it did not create the federal prison capacity to match these legal changes. By 2005 there were about 45,000 inmates sentenced under federal offenses, but the federal penitentiary system only had space for 3,500 inmates. This left the remaining 41,000 federal offenders in poorly functioning state prisons.

As late as the 1970s, three categories of institution could receive federal prisoners. First was the Lecumberri Prison. Second was Mexico's local and state prisons, institutions that were completely inadequate for Mexico's increasingly dangerous federal prisoners. Third were four facilities named for their cardinal locations: North, South, East, and West.

Despite the growing need for secure federal prisons, reformers took the capacity of the Mexican prison system in the opposite direction. The closure of Lecumberri Prison in 1976 represented this trend. The problem, stated Gomez, was that the campaign that closed Lecumberri was "humanism without transition." It was a transition *de golpe*, meaning in one fell swoop.

* See also Grayson (2010, pp. 109–111) on the Calderon administration's appointment strategies.

Two changes motivated the Mexican government to address the flaws in the corrections sector. First, the security situation worsened in the 1980s and 1990s as organized crime became increasingly complex, especially in northern Mexico. "The security situation changed, and the state penitentiaries did not do anything," said Gomez. Second, Mexico's transition to democracy in 2000 made the government more responsive to citizens' demands for security. "By the time that [President] Calderon and [Director of SSP] García Luna came to power, there was a crisis [in the penitentiary system]," said Gomez. "Previous administrations did not have a vision for the system. It had been abandoned for many years. [But] there was an expectation of security with the new administration."

Increased Resources

The first improvement was to increase resources. Gomez estimated that the federal system now has the capacity for 18,000 inmates, up from 3,500 in 2005, and will soon achieve space for 25,000. Though still 20,000 short of the capacity needed, it is a great improvement. Employees in the federal system have increased by 4,000 in the last few years, and an addition of 6,000 is planned. Gomez noted under the Calderon administration he was able to purchase new uniforms for OADPRS personnel and for prisoners. He had resources to establish a new training academy for prison personnel, the ANAP, in Jalapa, Veracruz.

Merit-Based Recruiting

Merit-based recruiting at the national level is the second major innovation that has recently emerged in the penitentiary sector. Merit-based recruitment includes an open announcement process in which SSP officials advertise thousands of potential openings through newspaper and internet ads.* In 2009, according to Gomez, the SSP received about 50,000 applications for the 4,000 posts that it filled. Applicants for positions ranging from prison cook to senior security posts must pass drug tests, fingerprint analysis, psychological examinations, aptitude tests, polygraph, physical fitness tests and have a physical inspection of their homes to assure that their material wealth is commensurate with that expected for someone from a given social background. This process assures that the majority of new hires are competent and not involved in organized crime.

* See comments by 17-year analyst of Mexico, Duncan Wood, on new police recruitment ads in the *Milenio* newspaper (Wood, 2013). "Reforming the Ranks: Assessing Police Reform Efforts in Mexico," 2/12/13, Woodrow Wilson Center, [http://www.wilsoncenter.org/event/reforming-the-ranks-assessing-police-reform-efforts-mexico#field_speakers].

Importantly, the military had a strong comparative advantage over other government agencies in this type of nationwide, logistically complex recruiting process. "The military had recruitment [of this sort. But] it had not existed in the penitentiary sector," Gomez said. Though formal policies for civil service exams had long been in place in Mexico, the rigorous implementation by the Calderon administration was exceptional.

When a nationwide recruitment was attempted for the first time in 2010, the process was plagued by unexpected challenges. "We had a national flu epidemic the first time we had a sit-in [standardized] test. It was difficult, but we did it anyway," Gomez remembered.

Enhanced Management Practices

The third major improvement was enhanced management practices. According to Gomez, these included the broadest possible professionalization of the sector through the creation or strengthening of various specializations: administrators, technicians (e.g., psychologists, dieticians), security personnel, and architects, among others. The new practices also included the creation of a National Registry of Penitentiary Information (RENIP). This database provides identifying information for inmates, including fingerprints, photographs, relatives, a tattoo registry and DNA samples.

Other techniques aim to minimize the possibility of prison employees' collusion with organized crime. For instance, through a system of checks-and-balances, administrators intentionally assign multiple individuals to the same task. One passes through multiple checkpoints manned by guards to enter into the inmate population area of Altiplano. These guard stations are monitored via closed-circuit television from the SSP headquarters in Mexico City, one and a half hours away. Organized crime groups wanting to corrupt prison personnel to allow illicit access would have to corrupt not only the local personnel, but also SSP officials in Mexico City.

However, checks-and-balances are not the only anti-corruption technique, and they may not even be the most important. Organizational identity is a crucial, if less intuitive, element in this fight.

Organizational Identity

The fourth major improvement has been to encourage organizational identity and pride in the corrections profession. Penitentiary officials are quick to point out that there is no level of compensation they can offer to public sector workers that would surpass that offered by organized crime. They cannot outbid the cartels. Instead, the employees must resist corruption for other reasons.

When employees are drawn together by a common culture and its physical manifestations, such as uniforms and symbols, they are more likely to think in terms of their participation in a group and see corruption as the betrayal of their common values. For instance, touring Altiplano one sees the organizational seal on walls, windbreakers, uniforms and in every imaginable place. The seal is circular with a blue background, and at its center stands the white profile of an individual standing upon a star between opening prison gates. The organizational names for SSP, OADPRS and Altiplano appear as an integral part of the seal's design. The prison director, Valentin Cardenas Lerma, said, "This identity [makes a worker] impervious to organized crime." He said that this emphasis was new and came "from above," from leaders such as Genaro García Luna, Patricio Patiño, and General Gomez.

Personal Correctional Philosophy

Two mutually reinforcing principles define the corrections philosophy in Mexico: rehabilitation and control.

Rehabilitation

The official name of the federal penitentiary system conveys the emphasis on rehabilitation: the Independent Office of Social Prevention and Rehabilitation.

The belief in rehabilitation rests on three antecedent beliefs about human nature and society. First, all individuals, even inmates, are dignified human beings deserving of ethical treatment. Gomez said, "The idea [of incarceration] is not to humiliate the individual." He empathizes with prisoners in their suffering: "One year inside is like 3 years outside." "If a prisoner passes much time inside [he becomes an institutional man]. He is somebody inside. But outside, no. [When he is] 60 or 70 years old, where does he go?" Similarly, Cardenas said, "The inmate is not an animal." "Many come from a situation of poverty. [But] society closes its doors to them and says, 'the ex-con is bad'." When I asked about the extent to which the philosophy of *lex talionis*, an eye-for-eye, might motivate incarceration policies, Gomez rejected this out of hand. "No," he said flatly.

One practical application of the principle of human dignity is seen in prison officials' attitudes toward an inmate's need to maintain family ties. All human beings need family ties to lead a full life, but how can the inmate achieve this if he spends extended periods in prison? "After 30 years in prison, [an inmate's] wife has remarried, his house is no longer there, his kids are nowhere to be found," said Gomez. Shorter sentences, when feasible, might encourage maintenance of these basic human relations. According to

Cardenas, 95% of the sentences in Altiplano are shorter now than they were in previous years. The shorter sentences give inmates hope for the future. Penitentiary officials further encourage inmates to recognize their children born out of wedlock and to marry the mother of their child. Officials encourage family visits in prison and look for innovative methods such as teleconferencing to promote them.

The second belief about human nature is that all individuals possess reason and can therefore make better decisions given the appropriate incentives. Gomez believes that you can influence inmate behavior through a system of carrots and sticks. "You give benefits for good behavior, and you give a proper punishment [for bad behavior]," he said.

A number of specific policies flow from this assumption of universal rationality. Gomez stated that a prisoner's sentence can be lengthened or reduced based on his behavior, and others spoke of reducing a prisoner's sentence by 3 months for a "model year," a year in which the inmate comports himself well. Educational resources are available to inmates under the assumption that a rational individual will use them to his benefit. Altiplano has a high school equivalency program and an inmate library. Inmates can check out books for 1 week and Bibles for a month.

The third belief on which rehabilitation is based deals with the needs of Mexican society. Rehabilitating inmates reduces the "cost to society," according to Gomez. Society saves resources by not having to incarcerate rehabilitated inmates and rehabilitated inmates become productive members of society.

Control

Control is the second principal element of corrections philosophy. Control has two dimensions. First, control is an internal characteristic of each individual. Self-control can facilitate an inmate's reintegration into society; its absence can impede his reintegration. However, self-control is incomplete in most if not all inmates in the Mexican penitentiary system. For instance, Gomez noted that inmates have been known to kill one another for tennis shoes. In the prison, inmates can use loose tools as weapons. Inmates illegally sell medicines as insignificant as aspirin, and this illicit activity can lead to fights or worse.

Compelling inmates to "respect rules" within the walls of the prison therefore furthers the goal of rehabilitation and also achieves the imperative of control, an end in and of itself.

Deference to the authority of prison officials is fundamental. When we passed three inmates being transported in the hallway in Altiplano, the inmates faced the wall with hands behind their backs and waited for us to pass. "You see, complete respect," said our guide.

Within the prison, an objective classification of inmates according to their level of dangerousness is essential to maintain control. The SSP has the flexibility to place the individual inmate at the required level of security (high, medium, or low) in order to increase security at the level of the prison.

Measures are taken to reduce the risk of prisoners fighting over unequally-distributed resources or over disputes related to trafficking. Providing identical uniforms and footwear to all inmates removes the motivation to take clothes by force, noted Gomez. The scrupulous accounting of medicines in the prison's pharmacy, tools and the chemicals that are stored on-site is fundamental. In the pharmacy, Cardenas invited me to randomly select one medicine from hundreds on the shelf. The pharmacist and I counted the boxes on the shelf, including pills in a partial box, and confirmed that the number matched his manifest perfectly.

The second understanding of control emphasizes the need to separate some dangerous inmates from Mexican society. This understanding of control is what scholars of criminal justice call incapacitation.

At the broadest level, all 115 million Mexicans benefit from the control of dangerous criminals. Housing over 40,000 dangerous convicts with links to organized crime in weak state prisons was a major threat to public safety. "[Practice has been] to put federal prisoners in local jails. This is a problem," said Gomez. For instance, Commandant Carlos Suarez Molina, chief of security at Altiplano, was able to name the prison breaks from state prisons by memory: "Matamoros, 2011, 40 inmates; Tamaulipas, 2 years ago, 600 inmates; Zacatecas, 53 inmates."* Gomez characterized state prisons as very weakly institutionalized.

In contrast, the federal system is capable of containing dangerous individuals. Federal prison directors accomplish this through several policies. General Gomez said of some limited cases. "In some cases we have to separate the [dangerous] inmate even from their family, from criminal contacts, from the outside world completely." This is so because organized crime contacts are almost always local. In limited instances, the SSP can transfer very dangerous inmates to a facility far from their homes, an impossible action for Mexico's 32 state prisons.

Strengthening federal facilities against external assaults further increases control. For instance, the personnel at Altiplano expressed approval of the construction of a barracks on site to protect against outside assaults. "This is very good," said the director of Altiplano. "We fear attacks from groups outside [such as those mentioned above]."

The logical extension of this thinking is that the more robust the federal system can grow and displace state capacity, the safer Mexico will be.

* These figures are on the whole correct.

Gomez summarized his comprehensive philosophy: "We aim for the security of our personnel, society, and the inmate."

Philosophical Coherence

Gomez holds these principles to be mutually reinforcing. For instance, an inmate's self-discipline helps assure safety of the prison staff and inmates and also promotes his reintegration into society. However, principles can conflict, as when the need to separate a dangerous prisoner from his links to organized crime—even if these links include his own family—can also impede reintegration into society at a future date. Gomez recognizes these contradictions as part of a complex set of imperatives that the SSP must juggle. However, the immediate safety of prison personnel and inmates and the safety of Mexican society take precedent. Gomez clarified, "Security is the highest goal."

Problems and Successes Experienced

The recent successes in the Mexican penitentiary system are many, and most are related to the growth of the sector described above.

However, this rapid growth has also created challenges. For instance, the strict standards applied to applicants have yielded high-quality hires, but also prevented OADPRS from meeting its numerical goals. Gomez pointed out that OADPRS still needs to hire 6,000 more corrections workers to reach its goal of 10,000. Clearly, expanding the sector and its personnel will be a challenge that dominates the institutions' efforts for the foreseeable future.

Gomez also sees a need to develop better post-incarceration institutions. These include registry and monitoring systems for sex offenders and "open institutions" such as halfway houses.

Another challenge is managing relationships with groups outside the penitentiary sector that emit laws of various types. In some cases, laws created by such groups can put individual rights into conflict. For instance, Gomez strongly disapproves of Mexican laws that mandate a woman's right to have her child with her in prison until the child turns six. "A woman arrives to prison already pregnant. In times past, the woman would have the baby and then pass it along to family members to raise while she served her prison term. But these days, the child can stay with her in prison until 6 years of age," he said. "It is very utopian [sentiment]." This policy has unintended consequences. First, it is an unfunded mandate. "There is no budget for this." Second, it is inhumane because "a prison is no place for a child."

The origins of this policy come from sincere but misguided efforts by legislators and their advisors. "There are a thousand books and speeches [from advocates for such policies, but the authors of these books and speeches] lack experience, [and lack] practice," Gomez said. Their motivations are rooted in what Gomez calls "humanism." "They are concerned about the rights of the mother, but what about the rights of the child?" he said. Other members of OADPRS echo this opinion of the policy.

Additionally, external groups can micromanage policy. Cardenas condemns some "laws [specifying] sanctions for inmates." For instance, if one prisoner removes food from another's lunch tray, this constitutes "indiscipline" and must be punished by a disproportionate 120 days of sanction (e.g., removing library or phone privileges). By contrast, at times the penalty specified is too light for a given infraction. Cardenas believes that prison administrators should have more discretion, though he does not use this term, in such cases.

Finally, social work of any sort, including prison work, is inherently challenging. Social work puts caring people in contact with individuals who do not always do what is in their best interest. The director of Altiplano recounted the story of a 39-year old inmate who died suddenly, only 8 days after being diagnosed with lung cancer. The inmate's mother, counseled by a lawyer, accused Altiplano of maltreatment, an accusation that occasioned a thorough internal review of the inmate's case file. This review revealed that during years of incarceration the inmate had not asked for medical treatment, though such services existed. However, he had repeatedly requested legal review of his case. "We made the entire contents of his file available to his mother. 'Come and see,' we said. She came to accept that we had not abused her son. She was not happy. No one wants to lose their son. But she was satisfied [that we had not mistreated him]," said Cardenas.

Theory and Practice

Most research that influences penitentiary policy in Mexico is of a very practical orientation. For instance, when asked about formal research, the director of Altiplano noted that his cooks take courses in nutrition. Dieticians have estimated the calorific needs of different groups of prisoners and have designed different menus, including a diabetic menu. Other trainings that the director mentioned included classes on secretarial skills, auditing and security training. One training dealt with the handling of combustible materials. OADPRS also commissions specific studies with local universities on applied topics of interest.

The SSP has the capacity to design its own curriculum internally in the ANAP academy. The academy includes staff with generic research and teaching skills, such as a political scientist, and individuals with applied knowledge, such as dieticians and hazardous chemicals experts.

The most pressing research need for the penitentiary system, according to Gomez, is in the classification of prisoners. Legal classifications, such as federal/state or processed/sentenced,* exist, but a system of risk profile classification for inmates in the system is also needed. Issues include diagnosing and treating drug addicts, appropriately grouping inmates to minimize the security risks, and separating those capable of rehabilitation from the incorrigible. Gomez complained that "there are not experts in such subjects [in Mexico]. There are theories [but not studies or experts]."

Evidence-Based Corrections

Gomez mentions the desirability of creating or strengthening "open institutions" such as supervised release, halfway houses, psychological treatment, and post release suicide prevention. Data from post incarceration treatment programs would also help prison managers track recidivism. Exposure to some of these ideas comes from study tours outside Mexico and from international institutions such as ACA and ICPA.

Mexican prison managers are receptive to any and all forms of formal training for themselves or their personnel. When I asked Cardenas if there were any useless or irrelevant trainings he had ever attended, he could not think of any that fit this description.

Transnational Relations

OADPRS policies originate from multiple sources. At the broadest level, the origins of policies may be classified as national or international. National-level policies come from local learning or from imitating the policies of other Mexican correctional institutions. For instance, as we walked in Altiplano's courtyard, the director pointed to a flagpole planted in the middle of the open area and a steel cable running to a nearby wall. Mexican correctional officials adopted the practice of placing the flagpoles in open spaces after learning of a botched helicopter escape attempt in the Lecumberri Prison in 1975. In contrast, international policies come from outside Mexican borders. For instance, Altiplano uses a system for tool inventory that was developed by the American Correctional Association (ACA). This is a bilateral relationship.

In some cases, national and international norms coincide, but the true origin of the policy is national. For instance, the federal prison system in Mexico has developed strict standards on the production and use of official

* "Processed" refers to an individual waiting for a sentence from a judge.

uniforms and official insignia. Though similar European Union technical recommendations exist, Mexican officials have in fact developed these policies autonomously in response to local imperatives. For instance, Vanesa Pedraza, Advisor for the Coordination of Advisors to the SSP, said, "It is not the case that the European Union arrived with these [technical] standards [for us Mexicans to implement]. I dare say that we originated these policies of our own accord."

National Influences

One of the most important sources of policy in Mexican penitentiaries is local learning. For instance, Gomez indicated that the impetus for major sector reform resulted from "the security situation in the country."

Similarly, the director of Altiplano related the origins of the fire safety policies that his team implements at Altiplano. "Lamentably, a few years ago we had a situation in which one prisoner sharing a cell with another set his roommate on fire. Our guards had great difficulty in getting to the burning prisoner because his attacker had jammed the locks. And when our guards finally did reach the poor fellow, our fire extinguishers did not work!" Based on this experience, Altiplano changed policies on locking cell doors to allow for emergency opening procedures and further implemented an inspection regimen for fire extinguishers.

Learning from quasi-local experiences, such as those of neighboring Honduras, can reinforce such lessons. The director and his team read newspaper accounts of a prison fire in Comayagua, Honduras, that killed approximately 300 inmates in February 2012 (Hernandez and Archibald, 2012). Knowledge of this event motivated the management team at Altiplano to ban all smoking in the institution.

International Influences: Bilateral

International influences can be further subdivided into bilateral and multilateral influences. Bilateral collaborations mentioned included ACA, the National Fire Protection Association (NFPA), and prison systems in many foreign countries.

Among bilateral collaborations, those with American institutions have been very influential. For instance, Altiplano officials found the collaboration with ACA exceedingly helpful. In additional to implementing the ACA tool inventory system, Altiplano has passed the ACA certification process, which has 127 separate rubrics. OADPRS officials adapted criteria to its local circumstances. For instance, the ACA recommends that at least one female guard be present at all times with female prisoners, which is not applicable to the all-male Altiplano. Managers at Altiplano therefore ignore this scoring criterion. Altiplano also employs a labeling regimen for dangerous chemicals in its storehouse promoted by the NFPA.

According to Gomez, ACA recommendations for the construction of prison plumbing, doors, surveillance systems, laundry facilities, furniture and other engineering and architectural facets of the built environment of prisons have been useful at a national level.

Bilateral assistance has also affected the Mexican penitentiary system. The Merida Initiative, a 2008 agreement between the US and Mexico to collaborate in the war on organized crime, has been influential. Through the Merida Initiative, Mexican penitentiary personnel have received technical training at the New Mexico Corrections Department Training Academy in Santa Fe, New Mexico. According to Gomez, visits to such facilities helped OADPRS create its own training academy, the ANAP. I viewed resources purchased through the Merida Initiative at Altiplano.

Gomez mentioned visits to penitentiary systems in Singapore, Chile, France, England, Italy and Germany. He found the English and Italian systems' emphasis on rehabilitation to be useful. By contrast, some policies observed in foreign nations would be wholly inappropriate for Mexico. For instance, Gomez was appalled by some German policies. "Due to cultural differences, there are super-excesses [in the German system from a Mexican perspective]. Germany builds houses for some prisoners. And furthermore, some prisoners have paid vacations," he said. This would never do in Mexico.

Gomez further emphasized not only what Mexican federal prison officials can learn from outsiders, but also what lessons they can impart to less institutionalized penitentiary systems within their sphere of influence. These include the weakly institutionalized prison systems of Central American countries such as Guatemala, Honduras and El Salvador, along with Mexican state prisons. The Central Americans in particular need information on construction techniques that the Mexican government and Mexican construction firms can impart. OADPRS periodically convokes meetings and trainings to make their lessons available to receptive prison managers.

International Influences: Multilateral

Multilateral institutions that the interviewees mentioned included the United Nations, the European Union and the International Corrections and Prisons Association (ICPA).

Gomez mentioned the UN minimum standards for prisons promulgated in 1957 and 1971, and, since the 1990s, the ICPA has had forums in Africa and Asia that have allowed prison officials from different countries to share experiences.

Some of the norms arising from the influence of such international institutions deal with very generic topics such as human rights. The Altiplano director was skeptical that such exhortations were meaningful at the operational level. "The public has fantasies [about the penitentiary sector]. They believe we treat inmates badly, that we deny them rights," he said. But this is not the case. For instance, a 2011 law explicitly added "protection of human rights" to the penitentiary system's goals. "But we already did that [here in Mexico]," he said.

General Assessments

Overall, General Gomez is pleased with the emphasis and resources that the penitentiary sector has received in the last several years. The director of Altiplano also said, "Without the resources [we have received], there would be no revolution [in the corrections sector in Mexico]." The one area Gomez would wish to see developed in the future is post incarceration rehabilitative programs (see Section 6).

On the whole, the prison sector is poorly understood by Mexican society. Its task is essential but not fully appreciated by the public at large. For instance, one of Gomez's employees, a medical doctor who had come to the prison sector from the health ministry, said he had never thought of working in corrections before and most Mexicans do not. "Very few people want to work in the penitentiary sector," he said. One reason is because people believe the work is unsafe. "But [to the contrary, the work] is 100% safe. There are no prison riots," he said. Very few workers in the sector have any complaints, and news of work in the sector spreads by word of mouth. "People recommend the work to others," he said. This medic additionally liked the grants offered by OADPRS for individual workers to receive more professional training. "The health sector [where he worked for years] does not do this for its employees."

Conclusion

Gomez seemed forthcoming and highly competent. The factual information he provided was on the whole accurate. In some instances, further research provided missing context for explanations. For example, Gomez asserted that Lecumberri Prison was closed in 1976 under hurried and rash circumstances, but the modern Santa Martha prison, opened in 1957, was created in part to relieve Lecumberri, though the transition was plagued by many pitfalls (García Ramirez, 1979). But any doubts raised by data of this sort are minor, and Gomez was obviously knowledgeable.

Themes

There are striking similarities between the public administration reforms made in the US Progressive Era (referred to by criminal justice scholars as the Professional Era) and the modern reforms in Mexico's penitentiary sector. The writings of August Vollmer and his student O.W. Wilson would be intelligible for Mexican penitentiary officials today.* Genero García Luna, while still director of the SSP, made explicit comparison between Mexico's situation and the US fight against organized crime in the 1920s and also favorably mentioned the more recent "Broken Windows" theory that informed police reforms in New York (García Luna, 2012).

Furthermore, the Mexican experience in prison reform is consonant with what political scientists know about modernizing regimes. Developing countries often initially rely on military personnel in instituting large and complex public administration reforms because of the military's relatively high capacity for merit-based recruiting, vertical social integration, national scope, and international connections (Huntington, 2006: pp. 192–263). For instance, the Japanese Ministry of International Trade and Investment (MITI), which so effectively vaulted the Japanese car industry to international dominance in the 1970s, actually began as a military bureaucracy in Japanese imperial wars with China in the late nineteenth and mid-twentieth centuries.† Similarly, General Gomez's experience with merit-based recruiting has been invaluable for the professionalization of the federal Mexican penitentiary sector.

Additionally, democracy had an important impact, even if at times this impact was ambiguous. Some interviewed criticized the democratic processes and the interest groups that it can empower. This is consistent with Peruvian economist Hernando de Soto's observation that impractical legal codes influenced by interest groups tend to force managers into stark choices between non compliance (called informality or illegality) or implementing bad policy (de Soto, 2000). But on the other hand, interviewees made little or no association between democracy on a national level and negative outcomes. For instance, it is difficult to imagine opportunities for new managers like Gomez without the alternation in power that democracy brought in 2000.

Scholarly Engagement

On the whole, the interviewees' comments echo the long-standing differences of perspective between analysts and practitioners. In 1833 Alexis de Tocqueville registered the skepticism of Elam Lynds, pioneer of the Auburn system, over the practicability of Edward Livingston's penal codes:

* Vollmer (1936); Mexico actually has a Spanish translation of Wilson and McLaren (1963).
† Francis Fukuyama, address, Johns Hopkins/SAIS, April 3, 2012.

"If Mr. Livingston, for instance, should be ordered to apply his theories of penitentiaries to people born like himself, in a class of society in which much intelligence and moral sensibility existed, I believe he would arrive at excellent results; but prisons, on the contrary, are filled with coarse beings, who have had no education, and who perceive with difficulty ideas, and often even sensations." (Beaumont and Tocqueville, 1833).

Nonetheless, there are opportunities for further scholarly engagement. Mexican officials were eager for guidance on the internal classification of inmates and therefore might be receptive to information on the Adult Internal Management System (AIMS). The high level of analytical capacity in the ANAP would allow Mexicans to engage with the underlying analysis of the AIMS and other EBP analyses. Mexican prison officials have clearly shown themselves capable of adapting relevant analysis to local circumstances. Finally, observing peer institutions has been important to policy in the Mexican penitentiary system (See DiIulio, 1987).

Glossary

ACA: American Correctional Association.

Altiplano: A maximum-security federal prison in Almoloya de Juarez, State of Mexico, about one and a half hours from Mexico City.

ANAP: National Academy of Penitentiary Administration. National training academy for the federal penitentiary system. Founded in 2009 in Veracruz.

***científico*:** During the modernizing Porfirio Diaz dictatorship (1876–1910), an influential group of intellectuals and public officials who believed in guiding public policy by scientific principles and the best methods and data available. Policy initiatives in Mexico included railroad construction, the first public health campaigns, and eugenics movements.

ICPA: International Corrections and Prisons Association.

INEGI: National Institute of Statistics and Geography. Mexican Census Bureau.

Merida Initiative: A 2008 agreement between the George W. Bush and Felipe Calderon administrations to collaborate in the war on organized crime in Mexico.

NFPA: National Fire Protection Association.

OADPRS: Independent Office of Social Prevention and Rehabilitation. The federal prison system in Mexico.

PAN: National Action Party. Founded in 1939, the PAN was the principal opposition political party in Mexico during the rule of the PRI from 1929 to 2000.

Plataforma Mexico: An integrated set of policies from the Calderon administration to address security concerns related to organized crime and narco-trafficking.

PRI: Institutional Revolutionary Party. Founded in 1929, the PRI was the only political party to hold national power in Mexico's single-party civilian authoritarian regime created after the Mexican Revolution (1910–1920). The PRI ruled continuously until 2000.

PRG: Procurator General of the Republic. Attorney General's Office.

SEGOB: Secretary of Governing. Mexican Executive Branch.

SSP: Secretariat of Public Security. Federal government entity responsible for federal police force, federal prison system, and some domestic intelligence functions. Abolished in 2012.

Keith Deville, Warden of Richwood Correctional Center, Louisiana, United States

9

ROBERT HANSER

Contents

Overview

This interview was conducted at Richwood Correctional Center, in Richwood, Louisiana, between Robert Hanser (the interviewer) and Warden Keith Deville (the inerviewee). Before discussing the interview itself, some overview information regarding corrections in the state of Louisiana will be provided within the following two pages. Later in this chapter, we will focus the remainder of our attention on the interview itself, highlighting input from Warden Deville throughout. In Louisiana, inmates are housed both in state facilities and in local facilities, with sheriff departments and/or private prisons helping to house the state's offender population. In 2012, there were 18,599 inmates who were housed in approximately 12 state facilities. Another 20,624 inmates were housed in local sheriff's facilities and/or private prison facilities throughout the state (LDPSC, 2013). Other inmates are located at separate and specialized assignments (such as the state police barracks) or at contract transitional work facilities throughout the state. As we will see later in this interview, private prisons are a substantial resource in Louisiana, but for now, it is probably just sufficient to point out that in Louisiana, there are 40,170 inmates and nearly half are in state facilities while the other half are housed in a collection of other types of localized or privately owned facilities (LDPSC, 2013).

The other segment of the correctional system in Louisiana consists of the Division of Probation and Parole. The adult division (my interview will focus on adult corrections, not juvenile corrections), has 21 offices strategically located throughout the state with a total of 511 officers allocated to supervise more than 70,000 probationers and parolees in the community, 99% of whom are felons (LDPSC, 2013). Further, about 2,700 of the 70,000 offenders are convicted sex offenders, many of whom require specialized supervision, treatment and compliance with registration and notification laws (LDPSC, 2013). The sentencing of sex offenders is taken very seriously in Louisiana as is their supervision. As such, Probation and Parole initiated a global positioning satellite (GPS) electronic monitoring program in 2007. Roughly 100 sex offenders in the highest risk category are monitored via the use of this GPS system (LDPSC, 2013).

In determining the state of corrections in Louisiana, it is important to consider the key tenets of the state wide mission for the correctional system. Essentially, the mission is to enhance public safety through safe and secure incarceration of offenders, the effective use of probation and parole supervision, *and the implementation of proven rehabilitative strategies that successfully reintegrate offenders into society* (LDPSC, 2013). It is important to note that this last statement is important for two reasons: Firstly, this statement demonstrates that we use *proven* strategies, which in and of itself should be an indicator to the reader that evidence-based practices are used in our state system and secondly, the state system emphasizes the use of *rehabilitative strategies* which are intended to facilitate the *reintegration* of offenders into society. This second point provides a clue as to the over arching correctional philosophy that currently guides the field of corrections in Louisiana.

It is important to first clarify these two points because later in this interview, we will talk about the use of evidence-based practices. In that section, an idea as to what should be considered evidence-based practice is provided as well as definitions and sources from the federal government. While this is important, the reader should know at the outset that the correctional system of this state is indeed committed to the use of such evidence-based practices. The very mission statement of the state's correctional services speaks to this issue. In addition, the Louisiana correctional philosophy is one grounded in reintegration and rehabilitation. In yet another section of this interview, the philosophical view of corrections, from Deville's perspective, is a combination of reintegration and rehabilitation of the offender population. Much of his perspective on corrections has, undoubtedly, been shaped by his experiences with this state's correctional system.

A large proportion of his 33 years of correctional service with Louisiana was spent at three facilities. These three prisons were Louisiana State Penitentiary at Angola (commonly referred to just as "Angola") which was his first assignment in 1978 (when he began his career in corrections). He then transferred to Elayn Hunt Correctional Center in 1979. He then worked at the Work Training Facility North for 19 years, and ultimately in 2007 ended up at the J. Levy Dabadie Correctional Center. He was promoted throughout the system and, along the way, transferred to these facilities over time due to position opportunities or promotions which resulted in his becoming a prison warden during the last 5 years of his career. When Deville retired from the Louisiana state correctional system, he was eventually hired by a private prison company, LaSalle Corrections, Inc.

LaSalle Corrections is a company that has built, developed, and operated correctional centers throughout the states of Louisiana and Texas. This company began providing assistance to law enforcement agencies that needed space for their incarnated population in 1997. LaSalle Corrections, as its own private system, manages 11 correctional facilities throughout Louisiana and Texas with a total population that exceeds 7,500 inmates in custody (LaSalle Corrections, 2013). The organization has over 1,100 employees serving at these locations. This private system consists of facilities that house minimum and medium-security inmates, providing correctional services for local, state, and federal law enforcement agencies (LaSalle Corrections, 2013).

For this interview, information regarding the two correctional systems in which Deville has worked is provided to make clear when either the State of Louisiana or LaSalle Corrections is referenced in this interview. Because many readers will either not be accustomed to the field of corrections or, even more likely, will not be familiar with the correctional system of Louisiana, this information was included as part of the introduction. Naturally, some of this information will either serve as a precursor to the section that follows or it may even overlap—slightly—with information that follows. If this is the case, it is still a good outcome as some information warrants repetition from different perspectives and in different contexts so as to adequately show the comparative nature of these multiple experiences that have occurred throughout the years of Deville's career in corrections. At this point, responses to numerous questions that were presented to warden Deville, in regard to his career and its development throughout the years, will be provided in the pages that follow.

Introduction

Selected for interview was warden Keith Deville, of Richwood Correctional Center, a medium-security prison in the Northeast Louisiana region. The interview was conducted in the warden's office, for the most part, but also entailed other interviews in different areas of the prison while he "made his rounds" from one place to the other throughout the facility. During this time, I was able to observe his day-to-day activities in a number of facets and capacities. During shift change and during supervisors' meetings, the warden would lead the meeting but would also have his Assistant wardens with him to disseminate information and provide leadership to security and auxiliary services staff. When in the work release sections or the substance abuse treatment areas of the prison, warden Deville exhibited an understanding of how different forms of programming were critical to aiding inmates who, without such programming, would have few, if any, skills with which to reenter society. Observation of day-to-day activities in other areas of the prison made it clear that warden Deville's job is one that is multifaceted and requires both broad and in-depth knowledge.

While conducting the interview itself, it was clear that the entire experience had been quite pleasant and informative. Staff were introduced and demonstrated professionalism that was both serious yet approachable in nature. Warden Deville was relaxed and made a point to make arrangements that were comfortable and conducive to effective interviewing. Upon learning some of the key areas of inquiry that would be relevant to students wishing to gain insight from a prison warden, he made a point of finding materials and documents that would ensure the accuracy of the information provided. This ensured that the interview itself was productive and that readers would be given appropriate and adequate information regarding prison operations in this practitioner's facility and the correctional system overall.

Career

My career with LaSalle Corrections began in 2011, shortly after I retired from my position as warden of the Dabadie Correctional Center. I was hired at the rank of warden and was assigned to Richwood Correctional Center, which is located in Northeast Louisiana in the town of Richwood. The total bed capacity for Richwood Correctional Center is 1,127 inmates and it is designated a medium-security facility (LaSalle Corrections, 2013). I currently supervise approximately 126 employees at my facility and have two notable programs, aside from those typically found in prison facilities, which are also under my watch. These two programs are our Work Release Program and our substance abuse treatment program which has been named the Blue Walters Substance Abuse Treatment Program.

Our work release program has consisted of a partnership between LaSalle Corrections and a regional poultry business. Other local sites also increasingly have requested inmates for employment under the work release program due to the successes that have been witnessed in the past few years and, as a result, it has become clear that our work release program addresses several market challenges, but the main problem that it assists in correcting is offender recidivism. According to the Re-Entry Policy Council, the recidivism rates of offenders who participate in vocational and educational training are lower by as much as 20%–60% than those who do not; participants also create fewer problems during incarceration and earn higher wages after release (LaSalle Corrections, 2013). This regionally focused work release program also positively impacts local economic development by providing employees who are regularly drug tested, show up on time, are well trained, and typically are pleased to be employed. Further, we provide evidence-based programming to aid offenders in their transition into the community. Our vocational and educational programs prepare offenders for the work release program by providing them with marketable skills that will be useful during and after incarceration.

Lastly, our substance abuse treatment program at Richwood Correctional Center is well known throughout the state. The Blue Walters Program is an 84 day intensive treatment program that provides good-time for offenders who complete this curriculum. Prior to beginning this program, inmates are given a battery of assessments that include a psychosocial interview, the Alcohol, Smoking and Substance Involvement Screening Test (ASSIST), the Mini International Neuropsychiatric Interview 5.0 (MINI 5.0) and, when appropriate, the Maryland Addiction Questionnaire (MAQ), and the Personal Experience Inventory (PEI). After completion of the assessment battery, inmates are then allowed to begin participation in the program (LaSalle Corrections, 2013).

This program is coupled with an additional program known as the Successful Treatment of Addiction and Recovery (STAR) Long-Term Program which is a year-long substance abuse treatment community. The STAR program is open to any inmate suffering from a substance abuse disorder with less than 4 years remaining on his sentence. Additional services in the STAR Program include, but are not limited to, addictions counseling, counseling for criminal thinking and behavior, mental health counseling, anger management, parenting classes, and more. Lastly, a variety of peer support programs are also simultaneously offered to participants (LaSalle Corrections, 2013).

I wanted to provide this information regarding the two correctional systems in which I work to make clear when I reference either the State of Louisiana or LaSalle Corrections to readers of this interview. Because I am aware that many readers will either not be accustomed to the field of corrections or, even more likely, will not be familiar with the correctional system of

Louisiana, I thought that it would be wise to include this information as part of my introduction. Naturally, some of this information will either serve as a precursor to the section that follows (my own career overview) or it may even overlap—slightly—with information that follows. If this is the case, I consider it a good outcome as some information warrants repetition from different perspectives and in different contexts so as to adequately show the comparative nature of these multiple experiences that have occurred throughout the years of my career in corrections. I will now proceed to address the numerous questions that I have been presented in regard to my career and its development throughout the years.

Initially, when I was young, I really had no plans to work in the field of corrections. I did have multiple family members who did work in this field, but I really had not seriously considered it as an option. But, as I approached graduation from high school, my father talked with me and encouraged me to work for the Louisiana Department of Corrections because I did not seem to have any other viable plans for my future. So, I basically entered this field because it was one that was accessible at the time, and because I really had not made any other plans otherwise.

My career began at the Louisiana Penitentiary at Angola and later I transferred to the Elayn Hunt Correctional Center, then later to Dabadie Correctional Center. I started as an entry-level correctional officer and worked my way up the ranks of security. Over time, I was provided with opportunities to work as a part of specialized teams and this is when my career became more interesting and rewarding. Indeed, at two different points while working in the security ranks, I actually worked in what I would call "dream" jobs. The first of these dream jobs was training bloodhounds and narcotics dogs. I was completely fascinated with the dog handling and dog training experience. Amazingly, I was being paid to do work that I absolutely loved. Later, I was promoted to Commander over the "chase team," which is a specialized team whose mission is to locate, apprehend, and bring back into institutional custody those inmates who escape from facilities. This resulted in over 200 felony arrests while I worked collaboratively with local, state, and federal authorities.

Later, I was promoted to Chief Investigative Officer and, with this promotion, I found myself becoming much more serious about the quality of work that we provided. During this time, I served as an expert witness in several criminal trials and also in multiple unemployment hearings. At that time, my highest goal had been to become Chief of Security or, perhaps, make the rank of Colonel. I really never expected to go further than this and certainly did not expect to be promoted to the rank of warden at Dabadie Correctional Center.

While I served as warden at the J. Levy Dabadie Correctional Center, I also served on the Board of Directors of the Department of Corrections Credit Union. Throughout my career in corrections, I was fortunate enough to receive several awards, among them most notably the Secretary of Corrections Award of Excellence, Lawman of the Year (which included nominees from corrections, local and state police), and the Honorary Senator award. I have always felt a bit humbled to have received these awards but I am grateful that others have seen my service as constructive, useful, and beneficial to the State of Louisiana.

Now, in 2013, I have worked in the field of corrections for nearly 35 years and I am retired from the Louisiana Department of Public Safety and Corrections (LDPSC). Upon retiring from the State of Louisiana, I was hired by LaSalle Corrections as the warden of Richwood Correctional Center. Thus, my career has been one with decades of service to the State of Louisiana and has also included over 2 years experience in the realm of private corrections. It is experience from both public and private corrections that I bring to this interview, including the ability to compare the two modes of correctional operation.

My career has been very different to what I initially expected. I never had thought that I would gain the promotions that I had obtained. I also did not think, especially in my early years, that I would become a warden. So, I can say that the differences in my career from those that I had expected have been due to good outcomes. Even further, I really had not anticipated that I would eventually work in the world of private corrections after completing my career with the state. In all honesty, the private corrections industry is much different from the public sector and, while I do enjoy the work, I have found pros and cons to each. In addition, I have had to go through a bit of an adjustment period as I transitioned from one version of corrections to the other. In speaking of this transition, I would first like to say that some of the adjustments were inevitable. After all, one does not retire from an agency after 30 years of experience and join another agency (whether public or private) without some need for adjustment and the need to acclimate to the different people, culture, and conditions.

The world of private corrections is one that moves much quicker than public service corrections and, of course, it is an area of correctional operations that is much more geared toward fiscally sound decisions. This has led to some differences in how one manages the facility but, in saying that, I must say that when something is needed by the facility, the system is capable of moving very quickly to correct the problem, much more quickly than the state system.

On the other hand, the state system is much longer established and due to the sheer size of the operation, coupled with the years of operational history that it has to build upon, has a variety of resources that exist, even when those resources may not be cost-effective. But this current economic climate has really harmed the state system, resulting in the closure of at least three state prisons. As a result, many of the programs and resources that once existed have been cut and, it would seem that the state, also, is having to operate in a more fiscally responsible and conscientious manner.

Changes Experienced

The most important change that occurred in Louisiana corrections over the course of my career has been when the Louisiana Department of Corrections became a part of the American Correctional Association and institutions were required to become accredited. Soon afterward the department began offering more rehabilitative services (i.e., job skills programming, substance abuse treatment programming, work release programs). These programs offered assistance to offenders who were nearing reentry into society and helped to aid them in their transition. There has been research that shows that these types of programs do lower recidivism. Thus, it was the push for ACA accreditation that ultimately modernized our correctional system's menu of offender programs.

Another extremely important change that has occurred in the field of corrections in general and in Louisiana corrections in particular is the adoption of technology. This is especially true with the implementation of computer technology. The transition to automated systems of data information and retrieval was not one that was smooth but it was one that was inevitable. As changes occur in society, they ultimately also affect the world inside the prison, albeit at a slower pace. Once computers had been introduced and successfully integrated into the Louisiana correctional system, administrators were able to make decisions at a pace that was much quicker and this allowed the system to operate in a much more nimble and strategic manner.

Another change that I have seen during the past 30 years in corrections was, during the 1970s and 1980s, an emphasis on inmates' civil rights. As I have noted previously, as changes occur in outside society, they eventually impact and change views, policies, and procedures inside the prison. In fact, the prison is a micro society whose barriers are permeated by the outside world. The civil rights movement of the 1960s affected society but was slow to have a direct impact on prisons which were largely left untouched by the federal courts. However, in the 1970s, federal courts began to make rulings on entire state systems, and many—but not all—of these states were in the southeastern United States. Included among these were Texas, Arkansas, and Mississippi, which all three surrounded Louisiana. It was completely foreseeable that the Federal 5th Circuit Court rulings would soon impact the Louisiana system as well.

It was during this time that entire state systems were scrutinized and, over time, this of course affected the Louisiana system as well. Angola, long known for the very hard time that was endured by inmates, went through changes wherein living conditions and standards of care were improved. In addition, programs related to therapeutic programming, education, and job training slowly became more common over the years that followed. These improvements slowly continued throughout the 1980s but were sometimes met with resistance by individuals within the organization. This was also during an era in which many people cited the *Martinson Report* (1974) as a means of touting the notion that treatment programming is ineffective. Thus, there was a considerable amount of conflict and debate regarding the worthiness of therapeutic programming. Amidst this, there was a very serious period of organizational change for many correctional systems and, as one might expect, there were challenges along the way.

Since that time, I have also witnessed a professionalization within the field of corrections and I attribute this mostly to the impact that the American Correctional Association has had upon the entire nation. This professionalization resulted in more emphasis on training for correctional personnel and I have seen our state provide increased amounts of pre service and in-service training to correctional officers. I have to say, overall, the quality of prisons and jails in the past 10 years has drastically improved through training of staff. Specialized training for issues such as suicide prevention, dealing with special needs offenders, and the emergence of the Prison Rape Elimination Act (PREA) demonstrate that humane conditions for inmates are a priority in today's world of corrections and this higher standard translates to the need for better trained correctional officers. As a result, I would have to say that at this time, in my own opinion, it is actually easier to be a correctional employee than in earlier years because employees are better prepared due to receiving intense training.

Personal Correctional Philosophy

It is my belief we should work toward offering an offender the opportunity to become a productive citizen upon returning to society. With that in mind, I will defer to the Louisiana Department of Corrections website which notes the following:

> Approximately 15,000 state offenders are released each year from Louisiana prisons to Louisiana communities—usually the communities where they were living when they committed their crimes.

To me, this is precisely why the problems observed in the United States continue to persist in regard to offender recidivism and the increase in offender populations behind bars. In Louisiana, offenders are cycling in and out of prison, going on to community supervision, and then returning back to prison again, in what appears to be a never-ending patter. Even more troublesome is the fact that in Louisiana, the recidivism rate after 5 years is almost 50%; a half return to prison. In my opinion, these results can be greatly improved.

As I noted in my opening statement, I do believe that we should work toward offering the offender the opportunity to become a productive citizen when they reenter society. Thus, I would guess that my primary orientation or philosophy regarding corrections is one based on reintegration and rehabilitation. To me, reintegration is focused on the reentry of the offender into society. The ultimate goal for reintegration programs is to connect the offender into legitimate areas of society in a manner that is gainful and productive. When used inside correctional institutions, this approach emphasizes continued contact between the offender and their families, friends, and even the community. This approach is set against the backdrop realization that the overwhelming majority of offenders will ultimately return to society. While reintegration efforts do emphasize offender accountability, the use of reintegration processes is focused on ensuring that the offender has a maximal set of circumstances that, at least initially, diminish the need or desire to engage in crime by cultivating the connections that the offender has to legitimate society. Reintegration efforts are intended to reduce recidivism among offenders. During the past few years, Louisiana has experienced an upsurge in interest in offender reentry programs.

I also support rehabilitative programming and have implemented a number of initiatives at my current facility, Richwood Correctional Center. To me, rehabilitation implies that an offender should be provided the means to fulfill a constructive level of functioning in society, with an implicit expectation that such offenders will be deterred from re offending due to their having worthwhile stakes in legitimate society; stakes that they will not wish to lose as a consequence of criminal offending. The use of vocational training, educational attainment, and/or therapeutic interventions is used to improve the offender's stakes in pro social behavior. I do want to make some distinctions, however, between reintegration and rehabilitation and will look toward some published work from Stohr et al. (2009) who have done this in a clear and informative manner. They note that the purpose of reintegration is rooted in the eventual reentry or restoration of the offender to society. They contend that reintegration is not very different from rehabilitation except that it is more practical in implementation and expectation. Reintegrative programs focus on concrete programs such as job training rather than changes in thought and/or attitude. Thus, reintegration efforts do have some distinction from a strictly rehabilitative approach in that external community-based issues are considered most important in preventing recidivism.

I also want to note that I am a very strong advocate of religious programming and I think that this should be the cornerstone of a facility's operation.

In my own facility, we offer a wide array of religious programs and activities and seek to cultivate the spiritual and moral development of men who are serving time. There has been research that does support the usefulness of this type of programming and has shown that it helps in offender reformation (Dammer, 2002). We have, at our facility, an individual who supervises our treatment programming and is also a university professor in Criminal Justice. At my request, he shared with me several studies that validate the efficacy of religious programming in transforming inmates and the lives they lead (Hanser, 2013). For example, research by Johnson et al. (1997) found that participants in religious programming had significantly fewer infractions while in prison than did inmates who did not participate in such programs. Even more convincing is the finding that inmates who participated frequently in religious programming services were less likely to be arrested when examined 1 year after their release.

More recent research provides continued empirical evidence indicating that religious programming reduces crime and recidivism among adult offenders (Hercik, 2007). For instance, Johnson and Larson (2003) conducted a preliminary evaluation of the InnerChange Freedom Initiative, a faith-based prisoner reform program. Results show that program graduates were 50% less likely to be rearrested and 60% less likely to be reincarcerated during a 2-year follow-up period. Thus, from this research I have just cited, it would appear that prison religious programs have both short-term and long-term positive effects while inside prison, and later, when offenders are released from prison.

Lastly, I think that it is important to note that religion has always been a central component of the correctional process. The word *penitentiary* is one derived from the religious meaning of penitence (Carlson et al., 2008; Dammer, 2002; Hanser, 2013). Throughout the history of corrections in Europe, the Church was always intertwined in the process of reforming offenders in an effort to save their souls from an even worse fate than that to which their bodies were subjected. In fact, one famous historical figure in correction was William Penn (1644–1718) who was the founder of the state of Pennsylvania and was also a leader of the religious Quakers. William Penn was an advocate of religious freedom as well as individual rights. He was also instrumental in spreading the notion that criminal offenders were worthy of humane treatment. William Penn, as well as other Quakers, was an early advocate of prison reform in America. Because the Quakers were a religious group, their correctional orientation was also religious in nature. Nowadays, it is still a large part of corrections in the United States and in Louisiana. At many facilities, including the one that I currently manage, the inclusion of religious volunteers is a commonplace practice.

The last point that I would like to make regarding my personal correctional philosophy is that regardless of everything that I have just said, my primary responsibility is to provide for the safe and secure incarceration of offenders. Throughout my career, I have been tasked with the charge of ensuring that inmates remained in custody until the expiration of the time that they are required to serve. Thus, all of the above thoughts on my own personal philosophy are prefaced with the point that my main mission, first and foremost, is one of public safety and security. It is only after that goal has been assured and secured that these other thoughts on corrections can be given appropriate time and attention.

I think that the public has typically viewed corrections as being primarily to do with the incapacitation of offenders. It is actually quite easy for me to make this assertion given that we have consistently held such a high rate of incarceration when compared to other states in the nation. Likewise, we have historically been a very punitive nation and I think much of this simply has to do with our cultural heritage in the southeastern portion of the United States. Many of those states have higher-than-average incarceration rates and are also more prone to use the death penalty.

Problems and Successes Experienced

During my career I have noted that warehousing an inmate without opportunity for self-help programming is not conducive to reducing recidivism. In contrast to that, the programming offered in the last 15 years has reduced recidivism but my fear is due to the present economy and budget shortfalls, offender programming will fall victim to budget cuts. By closing state prisons and warehousing inmates, rehabilitation programs will be lost which will give an offender fewer opportunities to participate in a variety of programs, including both professional programs and self-help programs.

When considering successes in corrections, particularly in Louisiana, I think that the attainment of ACA accreditation has been a great success. Likewise, I do think that the shift from an incapacitation model to a reentry model has been done well. Lastly, in reference to specific programs that I believe are successful, I have worked with transitional release programs, substance abuse treatment programs and faith-based programming. Each of these, in my opinion, has been very successful in treatment service delivery as well as outcomes that can be seen.

Theory and Practice

I would say that the relationship between theory and practice is one that is better understood in today's world of corrections than it was say, 20 or 30 years ago. I think that much of this has to do with the American Correctional Association's influence on professionalization of the field of corrections. Amidst the emphasis on professionalization, there is also a push for practitioners to gain higher levels of education. This acquisition of higher education among today's correctional employees results in a work force that is more exposed to both theory and research.

In fact, I can say firsthand that this occurs at my own facility because our officers are often students in the Department of Criminal Justice at our regional university. In addition, we often have students who are interns from counseling and criminal justice programs at the university who come here for their clinical hours and/or volunteer hours.

In many cases, we provide training that emphasizes the key theoretical differences between a model based on incapacitation and one based on rehabilitation. Our use of various types of treatment programming for substance abusers and for sex offenders, as well as our work release programs, our faith-based programs, and partnerships with outlying reentry organizations, demonstrates that theories related to restitution and reform are what we generally subscribe to at LaSalle Corrections. Anything less just amounts to simply warehousing offenders and that alone only fixes the crime problem while they are locked up, not once they get out. Being that the vast majority of our prison population will eventually be back out in society, we have to do more to reduce criminal behavior than simple lockdown.

When considering research, I do know that in the Louisiana Department of Corrections and also with LaSalle Corrections, research is routinely conducted. At my own facility, the director of our treatment programming conducts data collection and analysis on a routine basis with offenders who are in substance abuse treatment and with a program that we have established for sex offenders. I myself authorized our Sex Offender Treatment Program (SOTP) at Richwood Correctional Center and in that program we have an evaluation process that will allow us to evaluate how well the program changes thoughts and behaviors of sex offenders who are eventually released into society.

To me, our research on sex offender treatment and recidivism is very important for a number of reasons. First, the state of Louisiana has very few treatment services for sex offenders and has faced challenges getting them placed in the community when they are released on parole. Second, the public is very concerned about this group of offenders and will not stand for a lax approach of supervision for these offenders. Third, we increasingly face tight budgets but yet, at the same time, must provide a certain standard of care for offenders. Fourth, the state of Louisiana has the highest incarceration rate in the United States and this, alone, provides incentive for us to find alternatives to an approach that is only based on incapacitation. The state is hard-pressed to provide "good-time" incentives to sex offenders due to public perceptions yet, all the while, these offenders may languish within our facilities, only to eventually be released (sooner or later) into the world again. Because of these issues, we need research that can tell us what really works with these offenders in terms of programming so that we can maintain public safety despite tough budgetary conditions.

Another area of research that I think is useful and that should be conducted more frequently in our state systems is that related to religious programming. My own facility as well as other facilities with LaSalle Corrections provides an extensive array of religious-based interventions. We have found that offenders are very receptive to this programming. I am aware of some research on these programs and it is certainly promising. However, I really do think that more studies on this topic, perhaps of a longitudinal nature, would really be useful.

Evidence-Based Corrections

I can say that both the state and my current facility utilize Evidence-Based Practices (EBPs). To me, the key point for EBPs is that they are data-driven. In other words, future operations are based on data that guides the process of decision making, which again intermittently examines data that is assessed and evaluated as a means of further refining operations. To me, this is a process that creates a systemic loop whereby the agency is constantly assessing and evaluating itself. This is known as the assessment–evaluation cycle, which is the process whereby assessment data and evaluation data are compared to determine the effectiveness of programs and to find areas where improvement of agency services is required (Hanser, 2013). Agencies that successfully implement the assessment–evaluation cycle tend to use public resources more effectively and also are not prone to placing the community at risk of future criminal activity. In other words, agencies using the assessment–evaluation cycle will operate at an optimal level, avoiding harm to the community and the mismanagement of resources. On the other hand, agencies that do not successfully implement the assessment–evaluation cycle will be more likely to *both* waste agency resources and place the community at a level of risk that otherwise would be preventable.

I do read information on evidence-based practices from time-to-time. Much of the reading I do is from government sources, such as the National Institute of Justices' (2005) article entitled "Implementing Evidence Based Practice in Corrections," which outlines how these practices should shape correctional agencies. I also find examples of specific programs in professional magazines such as *Corrections Today* or even from just doing online searches. I likewise have a couple of academic staff who have terminal degrees and who often examine research in this field. I am able to consult with them on many occasions, if I wish, particularly in dealing with matters that are related to offender programming and/or rehabilitation. In fact, I have even incorporated them into some of our training initiatives as a means of ensuring that we have training based on what are evidence-based techniques that utilize evidence-based content.

I think that there are a number of programs that have been shown to work in the United States and are adopted as best practice. For example, I do think that the use of cognitive behavioral approaches in treatment have been shown to work well with the offender population. Likewise, as I noted earlier, I consider the use of religious programming to be evidence-based as well, given that I provided research that demonstrates its utility and effectiveness in an earlier section of this interview. Likewise, the use of technological applications in automated services has greatly transformed the field of corrections in a manner that has been easy to see and quite easy to measure. Lastly, there are a variety of programming approaches and curricular packages in prison education programs and prison treatment programs that have been shown to be effective. Thus, the recognition and adoption of evidence-based practices in corrections abounds in the United States in general and in Louisiana in particular.

Currently, the use of evidence-based practices is commonly touted in a range of human service industries and fields. This is true in corrections as well. I do think that this is a very good trend as it is a huge improvement over much of the "guess work" that often occurred in corrections in decades past. I see this as a natural part of the progression of maturity for the field of corrections and also see this as being consistent with what ACA standards support. To me, it would almost seem silly to not support evidence-based practices; the use of measurements of performance is something that should be part-and-parcel of the running of any organization.

Transnational Relations

With this area of consideration, it is easy to overlook the impact of the global community in areas that are not coastal, metropolitan, or do not have a large-scale immigrant population. However, my organization (LaSalle Corrections) is located in both Louisiana and in Texas. In each state, and in Texas in particular, there is a growing immigrant population and this, of course, is mirrored in our own correctional population.

Beyond this, I can say that the global movement toward concern with human rights demands has impacted both the Louisiana Department of Corrections (LDOC) as well as LaSalle Corrections. The state Department of Corrections is accredited with the American Correctional Association (ACA) and this requires that conditions within prisons meet standards that are in line with expected human rights conditions throughout the world. Further, the development of universal codes of ethics mirrors the emphasis on ethics that exists within LaSalle Corrections. I can also say that maintaining a high ethical standard of professionalism within an organization also has some costs. For instance, I find it necessary to sometimes dismiss or reprimand employees due to ethical parameters related to their behavior. Thus, the universal code of ethics has put a standard of behavior and professionalism into the field of corrections that is not met by every employee. This means that maintaining such a standard has a cost, both in terms of organizational change that routinely occurs as well as in terms of money and time required to hire and train these staff.

I think that international relationships with other countries have had only a slight impact on correctional policy and practice in Louisiana, but have had a greater impact on other areas of the United States. This impact is most readily apparent in the southwestern states where illegal crossings of Mexican and Central American immigrants have been experienced in massive numbers. Much of this illegal movement includes drug smuggling and trafficking, human trafficking, and the infiltration of gangs from abroad, such as Mara Salvatrucha (commonly called MS-13 in the United States) and other types of criminal groups. In Louisiana, we do not have as strong a representation of the Hispanic population as is encountered in western states, but when post-Hurricane Katrina construction and rebuilding of New Orleans began, members of MS-13 were reported to have infiltrated construction crews hired for this work. With this in mind and given the proximity of Louisiana to the Southwest, I do think that, over time, our correctional system will experience similar challenges in the future.

General Assessment

In general, I am satisfied with the way that the correctional field has emerged and been shaped during the past 30 or more years. This is a demanding field in which to work and it is very unique from most others. One key issue that existed in the past was the public misunderstanding of the intended role of corrections. Public sentiments and understanding today are much more balanced and educated and this has helped the field tremendously as it has matured and found its purpose within broader society. However, as I have previously stated, the economic climate has had a very bad impact on the ability of corrections to operate effectively and to avoid risks to public safety. My fear is that the economy will dictate where and how corrections will go in the future. With programming for inmates being a last priority in the budget, I do not expect we will continue moving forward but regress if these issues remain unattended.

The good news is that the state of Louisiana continues to make overt efforts to remedy this problem and officials do not deny the problems or hide from them. Rather, in our state system, reentry initiatives have been embraced at a level that is unprecedented. Granted, some of this is due to the economic circumstances that affect the state but, in all fairness, it is the society of Louisiana that ultimately influences how public offices will address matters like these. The public has, over time, seemingly become more accustomed to the idea that offenders will return to their community and, as a result, I see more grass roots initiatives to provide assistance to persons attempting to leave the life of prison behind them.

Conclusion

From this interview, it can be seen that the role of a warden in the Louisiana Department of Public Safety and Corrections is one that is quite encompassing. Along the way and throughout a career, most wardens in Louisiana have had stellar experiences throughout their careers that tend to set them apart from others within the organization. In addition, this interview does show that in Louisiana, it is possible for individuals to work their way up the entire chain-of-command, especially if they are willing to move to various areas throughout the state.

Likewise, the role of private corrections should not be discounted. This is a new and growing trend in corrections, both in Louisiana and throughout the United States. Many of the wardens employed in the private correctional arena were once state or federal prison wardens in their prior years. Their expertise is sought out among those companies that desire to provide correctional services in the competitive open market. This opportunity to work in the private industry allows many retired correctional personnel to further ply their trade while making the transition from one system to the other. This transition requires versatility and a willingness to continue to learn from individuals who take this path toward career progression, affording an entirely new and nearly limitless set of opportunities for those correctional administrators who are willing to take the challenge.

Glossary

American Correctional Association (ACA): The American Correctional Association is a recognized body that has shaped the state of corrections throughout the United States, both in terms of accreditation of institutions and the development of professionals who embark on correctional careers. The American Correctional Association (ACA) has well over 20,000 members within its ranks, including administrators, security personnel at various stages of career development, and programming personnel (ACA, 2011). The ACA provides a professional organization for all persons and groups, both public and private, that share a common goal of improving the justice system in general and the correctional system in particular.

Blue Walters Program: The Blue Walters Program is an 84-day intensive drug abuse treatment program that provides good-time for offenders who complete the curriculum and other activities required by the program. Dr. Robert Hanser is the Director of the Blue Walters Substance Abuse Treatment Program.

Disproportionate Minority Contact (DMC): The tendency for the justice system to process minority persons at rates that exceed, out of expected proportions, their representation in broader society. In other words, DMC means that more minorities, per capita, are behind bars than exist, per capita, in the outside community. There is a continuing debate among scholars and practitioners over whether this is due to racism within the justice system or other explanatory variables.

Global Positioning Satellite (GPS) Electronic Monitoring: This system entails a receiver that uses 24 military satellites to determine the exact location of a coordinate. Through the use of satellite monitoring and remote tracking, offenders can be tracked to their exact location. This type of monitoring is frequently used with the sex offender population in Louisiana.

Louisiana Department of Public Safety and Corrections (LDPSC): The United States consists of 50 different state bodies that are enjoined by a federal system of government. Louisiana is one of these 50 states and the LDPSC is the state's organizational body that administrates the law enforcement and correctional personnel for the statewide system, exclusive of small localized police agencies that may also have jail facilities under their own, fragmented jurisdiction. The state of Louisiana has the highest rate of incarceration of all the 50 states in Louisiana.

Louisiana State Prison (LSP), Angola: This prison is the largest maximum security prison in the United States, in terms of the number of inmates incarcerated at the farm. There are 5,000 inmates in LSP Angola and the prison farm sprawls over 18,000 acres of territory. Approximately 7 out of every 10 inmates at Angola are serving a life sentence. This is also where death row and the execution chamber are located for the state of Louisiana, meaning that all offenders who are put to death in Louisiana are put to death at LSP Angola.

Martinson Report (1974): An examination of a number various prison programs that included educational and vocational assistance, mental health treatment, medical treatment, early release, and so forth. The report was widely cited for the two decades following its release and was purported to indicate that few prison programs are effective in changing offender behavior. In fact, what Martinson (1974) claimed was that effectiveness for each program depended on a number of variables and also was determined by the means with which it was measured or evaluated. In essence, he had mixed findings. Anti-treatment pundits took this as proof that "nothing works," and publicly made this claim using his report as evidence.

Maryland Addiction Questionnaire (MAQ): The MAQ is a psychometric instrument used to measure intake evaluation and aid with treatment planning. The MAQ determines the severity of the addiction, the motivation of the individual in treatment, how to approach treatment, and the likelihood of relapse.

Personal Experience Inventory (PEI): The PEI is also a psychometric instrument used to assess all forms of substance abuse as well as related psychosocial problems including personal risk factors that may be possessed by the individual in drug recovery.

Prison Rape Elimination Act: The Prison Rape Elimination Act (PREA) of 2003 requires reporting by correctional systems of sexual assaults in correctional facilities so that a comprehensive statistical review and analysis of the incidence and effects of prison rape can be determined on an annual basis. This report includes but is not limited to, the identification of the common characteristics of both victims and perpetrators of prison rape; and prisons and prison systems with a high incidence of prison rape. PREA applies to all correctional facilities. Due to the sensitive nature of violent victimization and potential reluctance to report sexual assault, estimates of the prevalence of such acts do not rely on a single measure but include multiple measures on the incidence and prevalence of sexual assault.

STAR Program: The Successful Treatment of Addiction and Recovery (STAR) program is a long-term substance abuse treatment program at Richwood Correctional Center. STAR is open to any inmate suffering from a substance abuse disorder having less than 4 years remaining on his sentence. The offender benefits from a variety of services offered by the long-term substance abuse/re entry program. Services will be provided based on the need established in the assessment process and an individualized treatment plan will be developed for each participant. These services include, but are not limited to, addictions counseling, counseling for criminal thinking and behavior, mental health counseling, anger management, parenting classes, and more.

Gary Maynard, Secretary of Public Safety and Correctional Services, Maryland, United States

10

JACQUELINE RHODEN-TRADER

Contents

Overview

Public sentiments vary about the U.S. Criminal Justice System; however, there seems to be a consensus that the system is broken. Fraught with the belief of most of its citizens that harsh punishment is a deterrent to serious crimes, disproportionality of sentencing and the watering down of the trial by jury paradigm in favor of plea bargaining, the system has received less than favorable views.

In Maryland, the Department of Public Safety and Correctional Services is responsible for the management of correctional facilities throughout the state. The department operates 24 prisons and pre-releases centers and has an annual budget of more than 20 million (Division of Corrections Annual Report Fiscal Year 2011). Maryland (2010) has an incarceration rate that is approximately 4% lower than the national average of incarcerated per 100,000 adults in the population Guerin, Harrison, and Sabol 2011). The number of inmates housed in correctional facilities is just under 23,000. A significant percentage of those incarcerated in prison come from Baltimore County in Maryland.

Maryland's Criminal Justice System has experienced its share of criticisms from its citizens. Baltimore City, from where most wards of its correctional facilities hail, is widely known as Murder, Inc. (perpetuated by the media's love for the city as featured in some of the most-watched television shows on violence aired worldwide and statistically earned). As a port city in the northeastern region of the United States, nestled between Washington, DC, and New York City, Baltimore has been a hotbed for drug trafficking, illegal handgun possession, homicides, and gang warfare.

Introduction

I had the pleasure of interviewing Maryland's Secretary of Public Safety and Correctional Services at his Towson, Maryland, office. Charged with carrying out the governor's policies in the areas of public safety, crime prevention, correction, parole, and probation, the following interview illuminates his personal accounts and viewpoints on his journey to corrections, philosophy and leadership style, innovative approaches to critical issues, successes and failures, and resolve to serve the public by remaining an objective civil servant charged with carrying out the law of the land.

Career

Q: When did you get started in the field of correction?

A: Secretary Maynard's journey to corrections is ripe in passion, vision, and commitment. As a high school student in 1960, he knew what he was going to do for the rest of his life. His interest in corrections, prison, and jails consumed him and while in college, he majored in sociology and joined the Sociology Club. Fate would have it that the club desired a visit to the penitentiary and Maynard coordinated it. Seeing 2000 inmates on the yard and assessing the milieu was run by inmates rather than officers, his passion for the field burgeoned and he exclaimed to his friends upon return to campus, "That's what I want to do the rest of my life. I want that warden's job some day!" And thus, his journey began in 1962. In 1968, after earning his bachelor and master's degrees, he worked in mental health for a few years but kept his eyes on the pulse of happenings in corrections. When he learned of a schism between the Oklahoma Department of Corrections and the community over placing a work release center for inmates in an abandoned hotel, and the director publicly and unapologetically saying he would put the center there because "it's the right thing to do" even if it got him fired, Maynard thought "I want to work for this man!" As such, he made contact with the department and the following conversation ensued:

> "I'm Gary Maynard and I'd like a job in corrections."
>
> The lady said, "We don't have any jobs in corrections."
>
> "Well, I have a master's degree."
>
> She said, "We don't have any jobs for people with master's degrees."
>
> "Well, I understand. I know what I'm going to do the rest of my life, and I don't have any experience, so I'll work for nothing."
>
> And she said, "We don't have any jobs for people who want to work for nothing." So I said, "Well, if you take my name and phone number, if you ever have a job that nobody else wants and you don't have any money to pay them, would you call me?"
>
> She said, "Yeah, we'll call you."
>
> So the very next day she called and said, "Can you come in for an interview?"
>
> I said, "When?"
>
> She said, "Right now."
>
> So I drove from Norman, Oklahoma, to Oklahoma City and to the Department of Corrections. I reported in. I gave the lady my name and she said, "Mr. Pontesso wants to talk to you." She took me in to the director's office and he said, "Are you the young man that wants to work in corrections and it won't cost me anything?" I said, "That's right." He hired me right there. Of course, he paid me even though he knew I was willing to work for nothing. He knew I was committed.

The following timeline chronicles his mobility in corrections.

- 1997: Retired from corrections in Oklahoma
- 1997: Appointed as adjutant general of the Oklahoma National Guard
- 1997: Started the University of Oklahoma's Corrections and Public Safety Program in the College of Continuing Education

He was later hired as director of corrections in South Carolina when the previous director left. His accounts are as follows:

> When the director of corrections in South Carolina was removed due to sexual misconduct between staff and inmates and inmates and inmates, several different professional groups called and asked if I was interested in the job. I interviewed for the job and was hired. I took it knowing it was going to be a challenge. Susan Smith, the lady that drowned her two boys, was confined in the South Carolina women's prison. She was from Union in northern South Carolina. I'd seen that on TV, like everybody had. So I got there and found out part of the issue was sexual misconduct between her, a lieutenant, and a captain.
>
> The response of the department had been to lock her up, take away her good time, and put her on disciplinary status. They didn't discipline the lieutenant and the captain because they felt she had seduced them.

Believing there was inequity in the handling of Ms. Smith's case, Secretary Maynard restored her good time and placed her in the general population because she was under the authority of the officers. He also took disciplinary action against the two officers. His decision was based on the power the employees had over Ms. Smith rather than the reverse. His decision was shocking because the culture of that system had been to blame the inmate. He contracted with the National Institute of Corrections for consultants to work with staff to change the culture. The governor changed in 2 years and he looked at other state challenges. From there he went to a "small quiet system" in Iowa and stayed for 4 years. While there, he began reading about the problems of Maryland's correctional system. Being attracted to the challenge, he applied for the Maryland job. Two officers had been killed in 1 year in the Maryland system, which had not happened in the United States in 30 years. As shocking as those events were, Maryland didn't seem to have a solutions-driven plan. What they tried fell apart, and their system wasn't stable. He interviewed for the job, was offered it, and accepted it.

Q: What was your first plan of action?

A: I started work on 29th January 2007. I came to the office the first day. The second day I went to Jessup, MD, where the House of Corrections was located. It was one of the worst prisons I had seen in my career. Two days later, I went out to North Branch Correctional Institution in Western Maryland, which was to be a 1000-bed prison with four 250-bed quadrants. They had one quadrant open. The others were under construction, so I thought, "We have this coming online and this terrible prison in Jessup. Maybe we could do something."

There was a perception that the House of Corrections would be converted to minimum security in 3 years. One of the problems that made it so bad was that they had maximum, medium, and minimum security almost in the same prison. They had dangerous maximum-security inmates locked up and minimum-security prisoners running around doing their errands—carrying drugs, carrying orders, carrying hits—and all the power. This House of Corrections was really different to manage, because it had all those security levels. I briefed the governor and his staff and said, "We're going to convert to minimum security within 30 days." The governor asked, "What do you need?" I said, "Just your support." He said, "You've got it—full support."

So we started the process of converting this 1000-bed prison to minimum by moving out the maximum-security prisoners. After we had moved some out, circumstances caused me to move fast because on 2nd March, as we were in the process of converting to minimum, I learned we had an officer at the House of Corrections stabbed. He was at Shock Trauma in Baltimore, and I was told he might not make it through the night. I drove down there. On the way down, I called the governor, advised him about what had happened, and he said he would meet me there. When we got there, the corrections officers were having a candlelight vigil. There were TV cameras, and I interviewed with them.

After the governor and I visited with the injured officer, I was told that a number of other officers wanted to speak to me. I talked to them just briefly. I said, "We have a problem, a serious problem with the House of Corrections. I'm going to do something with the House. I don't know exactly what I'm going to do, but I need two things from you—your support and your patience." They had the look on their faces that I'd seen many times before in riot and hostage situations—this look of fear, anger, and frustration; but the one look that always impacts leaders, as it did this time, was that of questioning, that "What are you going to do to protect us" look. I told them that I needed their support and that I'd do something. I went around and shook hands with each of them. Each one said, "You've got our support, and we'll give you some time." I thought then, "That's a critical piece, to get that group support." Amidst this tragedy, they were giving and allowing responsibility to be placed on me, but they also gave me a lot of authority. On the way back home, I called the governor and said, "Governor, we need to close the House of Corrections." He said, "I agree. What do you need from me?" I said, "Just your support." He said, "You've got it." So, I came home that night. It was about 11:00 pm, and I called the deputy secretary. I told her, "You've got to get the smallest number of people together in the morning (this was Friday night). We're going to close the House of Corrections."

The next morning, with that seven-member committee, I shared the decision. Someone asked, "How long will we have to get it closed?" And without thinking, I said, "March 15th." They said, "This is March 3rd, so that's only 12 days. We can't do it in 12 days." I said, "We don't have any choice. If we don't, somebody else is going to get killed." And I could see they sort of understood … all of a sudden they snapped to the reality that we didn't have a choice.

I said, "You can't tell anybody. No one can know because if you let somebody know and an inmate finds out at the House of Corrections, somebody's going to get killed. You'll be responsible for that. So you can't do it. You can't talk to anybody. The only way it will work is if all of us agree that we will not talk to anybody unless it's agreed upon by this group, and that includes me." They all agreed.

At the start of the meeting, we were converting to minimum. Now, all of a sudden, we're closing everything. That means moving about 900 inmates out. I knew that if you moved the maximums out first, inmates and gang leaders would think, "Oh, they're just converting it. We'll still have the House. We're still in control of the House." And if I moved the mediums out, they'd still think, "Well, it's going to be all the mediums." Then, when it got to the minimums, we would really be under pressure to move.

We started moving the maximums and met secretly at nights and on weekends. Nobody knew. We didn't tell anybody. The governor asked, "When are you going to have it closed?" I said, "I can't tell you because if I tell you and the media asks, then you have to be dishonest or you have to tell them when." He said, "I don't need to know when."

After working about 12 days, it looked like we were going to extend it out maybe another day. We had a couple days to go and somebody in the group said, "We were checking the statutes and we don't have the authority to close a prison. Only the legislature can close it. We'll probably have to get permission from the legislature." I told them, "Well, I'll do that."

I called our corrections subcommittee chairs and told them that we were closing the House of Corrections. I stated that I knew we were originally talking about converting it, but that there was a serious problem. "So now, we're closing it." They asked, "When?" I told them that "I can't tell you when and you can't tell anybody, because if word gets out, somebody could get killed." They agreed they would not say a word.

We met again and I informed them, "I've advised the legislature, and it is fine. We now need to tell the Union." Everybody in the group said, "No, you can't tell them." I said, "We don't have a choice. I don't want them to read this in the paper. They've got to be part of it." After much discussion, everybody agreed that the union needed to be told. I called the union leaders and told them what we were doing and stated that "If you tell anybody, and an inmate finds out, a gang member, and an officer gets killed—one of your members get killed, you'll have some responsibility for that." They said, "We won't say a word."

So everybody agreed to keep it quiet, and they did. It came to the 12th day; we had about 400 inmates to move, minimums. When we started moving them, they realized what the movement was really about.

Our plan was leaking out to the media. I spoke to the governor and said, "We've got 400 to move and we can do it very quickly." We agreed to move the 400 on Saturday and have the press conference on Monday.

We moved that 400 in one day. We didn't have any resistance from any inmate, except one. "This is my home, he said. I'm not leaving." We picked him up by his arms, off of his bunk, and walked him out the door of the cell. Once he got outside his cell, he walked to the van.

Changes Experienced

Q: What changes have you seen?

A: From that point on, employees of the Division of Corrections felt there wasn't anything they couldn't do. It gave them a great deal of confidence. It sort of healed this whole system. From then on, it's been very positive, just working—trying to get a handle on the gang situation and violence.

Since closing the House in 2007, we've gotten a handle on the violence on inmates and staff. Violence on staff has gone down 65% over the last 6 years—68% actually—and violence on inmates has been decreased 47%. We're increasing the education. Even though we didn't increase any funding in education or treatment, we've increased the percentage of classes. When I came, the percentage of "fill" of education and vocational classes was less than 90% each. We're up—GED class is 98%, vocational classes are filled above 95%. So we have the same teachers, same classroom, same cost, but more inmates do our programs. We've actually increased in all the programs the number of inmates getting treatment, in the midst of a recession economy.

Q: How do you measure success?

A: It's hard to get a handle on measuring corrections. When I came, our recidivism rate was 50%. We release 10,000 a year, and 10,000 come in, so that's 5000 that, after 3 years, come back. That rate's been reduced 40.5%, which means, just in rough figures, about 800 people didn't come back or 800 people didn't commit crimes. That's a reduction in the cost to taxpayers with public safety benefits.

Q: To what do you attribute these successes? What policies have you implemented?

A: Closing the House of Corrections was significant to sort of restore confidence and empower leadership. We are working very closely with the union now; increased the number of inmates working in the communities in those restorative justice projects, doubled the number of inmates that are out every day; and increased programs. We're doing some innovative things. Our parole chairman is operating on a pro decision matrix that speaks to the likelihood to reoffend. We run the Baltimore City Pretrial Operation and use a risk assessment for pretrial also.

We are just implementing an electronic case management system that will connect all of those elements together. We will be one of the few systems in the country that connects police booking to corrections to the parole commission to community supervision. And that helps just to share information. We're doing a lot of sharing of information about gangs and security threat groups. That information is shared much more openly than it has been in the past. The governor has prompted us to work with other states in sharing criminal information. For example, somebody here in Maryland could go to New York and commit a crime. In the past, if they were held for 2 days, released and came back, we'd never know it. So now we keep them on supervision; whether they go to the gym, go to DC, it's a lot of running back and forth. We started sharing information with Virginia. If somebody gets arrested in Virginia, we know about it that same day. That information comes back to our parole database and notifies an agent. That agent starts the process of revocation, which is the same way in New York, Pennsylvania, Delaware, DC, and Virginia. We were the only state doing that kind of outreach, but now have expanded this information sharing along the I-95 corridor, which is the drug trafficking corridor.

This has helped to get a handle on the criminal element that's coming into our system. We have community supervision. We started the Governor's Initiative, called the Violence Prevention Initiative (VPI), which is used as a predictive analysis method. We analyzed the number of homicides in Baltimore City in a year and found 39% were under our supervision. We broke down those who were under our supervision, to what they looked like, where were they from, type of crime committed, and their history. To no surprise, they had a gun crime in their history, and with those whose first arrest came at the age of 14 or below, had 5 arrests in their history and were under the age of 29. So we took the criteria of these, and we applied it to the 70,000 that we had under supervision, whether they were suspects or victims. Two thousand were identified with that criteria and became our VPI for the whole population. We started intensive supervision twice a month then increased to 3 times a week. We conducted a personal face-to-face visit with that person and a urinalysis every week; drugs are a big problem. Those 2000, statewide, became our VPI. Out of that and over time, we said, "Well, some of these guys are behaving themselves." That was because we were supervising them closely. They were staying clean and they were staying in their programs, and doing better. As a result, we created the VPI-1, which is the highest, and then VPI-2, so they got moved down to regular supervision if they behaved themselves.

There are still about 2000 across the state—1300 of those or so in Baltimore City. I've supervised corrections in four states as well as parole and probation. This is the first time that our agents have really been recognized for the part they play in public safety. Law enforcement here embraces the parole and probation agents because of the governor's interest in helping our department become part of the crime fight. You typically don't see a correction system take that role. So that has been significant in changing this department. We have an extremely close relationship with the U.S. Attorney, the Federal Bureau of Investigation director, the Marshals' Service, and the Drug Enforcement Administration.

Q: In the broader correctional arena, what have been some of the most significant changes you've seen in your 40-plus years in the field?

A: It's kind of interesting. When I started in Oklahoma, the first director of corrections was interested in a work-release center. It was a new concept back then and he got fired for it. Then, as we moved into the 1970s, it got more violent and there was less concentration on rehabilitation. It was like Attica and McAlester in the early 1970s.

Among corrections directors across the country, there's a focus on reentry, transition, drug treatment, and restorative gestures, which is a good thing. People now see that restorative justice is, in effect, a public safety effort; that if you reintegrate somebody back into the community, they're not going to commit a crime, and that's protecting the public. So, one thing that I have brought with me wherever I go is a simplistic approach to the mission. In this business, we get criticized, but we focus very clearly on our mission. Years ago, when I was warden at the penitentiary (McAlester) and we had a riot, seven employees were taken hostage for 38 hours. During that entire time I was thinking, what is our mission here? So I changed the mission at the penitentiary. It had a long list talking about rehabilitation and protecting from escape. I changed it to "Our mission is to protect the public first, our employees second, and the offenders third."

Personal Correctional Philosophy

Q: Did your correctional philosophy emerge as a result?

A: Yes! Protect the public is first. Protect our employees second and offenders third. That's just the nature of the business. I put the sign up as you go into the penitentiary. Our mission: to protect the public, employees, and offenders.

When I became a director, I looked at the mission of the department and it didn't mention employees in it anywhere. I looked at 50 states—49 other states—only 3 or 4 of them mentioned employees in their mission. So I changed the mission of the Department of Corrections in Oklahoma to "protect the public, employees, and offenders"—in that order. I went to South Carolina, I changed the mission. I went to Iowa, I changed the mission. I came here, changed the mission. Our mission now is to protect the public, employees, and offenders—in that order.

And it's not because we're better human beings than offenders, because we're all equal. The public's no better than them. We're all equal. We're all human beings. What's different is the fact that the public hires us because they can't protect themselves. So they hire us. We're obligated to protect them first. The offenders are the nature of the business. We have an obligation to protect them—keep them alive and well, and do what we can for them. Employees are what we put in the middle here. I think our employees are in the middle. I think they should be part of our mission. Not many states mention employees in their mission. I think they're an integral part of it. So, if we change an offender's behavior so that they don't commit a crime, we end up protecting the public. I think our employees are in the middle and I tell them. I meet with every new employee in their initial training. I've met with 5000 in the past 6 years. I tell them. They know the mission. Everybody knows the mission. Everybody in this department—11,000 people—know the mission. But I explain the mission to those employees. I say, "This is why you're in the middle. You have an obligation to change these offenders' behavior, so that they don't go back to what they were doing." I think that makes a difference. I think they feel empowered by that. They feel responsible.

Problems and Successes Experienced

Q: What would you say is the most challenging issue facing corrections?

A: The thing for which we are being trained now is the Prison Rape Elimination Act of 2003 (PREA), a federal law that has been in the works for several years to prevent, detect, and respond to incidents of sexual abuse involving inmates and has finally gotten to some. Mental health is another issue. In just about every state, the corrections system is the largest holder of the mentally ill. We have probably 6000–8000 who have some mental health diagnosis in our system. There's not that many in the state mental hospitals. This is true in most states. We are getting better with the treatment of the mentally ill. I've tried to do something for years and finally, it's coming together. We are being proactive in terms of seeing that the mentally ill we have in prison are a public health issue and our ultimate responsibility because they come back. So in Baltimore City we have an electronic case management system. When somebody comes to prison, in the Baltimore City Jail, we take that identifier and match it against the Department of Mental Health—Baltimore City's mental health population that was receiving treatment. We then can find out if they were receiving treatment and we can start looking to continue the treatment they had going. We just started a couple months ago and in the first month, of the people who came into booking—and there's like 60,000–80,000 a year, so there's probably—how many is that a day? But the population that came in to Baltimore City, 49% of those had had contact with the Mental Health System in Baltimore, so half. When I say 30%, that's a conservative number and booking and pretrial may have a higher number as the people get rearrested over and over. Those who get in our system are a bigger number, but that's at least a solid number if 49% had contact with the Baltimore Mental Health System. In the future, we hope to be able to do this statewide. If we work with counties and make contact with the mental health providers, eventually, we will have a mental health history, instead of starting from scratch and trying to figure out what kind of medication and services they need.

If we have that information going in, we can ask them to be involved in the treatment plan for that person that's going to be with us a year or 3 years or whatever. We can do what they recommend—let them be part of the team—because when this person comes out, they're going back to them, too. They will know that this person's been treated with this regimen while they were here and that will be more continuity of care for them. No other state is doing that. Tying it to local community mental health is going to be the future paradigm for dealing with mental illness. When they come in, we'll offer treatment, keep in contact with them and have the person go back with the same treatment that they came in with so that we can keep that continuity of care.

Another issue being looked at nationwide is this whole question about administration segregation and disciplinary segregation. What do you do with the people who are so violent they have to be segregated? What kind of programs do they need to have? How do you have the step-down programs and all that? That's sort of on the table right now. I think restorative justice is going to be an issue in the future. It's on people's minds now about what you can do with restorative justice. The restorative justice model is something like helping to revitalize swimming pools in the neighborhoods in which you committed the crime or maintaining a historic cemetery in Southwest Baltimore, and so on. Anything can work. The recidivism rates of the inmates in restorative justice projects are way less than what we expect in the rest of the population. I see restorative justice as part of the promises and have made it a real part of our system.

Another big part of the future is partnerships. We're the biggest agency in the State of Maryland and cannot stand alone. We partnered with the Department of Veterans Affairs to identify veterans who were incarcerated and found 1500 in Maryland. We've partnered with the Department of Labor, Mental Health, Veteran's Administration, and others. We need help from everybody because we have people who are impacted in almost every agency in the state. The work that we do for the Department of Natural Resources by cleaning up the Chesapeake Bay is unbelievable. Fifty million oysters have been planted and each oyster filters two gallons of water each hour. Inmates have planted over a million trees along the Chesapeake Bay watershed.

Q: How does this impact your leadership?

A: I'm glad to be part of it because it empowers our department. My philosophy of leadership is taking responsibility because those things you take responsibility for, you have power over. The other day I was talking to someone and they were talking about being responsible for something. That person said, "Oh, you mean I'll be the fall guy." I said, "No, you're looking at it wrong. Being responsible doesn't make you the fall guy. Being responsible gives you the power to—gives you the opportunity to get things done." You can't get things done if you don't have the power.

I was talking to a leadership management group one time out at North Branch and this one man said, "Oh, I get it. You're in this job because you like power." It sort of shocked the class. I said, "Say that again." He said, "You got into corrections because you like power." And I said, "I think you're right. I figured out a long time ago, you can have a lot of good ideas about what to do, but if you don't have any power, you can't get thing anything done. If you have power you can get some good things done. So you're right. I do like power because power gives you opportunity to get good things done."

So my whole leadership theory is based on taking responsibility. I think I take more responsibility for what happens than anybody. Lawyers tell you, "Oh, you can't say that." Well, maybe not in court, but you do have to take responsibility. So it's huge. And what I try to do is develop that sense of responsibility.

Theory and Practice

Q: Do prisons work?

A: About 30 years ago a man who retired from the corrections wrote a book entitled, *Nothing Works*. He said, "I've been through this—30 years in this—working in these prisons and nothing works. These programs are not effective." [Secretary Maynard was referring to Robert Martinson's 1974 "nothing works" theory in which he posited few treatment programs reduced recidivism. As such, a more punitive stance on crime ensued in the 1980s and had full reign in the 1990s as evidenced by "get tough" policies such as "three strikes" and mandatory sentencing. Forty years later, Martinson's theory seems to be refuted as rehabilitation, restorative justice, and reentry policies dominate the corrections landscape.]

What I have learned over the years is that anything may work. I've seen people who were stabbed to within an inch of their life and it changed their thinking about the value of life and who they were, and it changed their behavior.

I've seen people whose mothers have died while they were in prison and it changed their thinking. It changed what's valuable in life, what's important—missing kids, families—all that, anything. I've seen inmates … if you want to see a grown man cry go to a graduation, a GED graduation. You'll see a 50-year-old man get a high school GED and cry because it's the first thing he's ever done that's significant.

So anything may work—anything. Drug treatment—someone gets drug-free for the first time in 15 years, it makes a difference. Church groups come in. People make religious conversions, get involved in health and exercise. People get involved in religion. It makes a difference. People used to be afraid. I used to get complaints from police officers. "Oh, those guys working out over there, you're building them up so they can hurt others." No. Those people that have a regimen; those people are taking care of their body, they're not going to hurt you. The one that's going to hurt you is the guy leaning up against the wall and smoking a cigarette. He's the dangerous guy. He was thinking about the next drug deal. This guy's not thinking about that. He's thinking about taking care of himself. You have to know what group you're dealing with. When people say they've had a religious conversion, I always believe them. I don't ever question anybody. I watch their behavior instead. You can tell if somebody's changed.

Q: How do you balance the law and practical applications?

A: When I was in Oklahoma, a controversial decision was made around capital punishment. I made a personal commitment that if I ever became a director, I would be involved, but I would never tell anybody what my feelings were about capital punishment, whether I'm for it or against it or how I felt about any law for that matter. In my role I have to carry out the law. So, I've carried that position through these four states. I've given the order and been present at seven executions. I went to Iowa. They didn't have capital punishment, and I didn't push for capital punishment. I just followed the law there. I come to Maryland. We have a law of capital punishment, but it's not carried out due to the moratorium. When I came here, I told the governor I don't have a public opinion on capital punishment and he put me on the death penalty commission. Another thing I don't do is contribute to political campaigns. I've never contributed to a governor's campaign. Each governor I interview with, I tell them that as a condition of employment. It's never been an issue with any governor I have worked for.

Evidence-Based Corrections

Q: Do you focus on the evidence-based practices?

A: It's hard to find good research but I'm very much interested. We did sort of the quick and dirty research on those inmates who worked in the cemetery and found their rate of return is a great deal less, but it's not pure research. So we need someone to do a study on restorative justice programs for different systems. That would be something that the long-term academics could bring too. I also just created a position last year for Director of Volunteer Programs whose job is to create volunteers all over the state to help us do our job. We would like to have interns and create research opportunities in colleges.

I was in a meeting of 38 directors in Aurora, Colorado, and three law students from Yale came and spoke to us about the benefits of prison visitation. (Two of them were based on research; one guy on actual experience. He had just graduated from Yale Law School. The other two were still in school.) He told us a story about visiting his parents in prison. His parents were infamous bank robbers of New York City and part of an antigovernmental group that wanted to fund their operations. The bank robbery went bad and they killed two security guards at the bank. So they went to trial. The man got life—federal prison life. The woman got– it was a husband and wife—the woman got 25 years. This Yale law student was the son of those two people.

He talked about the benefits of visiting his dad and mother when they were in prison. It was an emotional presentation for all of us. This kid was just as sincere as he could be and smart, and talked about visiting his parents in prison. He talked of going to the prison and how he was treated—sometimes very good; sometimes like he was an inmate—and how much difference it made to him as a young kid. So I asked him, "What do you think about going to video visitation in some areas of Baltimore?" He said, "Do it." He said, "Some of the most tragic times I had were times when I couldn't visit my mother for some reason or another, and she would send me audio tapes. I would play those over and over. Don't ever minimize the value of a card or a letter or a video visit. I would say do all you can. What you're doing there to help people connect that can't afford to drive, keep doing it." And so we've been thinking about video visitation here.

We've got a lot of inmates from Baltimore living in Western Correctional Institution (WCI), and their grandmothers and their mothers can't afford to drive 3½ hours out and 3½ hours back and all that. Phone calls are expensive. So we're going to set up free video visitation. We have a place in Baltimore City, a church or something, where we put in a screen and video conferencing capability and have the families visit the inmates. If families come in, we don't have to shake them down and they don't have to drive out. Maybe we're going the wrong direction. Maybe this personal contact is too much, but if we do video we move away from it. They're doing research on it to examine what difference it makes and some solid research shows those that got visits do better than those who didn't. Think about it! This young kid, a young law student, had both parents in prison when he was 6 years old. He graduated from Yale Law School. He still has a good relationship with his father and his mother. His dad's still in prison. His mother is out.

Transnational Relations

Q: Have any other countries contacted you, looking for insights?

A: I worked in South America and Paraguay when I was at the University of Oklahoma on several occasions looking at prison design and programs that might be helpful to them. Here in Maryland, I speak to groups from Mexico and the United Arab Emirates and other countries that are being trained at our Training Academy, about some of the programs we have started here.

Q: How have you used/are you using technology to make corrections operate more fluidly?

A: We got two vans that belonged to the Department of Labor that they purchased 8 years ago. That department never used them very much. I said I would like to have those two vans for our use. I'm going to use those for video visitation by taking them to different parts of Baltimore City so people don't have to come to the facility, especially those far away. We've got a lot of technology, and if we just keep pushing the use of it and we could hook up some video conferencing with the wardens and inmates, and maybe even do virtual tours.

General Assessments

Q: What is the milieu like in the prisons, from the maximum to the minimum? How do you engage inmates?

A: We think work is good and have increased the number of inmates inside the institution that are working. We try to get inmates involved in programs because idleness is the devil's workshop. We try to do it and we have. We've significantly increased the numbers involved in programs and in work.

We have some really good wardens in our systems who believe the mission. They believe that correction officers, as well as all staff, are part of changing offenders' behavior. We want prisoners to be safe in our seven medium-security big prisons and our one maximum-security prison that's in North Branch, Cumberland. The medium securities are generally open-yard, open activities. Inmates move from one program to another. Maximum security at North Branch is a, pretty much, lock-down institution. It's for the worst behaved. If inmates assault correction officers—serious assaults—they go to North Branch. They're involved in programs there. We still have education programs and drug treatment programs. It's just in a more controlled environment.

There are about 350 life without parole inmates out there and about 1300 life with parole, scattered though all the mediums. Our inmates who are sentenced to death, we have five, are out at North Branch. So North Branch is something in itself. Then we have the mediums with work-release and minimum security institutions, and we're trying to increase the number of minimums. We overbuilt in the maximum-security area and the mediums; we've underbuilt in minimums. So we're adding 1000 beds of minimum in the next couple of years.

Q: What are your thoughts on the public's notions that perhaps inmates have too many liberties?

A: I've heard that for 40 years and have an answer. One of our jobs is to create a safe environment for everyone concerned, our staff especially. So some of these programs are like occupiers of time. After they work, after they're in programs, they come back. It gives them something to do in the evenings with the TV or whatever. You have to earn a right to TV. It can be taken away based on behavior. They have to buy their own TV. The TV we provide is bought through the canteen. It's a see-through. You can see all the working parts inside—plastic, clear plastic, so you can't hide stuff in it. We don't want somebody to spend 20 years in prison and walk out and not know what's going on. So, the TV brings news; it brings sports and all the activities that make somebody more amenable to reentering and being successful outside. I've been dealing with this forever. For example, Oklahoma became a state in 1907, opened its penitentiary in 1911 and offered newspapers to its inmates. They had cartoons in them. But they had world history. It had all that information, so inmates have been getting newspapers forever. When radios came out in the 1930s, inmates got radios. When TVs came out, inmates got TVs. It's always been a practice in the prisons in the country to keep the population in touch with families; keep them in touch with the local, state, and world news. So, nothing's new. It's just offensive to some, but it's a part of the business. There is no system in the country that deprives its inmates, long term, of all of the things going on in the world.

We have a computer system set up for our women's prison. We started with them and now the male prisons, where we have closed Internet access to jobs across the state, so that women, in our women's prison, can go over to the lab and log onto this closed system. It doesn't put them on the Internet, except to that one site and that has all the jobs downloaded daily. We do that in the men's prison too, so they can learn to operate computers, because when they get out in the real world they're going to operate a computer to get a job, for the most part.

Conclusion

Secretary Gary Maynard is a principled man who does not shy away from responsibilities. In the interview he said he was responsible for any successes as well as failures. His conviction to carry out the law with immediacy and in a just manner void of personal sentiments makes him well suited for his position. Approximately a month postinterview, his leadership style and corrections philosophy were both tested when a corruptions scandal erupted. It involved a prominent gang (the Black Guerrilla Family) and in-prison operations, aided by more than a dozen female correctional officers, some of whom were allegedly impregnated by inmates, and made local, state, and national headlines. His response to the scandal was that of a true leader when he said, "The vast majority of our correctional officers do their jobs with integrity, honesty, and respect." Maynard further stated that he is partially to blame for this incident. "It's totally on me. I don't make any excuses … we will move up the chain of command, and people will be held accountable." Staff and officers have been disciplined and indictments brought against officers, some of whom have pleaded guilty. Secretary Maynard restored order to the Baltimore City Detention Center and then resigned from the Department of Public Safety and Correctional Services.

Glossary

administrative segregation: The placement of a prisoner in an isolated unit for the safety and security of the institution; a form of solitary confinement

Attica Prison riot: The most deadly prison riot in the 1970s. It occurred at the Attica Correctional Facility in Attica, New York, in 1971. The riot was based on prisoners' demands for political rights and better living conditions (Lohr, 2012).

disciplinary segregation: The isolation of prisoners from the general population due to violations of prison rules

McAlester Correctional Facility: In Oklahoma State, one of the worst prison riots in U.S. history occurred here. The riot was due to overcrowding (built in 1911 for 1100 and by 1973 housed 2200) and was the most expensive. Both Attica and McAlester led to a paradigm of more security and less programs.

security threat groups: "Any group of offenders a correctional facility believes poses a threat to the physical safety of other offenders and staff due to the very nature of said Security Threat Group." (Texas Department of Criminal Justice, 2007).

Western Correctional Institution (WCI): Opened in 1996 and located in Alleghany County, Maryland, this is a maximum-security facility designed to house approximately 1800 inmates.

III

Asia

Soh Wai Wah, Commissioner of Prisons, Singapore

11

SUSAN SIM

Contents

Overview

The physical amenities in Changi Prison in Singapore may be very basic, but inmates are offered a comprehensive suite of rehabilitation services, including skills training, and job matching and placement on release. In line with the risk–need–responsivity (RNR) principle, there is no one-size-fits-all approach. All adult prisoners are assessed and classified according to (1) general risk of reoffending, (2) criminogenic needs and specific risk of reoffending, (3) noncriminogenic needs, and (4) responsivity issues. Each inmate is then matched to appropriate rehabilitation programs and given a customized treatment plan called Personal Route Map (PRM) that allows his progress to be monitored throughout his stay in prison. Full-time psychologists and counselors run at least five treatment programs based on cognitive behavioral therapy (CBT) practices and motivational interviewing (MI) principles.

The treatment programs work to change inmates' belief and value systems, raise their motivation levels, and target their criminogenic needs. They are based on "what works" evidence-based practices adapted from successes elsewhere; there is frequent needs analysis evaluation to identify gaps in treatment, especially for high-risk offenders, and where necessary, programs are redeveloped to address the gaps (Leo, 2014).*

A government agency called SCORE runs several industries inside Changi Prison—including a laundry that is Southeast Asia's largest, a bakery that provides bread and pastries for several restaurant and grocery chains in Singapore, and a multimedia production unit, that offers inmates the opportunity to learn new skills and earn money for their postrelease needs. There is also a prison school that provides formal education leading up to the GCE A-levels (a milestone academic certification required to qualify for university admission in Singapore) as well as art and culinary workshops run by renowned artists and professional chefs.

The Singapore Prison Service also works with SCORE to run a volunteer CARE Network to help the 11,000 prisoners released annually reintegrate into society. A public education campaign called the Yellow Ribbon Project helps to mobilize volunteers to give released prisoners a second chance at life, including jobs. These efforts to involve the community in the rehabilitation of ex-offenders were recognized by the United Nations in 2007 for its ground breaking work.

Introduction

The interview took place just as the Singapore government began a 4-month public consultation on changes to prison legislation to introduce the Conditional Remission System and the Mandatory Aftercare Scheme. The amended Prisons Act, passed by the Singapore Parliament in January 2014, seeks to deter ex-inmates from reoffending by both strengthening aftercare support and expanding the responsibility of the Commissioner of Prisons to include postrelease supervision. Hitherto, prison inmates were granted one-third remission for good conduct and behavior in prison and released

* He notes that to ensure the classification capability remains robust and able to make accurate and systematic selection of inmates for rehabilitation, the Singapore Prison Service moved, in 2011, from the Level of Service Inventory–Revised (LSI-R) to the Level of Service/Case Management Inventory (LS/CMI) for assessments of the adult offenders. These assessment tools use a structured interview to assess the risk and needs of the offenders in eight domains that have been shown to have strong associations with the risk of reoffending: the four strongly established risk factors of reoffending—criminal history, antisocial personality pattern, antisocial cognition, and antisocial associates—and the four more moderate risk factors of reoffending—substance abuse, employment instability, family problems, and low engagements in prosocial leisure activities.

unconditionally, there being no parole conditions for those released at this point of their sentences. A legacy of the British Empire, this remission system was not changed after Singapore attained independence in 1965.

Career

A career police officer, Soh Wai Wah was seconded to the Singapore Prison Service at the end of 2009 to head the 2500-strong organization. He is also responsible for a prison population that in 2013 numbered 12,500, the majority of whom are incarcerated in the Changi Prison Complex in the eastern part of Singapore, with a land area of about 0.4 km^2. With what he considers to be an "extremely low" officer to inmate ratio of 1:6.25,* Soh runs what may be "the densest prison in the world" in the very densely populated island state of Singapore, where 5.4 million people reside on 716 km^2.†

In this interview, Soh sees himself not only as chief warden for Singapore, but also the chief corrections officer, responsible as much for the safe custody of every prisoner as for his rehabilitation and reintegration into society. "In Singapore, we are among the few agencies where both the prisons and corrections come under one responsibility. I think as a result we can talk about through-care and be more effective in our mission."

Changes Experienced

The new measures approved by the Singapore Parliament put the onus on prison officials to assess each inmate's risk of reoffending and to decide on which of three phases—halfway house stay, home supervision, or community integration—or combination thereof he should be placed in upon conditional release. The Commissioner of Prisons has the authority to administer punishments for minor breaches of the conditions, while the courts may sentence ex-inmates to imprisonment for major breaches.

These changes represent "a paradigm shift in our approach to aftercare, bringing us in line with practices in other jurisdictions," senior minister of state for home affairs, Masagos Zulkifli, told the Singapore Parliament.‡

* It is generally accepted that staff/inmate ratios alone do not determine adequacy of staffing levels as other variables such as facility design, level of security, and activity level have to be considered. But the Singapore ratio is low compared to the United Kingdom, where the officer to inmate ratio in 2009 was 1:2.9, and the United States, where nationally there were 3.9 inmates per correctional officer in 1993 (House of Commons Justice Committee report, 2014; Elias, 2014).

† Source: Department of Statistics Singapore (2014).

‡ Second Reading Speech on the Prisons (Amendment) Bill by Mr. Masagos Zulkifli, senior minister of state for home affairs and foreign affairs, 20 January, 2014, Singapore.

He made clear the impetus was the high rate of reoffending by drug addicts and those previously convicted of drug offenses; they made up more than 80% of repeat offenders, which comprised 80% of the prison population in 2013.

It should, however, be noted that Singapore's prison population has been declining in the last 10 years, while the recidivism rate has improved from 35% 10 years ago to 27.4% for the latest cohort of 2011.* But like the minister, Soh sees no room for complacency. "Singapore follows a crime control model that emphasizes the deterrent effect of the prison sentence and that has worked well for us all these years and I hope it will continue to work well for us," he notes. "There is thus a need for the effectiveness of our rehabilitation efforts to match up." As a prison leader, it is his job to prepare the prison service for challenges ahead and to champion creative solutions.

> We shouldn't just be comfortable to say that the recidivism rate is already very low. I think we may have a situation that can develop in the future where aged ex-prisoners are not deterred by any prison sentence. They are so used to it and they have nothing much to lose outside of prison. That is a phenomena I am trying to fight and that is why there is urgency. We have to do it now to prevent that kind of a scenario from happening 15–20 years down the road.

Personal Correctional Philosophy

While his personal philosophy is to "help another fellow human being in his journey of rehabilitation," Soh is also crystal clear that prison is also about punishment and deterrence. "The conditions in prison are very basic," he notes. And that is precisely why he is never short of volunteers prepared to help former prisoners. "Singaporeans are willing to help ex-offenders because they feel that the prisoners have been adequately punished. I think if they have doubts whether the prisoners have been punished, they will be less willing to help them. So that is why my prison must continue to provide only the most basic amenities. That is why my prison cells cannot look like, say, a student dormitory. That is why it still must be an unpleasant experience."

Crafting a New Vision Statement

In transitioning from police officer to chief prison officer, Soh developed a personal correctional philosophy informed as much by his previous job of

* Nur Asyiqin Mohamad Salleh, "More ex-inmates reoffend within 2 years of release," *Straits Times*, Singapore, 12 February 2014.

apprehending criminals as by the evidence-based doctrine of rehabilitation practiced in Changi Prison since 2004. He came to embrace and champion the concept of *through-care*, which he defines thus:

> It is a fusion of two words: in-care and aftercare. In-care means inside the prison and aftercare means outside the prison. It is common with many jurisdictions to view these two as dichotomous. The reason to be inside the prison is to be punished and the person suffers during his imprisonment. Then he is released and goes through some sort of parole and the caseworker could be helping him to reform in the aftercare program. But I believe in through-care, which means that I must begin with the end in mind: he is not to come back into prison again. So from his first day and to the last day of his in-care, I must bear that as the end in my mind. Of course there are other aspects I need to consider. His prison experience is meant to be a punishment for him. His safety and security is one of my core missions… But at the same time, I also know that how I treat him while he is in prison can affect his likelihood of coming back. This is the concept of through-care: that from the day of his admission, I must bear in mind that the end is not his release, but that he does not come back to prison, and thus his treatment during both in-care and after-care should support this end.

The key, Soh says, is to think about "what change we want to see in this person." As chief prison warden, he is aware that there is no consensus in the core correctional practice as to the role of prison wardens in the rehabilitation journey of prisoners. He is, however, convinced that prison officers have a role to play in instilling hope and guiding the behavior of prisoners.

> I think the prison guards and wardens have a role to change the thinking of prisoners. This is not just a one-on-one treatment but about the system and processes. If you are just running the prison system in the case of prison guards, you will just lock people up and give them X-box games so that you minimize their interaction. That is what some systems do because every interaction can be a liability and potential for danger. We can minimize the interaction of prisoners through X-box games or you can have a system where prison officers are encouraged to talk to them, to interact, and listen. That exposes the officers to a lot more work, liability, and danger. But it is essential for the prisoner to feel that he is not just being locked up in jail. He should be made to feel responsible for his own rehabilitation journey.

The risks Soh speaks of were demonstrated the week before the interview when an officer was stabbed by a prisoner. The mental resiliency of officers is thus "tested every day," and as Soh puts it, the counseling skills of his psychologists and counselors are "being practiced on a day-to-day basis."

Importantly, the organizational ethos has also been strengthened by involving all staff in developing a new shared vision statement that seeks to inspire them toward the lofty goal of zero recidivism and places their work and aspirations within the larger societal context.

> Our previous vision statement* was articulated at end 1999, beginning of 2000. It has been 12 or 13 years since. It has served us very well but as soon as we started thinking about it, we realized that it needed to be changed. One clear yardstick is that when the vision statement was first crafted, there were people back in 1999 who would say that was impossible, and it was an effective vision statement because it was incredulous then. So when we looked at this last year—I commissioned a team to look at this last year—the obvious thing was to see how comfortable we had become with this concept of Captains of Lives. We say we are Captains of Lives and it doesn't sound incredulous anymore. This means the vision statement has run out of its ability to inspire, so we said let's start and get a new vision statement.
>
> When I said I wanted a new vision statement, I also wanted everyone to be involved. With 2500 people how can everyone be involved? Well let's do a survey as everyone can participate in the survey. All 2500 did the survey with a few simple questions. We identified what was close to the heart of my officers. Safety and security is still a key ingredient of their work. But in addition, they also want to do more rehabilitation and they want to do more aftercare. From this survey I formed a smaller team that crafted a few drafts. I was prepared to take a long time for this to be done so I said, "Let's come out with a few drafts and bounce those drafts against focus groups." About 2500 were in the survey and about a thousand people participated in the focus groups, during which they gave comments on the various drafts. I attended one of those focus group discussions. One of the drafts said something like we want to rehabilitate everyone. I remember one of the responses was, "This is ridiculous and it is unachievable." That moment struck me because I thought, "that is what the vision statement is supposed to do." We are supposed to come up with something that when people look at it, half of them will say it cannot be done. That must be the essence of a vision statement and that struck me at that moment. From 1000 people involved in the focus group discussions, we did a bit more fine tuning and we finally arrived at the vision statement: As Captains of Lives, we inspire everyone, at every chance, toward a society without reoffending.
>
> I want as many people to identify with this statement as possible. There are people in my system who are involved directly in rehabilitation. They are the counselors. They will identify with the statement immediately. Why? It is because it sounds rehabilitative.
>
> I also want the statement to be applicable to the prison guards who are the front end of the incarceration process. They are actually not dealing with

* The 1999 vision statement read: "We aspire to be captains in the lives of offenders committed to our custody. We will be instrumental in steering them toward being responsible citizens with the help of their families and the community. We will thus build a secure and exemplary prison system."

direct rehabilitation work. The priority for them is safety and security. When I use the word inspire, it is very broad. It can be inspiring rehabilitation but you can be inspiring good behavior too.

Therefore my vision statement is not just about rehabilitation. It is also about good order, about discipline, about safety and security. It is not a one-sided vision statement. It applies not just to the soft side but also the hard aspects of our work. That is why it applies to everyone. The vision statement is also crafted so that it is relevant even to staff not dealing with prisoners, such as those involved in mobilizing the public to support our work in rehabilitation and giving second chances to released ex-prisoners.

Problems and Successes Experienced

How Much More Can the Recidivism Rate Be Lowered?

Soh is candid that he does not "feel I'm charting an entirely new path"; his predecessors, the last two also former police leaders, one of whom left to become commissioner of police, had initiated and emphasized the role of volunteers in postrelease support. One of Soh's major speeches soon after taking over the Singapore Prison Service leadership in 2010 was to celebrate the Yellow Ribbon Project (YRP), a community engagement campaign established in 2004 "to provide a concerted and coordinated approach to create awareness, generate acceptance and inspire action within the community to support the rehabilitation and reintegration of ex-offenders" (Soh, 2010).

By Soh's account, the YRP has become so successful—a public perception survey commissioned in 2007 showed 94% of the respondents were aware of the YRP—that he is "not short of people willing to come forward" although "I can always do with more."

He has also received "tremendous" support from the Ministry of Home Affairs. "There is a realization that you need to invest in rehabilitation, and resources have been forthcoming for me to be able to do what I have been doing."

Theory and Practice

The Starfish Moral

In improving on his rehabilitation mission, Soh has transformed his organization, increasing the number of civilian staff on the frontlines. The drive to be evidence based in prison practices has culminated in the formation of two divisions—the Rehabilitation and Reintegration Division (RRD) and the Psychological and Correctional Rehabilitation Division (PCRD)— to develop policies and frameworks and promote collaboration with external partners. The PCRD also functions as the scientific think tank, to assess and deliver criminogenic interventions to offenders, provide specialized training and support to prison staff and community partners, and conduct research and program evaluation (Leo, 2014).

> I have about 2000 officers in uniform but also a substantial number, about 500, who are civilian. Civilians in the past used to be associated only with support functions. But now they are engaged in what I call frontline work providing case work interaction between the prisoner and counselor. My organization must now see itself as one where frontline work is not done only by staff in uniform, but also by professionally trained civilians, and there must be a cohesive shared culture between them.
>
> It is an interesting situation because in many institutions and jurisdictions that I know overseas, prisons and corrections are kept separate. A prison is run by wardens. Corrections is done by a different group of people—usually civilians—and they may even report to a different head. In this sort of setup, it is very difficult to talk about through-care because it involves two different groups of people. Whereas in Singapore we are among the few agencies where both the prisons and corrections come under one responsibility. I think as a result we can talk about through-care and be more effective in our mission.

But the mission, he repeats through the interview, is twofold, and he expects his staff to carry out both, using the latest research theories but never forgetting the operational realities of where they work.

> It is not just rehabilitation but also safety and security. My officers are not only skilled one way or the other. They have a very difficult job having to bear both in mind. I have a growing group of psychologists and some among them have doctorates. I place high value on research and evaluation because we are talking about resources and there is accountability and I have to assure myself and assure the government that the resources given do yield results. The people who evaluate are people with experience on the ground. They are not lab technicians wearing a white coat. They are people on the ground doing their work and at different points in their career they do evaluation. This gives a good sense of confidence that they are doing the real stuff and are not just armchair researchers or practitioners who have no sense of theory.

Yet, Soh wants his staff to remember the individual, not just the numbers, in the quest for lower recidivism rates. Asked how he measures success, he says:

> I definitely see objective measures for success. One of my officers likes to tell the starfish story. This starfish story says there is a boy at a beach and he sees many starfish on the beach. The starfish are dying and he needs to throw them

into the sea to save them. There is a man looking at the boy and he says, "Look, you are only one boy and there are many starfish on the beach. How many can you throw and save? What difference can you make?" The boy answers, "Well at least I made a difference for this one."

The moral behind the story is that we shouldn't be overwhelmed with the idea that we can't save everyone, because saving even just one matters. I think that is a good story but we can go beyond it. I think we can look at the recidivism rate as a measure of how well we are doing because everyone is important. I would like to save them by the thousands.

General Assessment

The implicit conundrum for a correctional leader in his position is how do you build on success, especially in a system heralded for lowering recidivism rates by some 15% over 15 years? Soh's approach is to take on more work.

> In a sense my prison work has extended on both ends. Extended on the aftercare and pre-in-care.

Inspired by the work of religious counselors in prison, Soh believes they fulfill one of the RNR principles, which is that "prisoners need a close social network."

> What we learn in RNR is that if they have multiple needs, just addressing one of his needs is insufficient. He needs work but he also needs counseling to change his mental attitude, so if you give him work and do not change his attitude, it won't be enough. He also needs prosocial friends. That is something the government cannot do. What we can do as an authority is to mobilize willing members of the public to be the prosocial friends.

He thus began a program to train and bring more volunteers into prison to befriend prisoners, in essence starting their aftercare months before their release.

> I have seen among volunteers who come to do religious counseling, they are people who can potentially make friends with the prisoners. So they should see themselves coming not just to provide religious counseling. I hope they will see themselves as being prosocial friends of the prisoners. So I came up with a prerelease regime. In the prerelease regime, prisoners about to be released are grouped together for a 10-month experience.
>
> During this prerelease regime, they are prepared for work outside and whatever training they haven't received they will receive it during these 10 months. We also ensure everyone receives what we call integrated criminogenic programs. During the 10 months, we will have an intensive period

> of reestablishing family contact. For the religious counseling, more emphasis is put on helping the friendships to develop. So the religious counseling takes on a different character. For instance, religious volunteers providing the counseling are specifically told that their key role is to begin and maintain their friendship with the prisoners after their release. Of course in Singapore's multiracial context we make sure that the religious volunteers will only have access to those of the same religion. So you don't have, say, a Muslim prisoner being provided Christian counseling. I also mobilize volunteers who befriend prisoners on a nonreligious basis. All these are to provide released prisoners with prosocial friends to help in their rehabilitation journey.

At the same time, Soh is conscious that although he has been able to double the number of counselors on his staff from 70 in 2012, the man power crunch that Singapore is facing nationwide affects his service too.

> While I say I have more resources for the new work that I do, I am also expected to be productive in the current work that I do and to be able to do it more efficiently. So on one hand, yes, I am given the support; on the other hand, I need to show productivity and efficiency.

Infrastructure design—Changi is modeled on supermax facilities in the United States with prisoners housed in self-contained clusters—means the prison can be run very efficiently, with each officer responsible for six inmates. Soh expects that he will have to explore the use of more technology and improve on processes. At the moment, however, he is seized by the tangible and intangible costs of incarcerating a person and what his service can do to ameliorate some of these costs.

> Being in prison comes with a cost. Firstly we have increasing healthcare cost. The cost of running a prison. We cannot run away from the fact that I don't have all healthy prisoners. Prisoners become sick like everyone else. There is also a cost to society in terms of dysfunctional families, in terms of the next generation of prisoners as a result of absent fathers and mothers. There is also a cost to society in terms of the economic output of the otherwise incarcerated prisoner; we talk about shortage of labor and the need for foreign workers. Can we be creative in how we punish offenders while maintaining the deterrence effect of the crime control model? So we may have to think of new ways of punishing people that are effective but cost less to society.

Alternatives to imprisonment known as community work orders were introduced in 2011 and, according to Soh, have been quite well received over the last 2 years. He thinks Singapore can do with more community-based sentencing.

> One part of it comes under my direct administration which is a day reporting order. Instead of coming to jail, the offenders come to my counselors or

caseworkers. I think more can be done in this area. More people can be put through this system.

Some of my charges are not in prison and in lieu of a prison term, they report to my caseworkers regularly. They tend to be first timers who have committed relatively minor offences.

As for families made dysfunctional by the imprisonment of a parent or breadwinner, Soh is mobilizing volunteers to look after their families. He calls them the Yellow Ribbon Champions.

What we have started during my term is what we call the Yellow Ribbon Champions at the grassroots level. With the consent of the prisoner, we connect the grassroots with the prisoner's family. The prisoner could be in prison but his family may be in dire need. I identify Yellow Ribbon Champions among the grassroots and neighborhood who will then render help to the families who are in need. That is to stop a next generation of criminals from being spawned and of course it maintains the family integrity so that when the prisoner is released, he can return to a family that is functional.

In accordance with the RNR concept, it is the people with the higher or highest risk who need the most help. So the people with the highest risk generally tend to be those serving the longest sentences, the people with dysfunctional families, those with employment problems, the people with long-term drug problems. These are the people who need the most help and these are the people we need to render help to. It is not like a low-lying fruit concept. The low-lying fruit just needs to be plucked. Those that are right at the top are where an effort is needed to reach up to them.

In the last 2 years, Soh has covered a third of Singapore, helping hundreds of families with the aid of the Yellow Ribbon Champions.

Conclusion

Of the five Singapore Prison Service chiefs appointed since 1988, four have been senior police leaders and one a former director of the Central Narcotics Bureau. Two went on to become commissioners of police.

Cross-postings of uniformed and civilian officers to different departments are not unusual within the Singapore public service, especially for those in the elite administrative service, whose members are recruited and groomed to assume the top posts in the civil service. The Home Team—which comprises the law enforcement and emergency services that report to the minister for home affairs—uses postings not just for career development purposes, but also to nurture what it calls the Home Team Plus officer. The idea is to create a community of professionals and practitioners with diverse skills, bonded by common experiences and dedicated to a shared mission of keeping Singapore safe and secure while able to think and act beyond organizational silos.

Despite being parachuted in from outside the prison service, it is a police leader who is credited with changing the organization's culture and mission. In 1999, Chua Chin Kiat, then in his first year as director of prisons (as Singapore's top prison warden was called until 2014*), organized what the prison service called "a visioning exercise … to collectively craft a shared vision and conduct a review of its mission to better accommodate the changing needs and expectations of its stakeholders and the public."† Prison officers became Captains of Lives, with a mission to Rehab, Renew, Restart the lives of their charges. By the time Chua retired from the service in 2007, the Yellow Ribbon Project was in full bloom, with thousands of volunteers signed up to help former inmates "unlock the second prison."

Soh Wai Wah is the latest of this tribe of Singapore police officers turned jailers and, more importantly, champions of second chances for criminals. This interview provides insights into how such a transition benefits the prison service leadership. As Soh puts it, seeing criminals he caught and sent to prison coming back again spurred him to think about the pathology of criminal justice and the importance of rehabilitation in addition to punishment as deterrence.

Indeed, Soh never loses sight of the fact that prisons have to be about punishment and discipline and it is this sense of just deserts that makes rehabilitation possible at operational and strategic levels. As he emphasizes several times, his prison offers only very basic amenities. This environment of strict discipline provides the safe and secure backdrop that makes counseling and vocational training of inmates possible.

It also allows the prison service to draw on resources beyond the wire. As Soh observes, people are more prepared to give offenders a second chance if they are convinced they have been duly punished for their crimes.

Soh is overseeing a pivotal transformation of the prison landscape, where prisoners released early on remission are for the first time subject to probation and sanctions. "It will be a Singapore variant of what the Americans call the parole system," he says, adding: "It is additional work. And that is what we want to undertake. Because if we believe in corrections, if we believe that prisoners can be rehabilitated and we have a role to rehabilitate them, then we must extend our work outside of the prisons."

* The change in job title from director to commissioner of prisons was legislated in the amendments to the Prisons Act passed by the Singapore Parliament in January 2014. No reason was given for the name change, but as several of the other Home Team departments use "Commissioner" for their top leadership position, this change might just be to standardize job titles.

† The Singapore Prison Service website, retrieved from www.prisons.gov.sg.

But beyond the prison walls also means the absence of the secure and safe environment in which prisoners and prison staff have been accustomed to interacting. The operational challenges are at this stage unclear. Yet asked if his work is exciting, Soh answers "it is."

Glossary

Captains of Lives: The tagline first introduced by the Singapore Prison Service in December 1999 to motive its officers to "aspire to make a difference in the lives of inmates." As Captains in the lives of inmates, their interactions have a direct impact on their journey of rehabilitation. They are thus to be fair yet firm in the treatment of inmates and to carry themselves as role models. "We believe inmates have the potential to turn over a new leaf but the motivation to change must ultimately come from within themselves," officers are exhorted. Three broad principles guide them:

- *REHAB*: a commitment to programs and services within the prison system to support inmates who have proven they have the inherent desire to change.
- *RENEW*: a commitment an inmate makes to change his/her life for the better. Looking beyond their imprisonment, they demonstrate a willingness and desire to renew their lives.
- *RESTART*: a commitment to garner the support of the community. Through the CARE Network, offenders are given opportunities to restart their lives.

CARE Network: Community Action for the Rehabilitation of Ex-offenders (CARE) Network. Started in 2000, it has more than 100 partners, with a secretariat based in SCORE, which engages the community in providing coordinated aftercare for ex-offenders. It believes that better awareness and understanding will generate greater acceptance and more second chances for ex-offenders. Its signature public awareness campaign is the *Yellow Ribbon Project*. In 2013, the CARE Network announced that to improve rehabilitation and reintegration prospects for high-risk offenders released from prison, it will roll out a new competency framework to enhance the capabilities of its aftercare partners. They will be equipped with specialized skill sets and knowledge to handle the changing inmate profile, as many high-risk inmates have a long history of substance abuse and long-term incarceration, with multiple and complex reintegration needs.

Changi Prison: Built and operationalized as a maximum-security prison by the British colonial government in 1936. Even then it espoused a philosophy of reform and rehabilitation: "It is hoped that in due course this prison may become a training ground for the misfits of society, rather than a purely penal institution," said Inspector of Prisons OC Hancock at the opening of Changi Prison on 4th January 1937. Redevelopment of the Changi Prison Complex began in 1999 to model it after several high-security prisons overseas. When fully redeveloped, it will have four clusters featuring technologically sophisticated security systems to make prison supervision a safer job, as well as to allow greater focus on rehabilitation and create more employment opportunities for inmates. Southeast Asia's largest laundry is based in one of the two modules already open and functioning.

SCORE: The Singapore Corporation of Rehabilitative Enterprises, a government agency under the Ministry of Home Affairs. SCORE's stated objective is to build bridges of hope by giving ex-offenders and their families a second chance at life and by inspiring people to become more accepting and compassionate toward ex-offenders. Apart from public relations activities such as an annual art exhibition featuring the work of inmates and publications by and about inmates and their rehabilitation, SCORE, as its name implies, runs a range of industries and job skills programs:

- Industries from food manufacturing and laundry services to multimedia production and subcontracting offer inmates the opportunity to learn new skills and to be productive during their stay in prison. By working closely with both private companies and government agencies, SCORE helps inmates spend their time meaningfully and save money for their release. Income earned by SCORE enterprises are donated to halfway houses, the Singapore Anti-Narcotics Association, and aftercare associations.
- Training programs equip offenders with the skills they need to start new lives free from crime. Since training alone will not guarantee that an inmate will actually land a job upon release, SCORE also has a "Train and Place" scheme to ensure trainees are placed in jobs.
- An Employment Assistance Unit has a database of 1500 companies from various industries that are willing to offer jobs to ex-offenders.

Yellow Ribbon Project: Officially launched in October 2004 by the president of Singapore. An annual campaign aimed at changing society's mindset toward giving ex-offenders a second chance in life, it takes its name from the 1970s hit song, "Tie a Yellow Ribbon Round the

Ole Oak Tree," which describes a released prisoner's desire for forgiveness and acceptance. Each year, the project promotes a different theme to move the level of engagement upwards; from creating public awareness, subsequent campaigns have widened and deepened the message through use of celebrities and Rehabilitation Ambassadors, and mobilizing inmates and reformed ex-offenders to give back to society. Its signature message of "Help Unlock the Second Prison" and the Yellow Ribbon logo are now widely recognized in Singapore as a symbol of giving hope and second chances to ex-offenders. A public perceptions survey in 2007 showed that 94% of respondents were aware of the project, and more than 60% had generally positive attitudes toward ex-offenders, with most agreeing that ex-offenders deserve a second chance and hence were willing to accept them back into society.

12

Ayuth Sintoppant, Warden, Thonburi Remand Prison in Nonthaburi Province, Thailand

ATTAPOL KUANLIANG AND
SRISOMBAT CHOKPRAJAKCHAT

Contents

Overview

The evolution of corrections in the Kingdom of Thailand has a long history. The development of correctional systems and practices in Thailand has been influenced by a variety of political, economic, and social factors that have affected the current state of affairs in corrections. This has been true during each era or phase of correctional history in the nation. Prior to the reign of King Rama V (1868–1910), prisons and jails were unsystemized and widely dispersed in all important cities under the administration of various agencies, like the Ministry of Justice, Ministry of Interior, and Ministry of Defense.

During this early period of history in the correctional systems and practices in Thailand, the correctional system was divided into two parts. The first segment was in Bangkok and was composed of two types of facilities: the *khuk*, which is administered by the Ministry of the Metropolitan and was designed to house offenders who receive a sentence of 6 months or longer; and the *tarang*, which was designed to hold inmates who receive a sentence of less than 6 months. The second segment of the Thai correctional system consisted of those facilities in outlying provinces, outside of the immediate vicinity of Bangkok. In this segment, tarangs were the most common type of facility and they were managed by the governor of that given district. In most cases, offenders who receive sentences longer than 6 months are sent to a khuk that will be located in Bangkok. Today, in the contemporary correctional environment, the khuk is now referred to as the felony division and the tarant is referred to as the misdemeanor division.

From a historical point of view, it is perhaps the Correctional Institution Act of 1901 that was most profound in shaping the correctional system that exists today in Thailand. This act was crafted with the desire to improve the correctional system in Thailand. Later, in October of 1915, during the reign of King Vajiravudh (Rama VI) the Department of Correction Act was enacted to officially establish the Department of Corrections. During the year that followed, like many other nations during the World War I era, Thailand experienced a serious economic crisis, which affected a number of spheres in government, including corrections.

Political upheaval in the country, aggravated by financial crises, led to the collapse of King Prajadhipok's (Rama VII) regime. While the king continued to hold his position, the actual workings of the government were significantly reorganized. As a result of this reorganization, the Department of Correction was placed under the Ministry of Justice. Then, a few years later, the Department of Correction was renamed the Division of Corrections and was placed under the Ministry of the Interior.

Later in 1932, the Siamese Revolution occurred. This was a nearly bloodless coup d'état in which Thailand moved from being an absolute monarchy to a constitutional monarchy. This revolution occurred at the hands of a small group of military and civilian persons who would ultimately create Thailand's first political party. After this revolution and amidst other governmental change, the Thai correctional system was once again named the Department of Corrections. This was followed by the Correction Act of 1936, which mandated the role and function of prisons and jails in Thailand. This act also outlined procedures and guidelines for facilities throughout the nation.

More recently, in 2002, extensive bureaucratic reform occurred and this resulted in the Department of Correction, once again, falling under the purview of the Ministry of Justice. During this time, the Department of Corrections experienced a serious overcrowding crisis as the total number of inmates stood at 254,070, which exceeded the overall total capacity of this correctional system, which was designed to hold 100,000 inmates. As a result of the extensive reorganization and the desire to decrease the number of inmates housed in the correctional system, a number of strategies were employed that included the Royal Pardon, the Narcotics Rehabilitation Act 2002, and the Vivat Polamaung Rachatan School (Correctional Boot Camp). As of 2008, the correctional population had slowly been reduced to 166,338.

Modern Correctional Standards in Thailand

Presently, the Thai Department of Correction has set forth initiatives intended to both control and correct offenders. Rehabilitation both mentally and physically is emphasized to make sure that prisoners will become productive citizens of society and will not reoffend. According to the Ministry of Justice's ministerial regulations (2002), the Department of Correction has the following responsibilities:

1. Treat prisoners according to their sentence or other related laws
2. Set guidelines for the treatment of offenders under relevant laws and regulations, penological practices, and the United Nation's Standards on Treatment of Offenders
3. Manage the welfare of inmates within the system
4. Other tasks that mandate bylaws and regulations of the ministry or orders from a minister at the Department of Corrections, n.d.b)

Within the Department of Correction (DOC), there are four deputy generals managing tasks related to general operations, prison administration, offender rehabilitation, and educational services. These deputy generals are tasked with maintaining standards of care and service, in their respective spheres of responsibility, to ensure the appropriate treatment of offenders. These prison standards include the following:

> *General Prison Standards*: This set of standards covers 10 aspects, namely, Managerial Administration, Qualified Staff, Physical Plants, Prisoner Classification, Custody, Work and Labour Force, Education and Vocational Training, Disciplinary Procedure and Punishment, Prisoners' Services, and Prisoner Activities and Privileges.
>
> *Prisoners' Living Standards*: According to these standards, each prison facility is required to achieve a minimum of four out of five of these standards, namely Standard of Sleeping Material, Prison Kitchen, Canteen, Medical Centre, and Garbage Treatment.
>
> *Prisoner Transparency Standards*: This set of standards emphasizes the transparency of prison administration and concern management including Standard of Rice, Food, Prisoner's Work, Welfare Shop, and Managerial Administration.

Next, in relation to demonstrating transparency and a willingness to maintain, the DOC has an additional branch, the *office of internal affairs*, which inspects and investigates complaints and allegations. This office also audits the performance of various components of the department. The office of internal affairs is important because it helps to ensure that the agency is in compliance with numerous requirements, such as the United Nations Standard Minimum Rules for the Treatment of Prisoners, the International Covenant on Civil and Political Rights (ICCPR), and the Convention against Torture and Other Cruel, Inhuman or Degrading Treatment or Punishment (CAT).

Structure of the Prison System and Demographics of Inmate Population

The Thailand DOC is divided into two key segments of prison operation: the central and provincial components. In the central segment, there are a total of 67 prisons, jails, and correctional institutions. In the provincial segment, there are total of 50 provincial prisons along with another 26 district prisons that are in the jurisdiction of one province or another throughout the nation.

In regard to the prison population itself, it can be seen in Table 12.1 that approximately half of all convicted offenders received a sentence between 2 and 10 years. Further, the majority of these inmates are between the ages of 21 and 35 years old. There were about 1.52% of inmates sentenced to life in prison and about 0.04% are death-row inmates (see Table 12.1).

In 2012, the Thailand DOC employed 12,332 correctional officers and staff, with 8,402 being male and 2,147 being female. In 2010, the ratio of correctional officers to inmates was 1 officer to every 17 inmates. There were

Table 12.1 Number of Prisoners by Length of Sentence

Length of Sentence	Male	Female	Total	Percent
Less than 3 months	923	109	1,032	0.61
3–6 months	2,546	677	3,223	1.91
6–12 months	6,609	1,362	7,971	4.72
1–2 years	22,677	4,321	26,998	15.98
2–5 years	45,484	8,547	54,031	31.97
5–10 years	30,164	4,188	34,352	20.33
10–15 years	11,417	1,544	12,961	7.67
15–20 years	8,578	1,215	9,793	5.79
20–50 years	12,979	3,012	15,991	9.46
Life sentence	2,324	245	2,569	1.52
Death sentence	69	7	76	0.04
Total	143,770	25,227	168,997	100.00

Source: Department of Corrections, *Prisons and Correctional Institutions*, Thailand Ministry of Justice, Bangkok, Thailand, 2012.

168,997 inmates: 143,770 male prisoners and 25,227 female prisoners. The majority of inmates in the Thai system are convicted of drug offenses (86,669) followed by property offenses (36,726), homicide (10,983), sex offenses (6,640), physical offenses (5,261), and other offenses (6,871), respectively. Moreover, there are 27,215 inmates who were involved in some sort of appellate process. In addition, another 11,633 inmates were waiting for their official sentence, as well as 12,738 jail inmates who were waiting for their trial, not yet having been found guilty of the crime with which they were charged (Department of Corrections, B. E. 2555).

Drug Offenders and the Prison System

In 2003, the Thai government launched a War on Drugs similar to that in the United States. It was designed to suppress drug trafficking and prevent drug use. However, in Thailand, the primary drug problem was not stimulant drugs (as crack cocaine was in the United States) but narcotics from the opium fields that can be found in various parts of Southeast Asia.

The drug enforcement policy that followed increased penalties in drug-related offenses and also doled out more sentences of life imprisonment than had been observed in times past. Likewise, this policy led to an increase in death penalty–eligible offenses. This shift in policy proved to be quite significant and, as a result of this policy, there was an increase in the inmate population, despite the fact that the prison system had traditionally been overcrowded. Most of the swelling numbers of inmates were those who

Table 12.2 Number of Drug Offenders by Type of Drug

Type	Male	Female	Total	Percent
Heroin	2,745	335	3,080	2.68
Marijuana	928	142	1,070	0.93
Opium	1,406	34	1,440	1.25
Methamphetamine	86,784	20,297	107,081	93.05
Inhalants	36	6	42	0.04
Morphine	814	71	885	0.77
Cocaine	28	167	195	0.17
Other type of drugs	890	393	1,283	1.11
Total	93,631	21,445	115,076	100.00

Source: Department of Corrections, *Prisons and Correctional Institutions*, Thailand Ministry of Justice, Bangkok, Thailand, 2012.

violated some type of drug law. According to a DOC report in 2012, the majority of prisoners (115,076) were convicted of drug-related offenses (see Table 12.2). The report shows that there were 69,800 inmates who committed distribution and trafficking offense. The most drugs-related offenses involve methamphetamine (Department of Corrections, B. E. 2555).

In 2002, the number of drug offenders reached a height of 110,778 and since that time, has gradually decreased; this is no accident. Rather, this is the result of various countermeasures that were operated to alleviate prison overcrowding and the enactment of the Narcotics Addict Rehabilitation Act 2002, which assigns drug addicts to receive compulsory treatment instead of being sentenced to prison. Nonetheless, there still are a number of drug-related offenders with drug-abusing backgrounds.

Introduction

The interview was conducted with Warden Ayuth Sintoppant, the prison commander at Thonburi Remand Prison in Nonthaburi Province, Thailand. The Thonburi Remand Prison was established in 1994. It is one of the three remand prisons in the Bangkok area. This facility has custody of both remandees and convicted offenders. Among the convicted offenders are those whose sentence is at least 7 years and no longer than 14 years old. The maximum of 14 years applies to elderly offenders.

According to Warden Sintoppant, there were 3396 prisoners and 256 prison staff at Thonburi Remand Prison. The prison has been recognized for its outstanding public management, prison cleanliness, prison diet, meaningful treatment programs, and community relations, of which Warden Sintoppant noted he is quite proud (Department of Correction, 2010). In addition to security priorities, Thonburi Remand Prison also provides several rehabilitative programs for prisoners, such as therapeutic community for drug-addicted prisoners, programs for violent prisoners, programs for elderly prisoners, and arts classes (Department of Correction, 2010). The prison also creates the One-Stop-Service program. This program allows prisoners' relatives to easily acquire information on the prisoners such as their building number, visiting schedule, classification, good-time-allowance days, and parole estimation day (Department of Corrections, 2010).

Career

Warden Sintoppant started working for the DOC in August 1986. At that time, he started as a correctional officer at the Chachoengsao Provincial Prison and, after a short time, was transferred to work at a Bangkok Special Prison. He has worked for the DOC for almost 28 years and has had the good fortune of having a successful career. Nevertheless, Warden Sintoppant noted that, in actuality, the field of corrections is not what he had originally hoped to have as a long-term career.

When he was a young adult, he actually had hoped to be a pilot for Thai Airways or, if that did not work out, a career soldier. However, due to honor-based norms and expectations of his family, he was encouraged and, in fact coerced, to apply for employment in the DOC. As it turned out, his father was also employed by the DOC during that time and wanted his son to follow in his footsteps. Initially, he detested the job and the field of corrections, finding it to be a bit dismal. However, as time went on and he gained experience as well as his pursuit of an advanced degree in criminology, he began to develop a knack for this type of work. Further, he also became immersed in the workings of the Thai DOC and also developed strong relationships with his fellow coworkers.

Warden Sintoppant likewise added that the Thai correctional system went through a series of developments and transformations that, in many respects, were reactionary to the crime and social problems emphasized during a given era. Further, he noted that in the past, the general perception was that people who committed crimes came mostly from lower socioeconomic backgrounds. However, in more recent times, particularly as a result of technological developments in communication and travel, as well as the impact of globalization, Thailand is now faced with more complex and advanced criminal issues, such as computer crimes, more sophisticated drug manufacture, white collar crime, and networking of criminal groups on a transnational level that requires coordination with police and correctional personnel from multiple countries. Further, as a result of these developments, there is more diversity in socioeconomics, ethnicity, and criminality among inmates in

Thai prisons. In tandem with these changes has been the need for the department to appropriately adjust inmate treatment programming and supervision practices to correspond to this change in the offender population.

As an example, consider the advancements in cell phone technologies, which have created a very challenging problem for security personnel in Thai prisons. Cell phones are now not only smaller but have more usable functions as well as the ability to store large data files. This cell phone problem is not restricted to Thailand but extends to other countries as well. Therefore, Warden Sintoppant indicated that correctional officials need to consult with one another to help each other reduce or even solve this problem. Further, he has noted that in Thailand, the screening process for visitors and employees entering an institution needs to be revamped so as to include more intensive scrutiny.

As will be clear from this interview, the two primary challenges to corrections in Thailand revolve around limited human resources and more restricted budgetary allocations. Even though the number of inmates is continuously increasing, the number of correctional officers has remained unchanged or even been reduced in some facilities. In addition, the national budget for prison operations has remained stagnant, not accounting for inflation or higher demands in responsibilities. Amidst these realities, the DOC is expected to supervise inmates and provide meaningful programming that includes occupational, education, rehabilitation, and spiritual programs. In addition, the DOC is responsible for ensuring that staff are given training and that they have access to education.

Because of these various and sometimes competing demands, Warden Sintoppant perceives correctional work today is more complicated than the past. As mentioned, the challenge in inmate supervision is more difficult. One reason is the human rights movement, which keeps a close eye on correctional officer treatment of inmates, ensuring that they are treated humanely and in accordance with the minimum standards on human rights. Another key challenge is the increased number of offenders, especially drug offenders, who are affiliated with organized crime organization, having outside influence through which they can sometimes intimidate correctional officers and use that influence to benefit them inside institutions. This issue shows, all the more, why it is important for correctional institutions to network with outside law enforcement in crime reduction measures as well as criminal investigations.

Personal Correctional Philosophy

Personally, I think that a prison is simply an institution reserved for violent and chronic offenders. Those who are first-time offenders or commit misdemeanor offenses should not be in these institutions. We should find or implement an appropriate punishment such as diversion programs and intermediate sanctions. This can also resolve overcrowding problems and will make correctional supervision easier. Essentially, Dr. Sintoppant espouses a design that reflects a selective incapacitation model of corrections.

In selective incapacitation models, prison space is utilized for those offenders who are identified as the most dangerous or most likely to recidivate. Selective incapacitation is implemented by identifying those inmates who are of particular concern to public safety and by providing those specific offenders with much longer sentences than would be given to other inmates. The idea is to improve the use of incapacitation through more accurate identification of those offenders who present the worst risks to society. This then maximizes the use of prison space and likely creates the best reduction in crime, dollar-for-dollar, since monies are not spent housing less dangerous inmates. This type of incapacitation bases sentencing on predictions that some offenders will commit serious offenses at a higher rate that others convicted of the same type of crime.

Thai Correctional Organization

When asked, Warden Sintoppant noted that the correctional organization in Thailand is organized systemically according to primary duties or function of a given group within the organization. He also pointed out that the organizational structure is very similar to many in other countries around the world. As can be seen in Figure 12.1, the director general is the top administrative official of the Thai DOC. Next follow five deputy directors who each have responsibility for some primary sphere within the Thai DOC (Operations, Rehabilitation, Administration, Academic, and Office of Internal Affairs). While the organizational structure of the Thai DOC reflects those of similar organizations in other countries, Warden Sintoppant noted that, in reality, this organizational structure lacks some very important components that he and other colleagues throughout the DOC have observed as being lacking.

Warden Sintoppant commented in detail on these observations and indicated that, in addition to the divisions that currently exist, there should be an Aftercare Division that would have responsibility to oversee prisoners after they are released back to communities. He noted that if they had this unit, the department would be better suited to offenders in obtaining jobs or housing and this would allow a smoother transition for offenders who are returned back to communities. Warden Sintoppant added that this component of the organization is one that exists within most other more modernized correctional systems, particularly in Western and/or industrialized nations, and he pointed out that this addition of services would likely see a further reduction

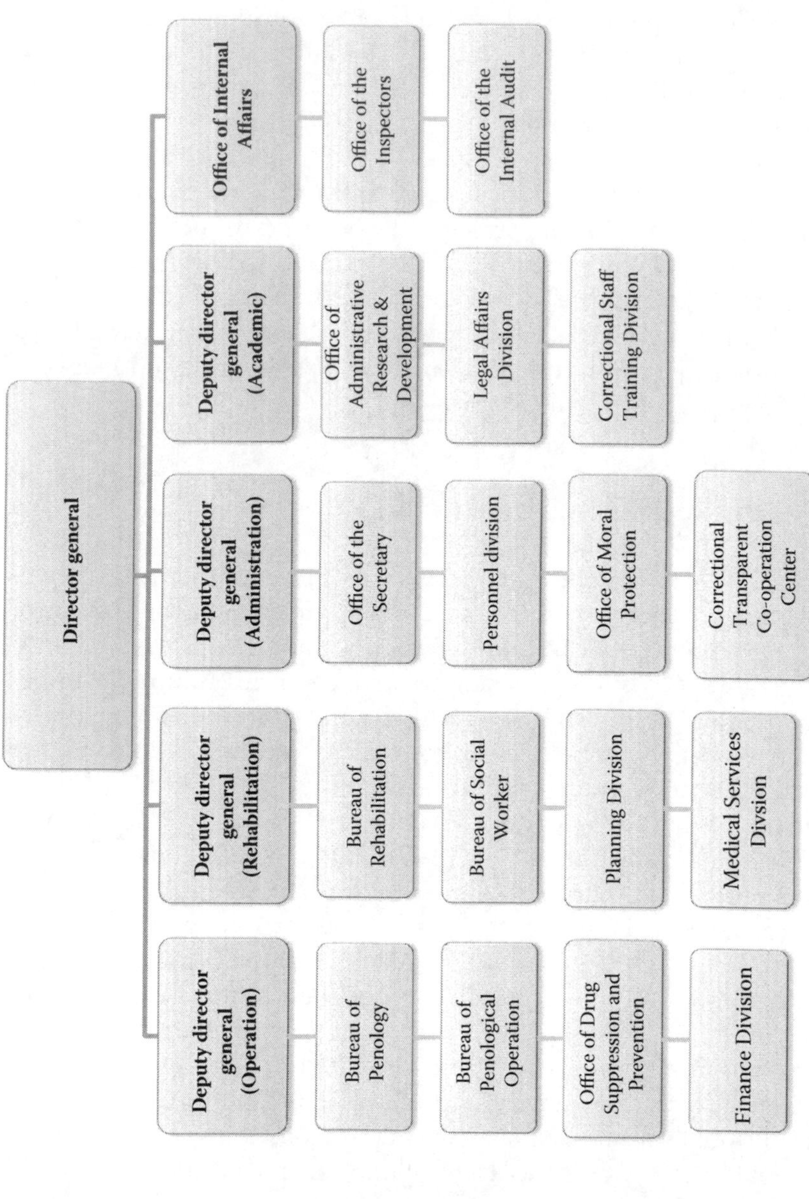

Figure 12.1 Organizational structure of managerial offices for Thailand DOC. (From Department of Corrections, *Prisons and Correctional Institutions*, Thailand Ministry of Justice, Bangkok, Thailand, 2012.)

in recidivism among offenders who are released. It was his contention that such an addition would pay for itself through a reduction in victimizations and a reduction in future arrests, alone.

He also pointed out that the Thai correctional system needed to have many more psychiatrists and psychologists, as well as other mental health professionals, rather than laypersons and paraprofessionals. He indicated that Thai correction has limited numbers of full-time psychiatrists and psychologists, and that the current number is not enough to provide sufficient services to prisoners. Some prisoners who have psychological problems never receive proper care and screening. These inmates create a disproportionate number of incidents and infractions within facilities and this is a drain on institutional resources. He speculated that, while hiring more mental health professionals could be costly, it might be offset considerably by the reduction in behavioral problems inside institutions as well as the reduction in future criminality that often results in their return to prison after release.

Dr. Sintoppant also noted that there should be more official allocations for intermediate sanctions—criminal sentences that fall between traditional probation and incarceration. He noted that in Thailand, these sentencing strategies exist on paper, but in practice this strategy is not widely implemented. For example, when considering the use of house arrest or home confinement, there is a law supporting this sanction, but in reality there is no one in Thailand who receives this sanction as an alternative to incarceration. He speculated that this is possibly due to the fact that the procedure to implement this technique is still ill equipped, both in terms of community supervision personnel and in terms of supervision equipment. Nevertheless, he did note that there are examples where this type of sentence proves quite successful and is much less costly than incarceration, particularly for nonviolent offenders (Hanser, 2013). Dr. Sintoppant further noted that, instead, these offenders are more likely to get a sentence of prison or jail. Further, he indicated that diversion programs are also rarely used in Thailand, even though these programs exist in a variety of fashions in other countries around the world (Hanser, 2014). Thus, as we can see, sentencing options are very limited in Thailand. These oversights undoubtedly contribute to overcrowding problems that persist in the Thai correctional system.

Problems and Successes Experienced

Warden Sintoppant indicated that it is difficult to evaluate policies and programs in the Thai DOC so as to determine problems and successes throughout the organization. One reason for this is, as will be seen later in this chapter, that evidence-based practices are lacking, for the most part, in the Thai DOC. There is a dearth of research and/or data-driven analyses on the effectiveness of Thai programming in the DOC. This is a problem, unto itself, as it makes it difficult to answer questions such as the one presented. In addition, Dr. Sintoppant noted that it is probably unreasonable to think that an organization can be managed at optimal levels if it does not adequately and accurately measure its own performance and progress. The lack of sound methodology, scrutiny, and rigor in evaluation of the department means that, in truth, nobody truly knows if the department is or is not effective and efficient in carrying out the tasks to which it is charged.

However, from his own experience, most policies and programs implemented seem to be successful at some level, but this is, of course, an opinion. Warden Sintoppant noted that many in the Thailand Department of Corrections consider the department to be successful, but that there is little in the way of comparison to confirm this. Rather, as long as there is nothing significant found to the contrary, it is fairly well presumed that the system is successful in how it conducts business on a day-to-day basis. This is, of course, fraught with potential mistakes in perception.

Consider, for example, the means by which the Thailand DOC measures recidivism rates in the country. The process entails a random sample of only 14% of released offenders who are supervised in the community. Warden Sintoppant noted that while it is hoped that these statistical data represent a true picture, in reality, it is not known exactly how many offenders do recidivate. Because of this, he contends that it is difficult to judge what programs or policies achieve their objectives since any empirical measures that do exist have faulty methodologies and since there is no assurance that the data are valid and reliable.

One thing is clear, according to Warden Sintoppant: the DOC will not honor requests to increase the number of correctional staff. Because these staff are considered government employees, the Thai government centralizes human resource projections and allocations to a total number of employees that is mandated each year. These caps on government employees are rigid and corrections is not considered an exception. Therefore, it is very difficult or almost impossible for the DOC to request increases in correctional staff. This is regardless of the evidence of such a need, the circumstances regarding potential public safety, and the conditions that exist within correctional facilities. Thus, it would appear that, regardless of how well or how poorly one might evaluate the state of correctional services in Thailand, there simply is no existing budgetary ability (or desire) to improve the circumstances if such requires additional budgetary resources.

Theory and Practice

Warden Sintoppant mentioned that, when considering theory and practice, he believes it is important for practitioners and scholars to work together closely. This was not a surprising answer given that he is a corrections practitioner who holds a doctorate degree in criminology. With that noted, he went on to add that most correctional officers in the Thai correctional system consider theories to be impractical. This is in contrast to researchers who contend that such theories should be part of the routine practice of a correctional system.

This divergence between theory and practice is considered problematic by Warden Sintoppant and he noted that this can and should be corrected by providing training to practitioners that integrates both the procedural aspects and the ideological rationale upon which the correctional system operates, so as to provide perspective on the reasons for why and how the system operates as it does. Further, Warden Sintoppant noted that training curricula within the department are not sufficient and, in that training, the opportunity exists to integrate theory and practice, if done correctly. Warden Sintoppant stated that even though numerous correctional officers have a master's degree or doctorate, there exists an organizational norm to resist change and this has discouraged even this elite group from innovatively applying theories or develop new policies. Warden Sintoppant noted that it is very difficult to change organizational culture, and that is precisely what is needed if theory and practice are to be better integrated. He further indicated that many correctional officials are not familiar with criminological thought due to the fact that many have educational backgrounds in various other disciplines. Warden Sintoppant suggested that the Thai DOC should consider the development of a special task force to encourage both practitioners and researchers to work collaboratively to improve policies and to ensure that they are implemented at the procedural level. Given the dearth of effective research that is available throughout the organization, Warden Sintoppant found this to be a very practical means to improve the organization, both in terms of strategic planning as well as overall operations of the organization on a day-to-day level.

It would seem, from Warden Sintoppant's comments, that if a correctional program is to be effective, it must have a clear theoretical and philosophical grounding. Numerous criminological theories exist that are used to explain why crime occurs and to explain how one might predict crime. The ability to predict crime allows an agency to find those factors that lead to crime and therefore give guidance on what should be done to prevent crime (Hanser, 2013). In addition, if practitioners are able to explain why crime occurs, then they should be better able to determine those factors that must be addressed to correct aberrant tendencies toward criminal behavior. Thus, appropriate grounding in theoretical underpinnings to criminal behavior can improve any correctional effort. However, theoretical applications may not always be quite so clear in the day-to-day practice of corrections. Warden Sintoppant believes that more effective and more specific training, along with changes in the organizational culture, are the key to making more clear the role of theory in day-to-day practice.

Evidence-Based Correction

Warden Sintoppant noted that, in Thailand, there remains a lack of evidence-based programming. Because of this and due to the lack of reliable evaluation information, it is difficult to know whether the Thai correctional system is a success or might be classified otherwise. Warden Sintoppant noted that much more research was needed in various areas of the correctional system. This is actually quite important because as it stands, currently, it is unknown whether prisons contribute a long-term benefit to reducing recidivism or contribute toward further criminality.

As with many countries around the world, funding constraints have impaired many of the programs and services within the Thai DOC. Financial restraints have also affected the ability of this nationwide agency to implement processes to implement evidence-based practices and processes. While data exists and assessment and evaluation do occur, the actual use of this data to later revise correctional processes is limited, largely due to the lack of money available for additional staff training, resource development, and implementation of changes within the organization.

For now, according to Warden Sintoppant, it has been considered a priority to focus on improvements of inmate treatment within the correctional system as consideration for human rights issues has gained the attention of top administrators and government officials. In addition, it would seem that the Thai government has also placed more emphasis on building new correctional facilities that have modern technological, architectural, and construction features that are better designed for housing violent offenders as well as members of various extremist groups. This challenging inmate population is difficult to house securely and requires a disproportionate amount of budgetary expenditures to ensure public safety.

The point could be made, perhaps, that the use of these new measures in security are an example of some type of evidence-based corrections but, in reality, evaluations are seldom consulted when deciding on these technologies. Rather, the Thai DOC tends to simply buy the most secure and up-to-date technology for housing violent populations. While this is thought to increase security, there is not necessarily any specific data-driven evidence of this, as would be typical of an evidence-based model of corrections. Lastly, the use of improved technologies has, on the one hand, saved some funds in terms of human resources but have, on the other hand, generated expenses that are quite costly and not negotiable if the correctional system is to keep these dangerous elements out of Thai society. This has also resulted in a larger-than-expected drain on the correctional budget.

Transnational Relations

According to Warden Sintoppant, international relationships are very important to the Thailand DOC. Thailand, being a country that borders several other nations in Southeast Asia and being a nation through which a substantial number of foreign visitors frequently appear, finds itself working in tandem and in alliance with numerous other nations throughout the region. Further, much of the crime experienced in Thailand results from activity that is porous in terms of geography; criminals tend to cross from one country to another with ease and also commit criminal acts in a variety of countries. This is particularly true in regard to drug trafficking, human trafficking, and similar activities. Thus, international relations are important for the correctional system of Thailand.

In particular, the Thai government has focused on the important role of the Association of Southeast Asia Nations (ASEAN), in which Thailand has committed to increase all government entities to meet, agree, and follow with ASEAN standards, treaties, and agreements. The goals of this association are to foster economic growth, social progress, and cultural development among its members. Further, this association seeks to promote regional peace and stability, and opportunities for member countries to peacefully discuss differences (ASEAN, 2013). The ASEAN agreement encourages relationships among member countries in both governmental and private sectors. It also allows citizens of country members to travel within Southeast Asia freely (ASEAN, 2013).

However, one drawback to this freedom of movement throughout and within these various countries is that it can also open doors for criminals to engage in criminal activity throughout these various member countries. Therefore, criminal justice agencies, including corrections, have to work together to prevent and deter criminal activities among nation members. Membership in ASEAN does create another challenge for the Thai DOC—the likely increase in the number of offenders who are from ASEAN nations ending up in the Thai correctional system (ASEAN, 2013). Another challenge that has and will continue to emerge is the multiple language barriers between correctional officers and inmates, and even between inmates and their fellow inmates. The member ASEAN nations tend to have quite different languages that will result in fragmentation of the population but will also create additional demands upon the organization. One last issue includes the need to be adept with addressing the cultural and ethnic diversity that is increasing throughout the correctional population. This diversity can put burdens on correctional management, which must contend with diverse dietary requirements, a variety of religious and spiritual orientations, and so forth. In 2012, there were 10,291 foreign inmates in the Thai DOC (กรมราชทัณฑ์, B. E. 2555). The majority of foreign inmates come from ASEAN nations (see Table 12.3).

Warden Sintoppant also mentioned that, when considering the international inmate population that is held within the Thai DOC, it is important to ensure that political influence is minimized within an institution. Because some inmates from other countries may have influence from external bodies and advocacy, it is important to ensure that all are held accountable, equally, in serving their sentence while in the facility. In addition, it is important to ensure that inmates of Thai descent are not given treatment that is better than non-Thai inmates, as this bias can build resentment and discord among the inmate population, cast an unprofessional light on the correctional staff, and lead to problems in relations with surrounding countries.

Warden Sintoppant also noted that another transnational issue that sometimes emerges is that fact that punishments in other countries may be substantially different from in Thailand, making the outcome in sentencing quite disparate from what the a noncitizen might have otherwise received. This, too, can strain international relations with neighboring countries as well as countries in distant areas around the globe. Examples abound where citizens of Australia, the United States, and other industrialized countries have received punishments that are fairly routine in Thailand but are considered unusual in the countries of origin for the offender. As an example, consider that capital punishment in Thailand is currently utilized despite

Table 12.3 Number of Foreign Prisoners by Country

Nationality	Number
Burma (Myanmar)	3048
Cambodia	2418
Laos	2358
Malaysia	320
Nigeria	240
China	179
Iran	164
Vietnam	140
Taiwan	134
Nepal	10

Source: Department of Corrections, Observation tours on Thai prison during the 11th UN Congress (Bangkok 18–22 April 2005). Retrieved from http://www.correct.go.th/comnet1/un/pv1.html, 2005.

the fact that some countries may look at this punishment as barbaric and in violation of contemporary views on human rights. In fact, the use of this sanction is sometimes even questioned by other countries that also use this sanction, implying that somehow Thailand's use of this sanction is perhaps not as sound, fair, and balanced as it is in other nations.

In reality, it is not fair to simply assume that Thai correctional systems and practices are horrific based on the implementation of the death penalty (Finch and Tangprasit, 2012; Union for Civil Liberty, 2005). Punishments, including the death penalty, are required to go through a rigorous process that is accountable to the Rule of Law and is not capricious in nature. Warden Sintoppant explained that because of this, other countries need to respect the Thai system of death penalty application (Finch and Tangprasit, 2012; Union for Civil Liberty, 2005). He further noted that the DOC is not the organization that makes the decision as to who does or does not receive the death penalty. It is the law in the books that sets these rules and punishments, interpreted through the judiciary (Finch and Tangprasit, 2012). Thus, it is not realistic to cast judgment on the Thai correctional system for the application of the death penalty, as it is the role of the DOC to simply follow the instructions set forth through rule of law. Despite this, Warden Sintoppant did note that there is substantial international pressure to change these laws and to eliminate this sanction.

In regard to the actual use of this penalty, it should be noted that the Department of Corrections reported in 2012 that there were 76 death-row inmates in Thailand, with 69 being male offenders and 7 being female offenders (Department of Corrections, B. E. 2555). Thus, this is a miniscule number of offenders in comparison to the entire inmate population. This same demographic and statistical characteristic is similar to other countries that utilize the death penalty. Regardless, Warden Sintoppant again noted that international pressure will likely result in Thailand modifying or eliminating its use of these laws and this form of punishment. As an example of how capital punishment has changed in Thailand over time, Warden Sintoppant pointed toward the use of the firing squad as a method of death penalty in times past (Finch and Tangprasit, 2012; Union for Civil Liberty, 2005). Years ago, inmates were placed behind a screen, tied to a pole and blindfolded while holding a bunch of flowers, joss sticks, and a candle as part of their final rite. The executioner would then ask for forgiveness from the inmate. A target was painted on the screen that was placed between the prisoner and the submachine gun stand, thus allowing the executioner to pull the trigger and fire a hail of bullets through the bull's eye, allowing the executioner to be relieved of viewing the shooting of his real target (Union for Civil Liberty, 2005). After substantial debate and consideration in 2003, Thailand introduced lethal injection as a method of execution (Finch and Tangprasit, 2012; Union for Civil Liberty, 2005).

Warden Sintoppant noted that the death penalty is a very sensitive subject and there is no homogenous opinion among the general public. Throughout the Kingdom of Thailand, there are some groups that support death penalty and some groups that are against it (Finch and Tangprasit, 2012; Hanser, 2013; Union for Civil Liberty, 2005). It is still a talking point among policy makers and scholars. The controversial nature of this sentence has led to more frequent use of extradition for offenders from other countries; this tends to also be good for international relations. Keeping strong alliances with countries that are crime-fighting allies is important and, as it turns out, the reciprocation of correctional policies and practices make the extradition process a favorable option that, at the same time, takes the burden from the Thai correctional system. In 2012, the DOC extradited 959 inmates back to their country of origin (กรมราชทัณฑ์, B. E. 2555). It is expected that the use of this option will continue in the future, particularly as Thailand continues to partner with other countries in the crime-fighting process.

Role of Corrections

Warden Sintoppant noted that, unlike in the United States, the Thai public typically has high expectations of the DOC. It would seem that these expectations come in the way of expecting the department to provide treatment and rehabilitation services for inmates as well as occupational training and educational programming. Among these programs, one of the most widespread types of treatment is that of drug treatment. Indeed, the Prime Minister's Order on Treatment of Drug Offenders was passed in 1998 and serves as proof of how serious this issue is considered in Thailand (Kuratanavej, 2001). As it stands, drug offenders are the most common type of offender in the Thai correctional system; most offenders in prison are drug offenders. Out of concern for this and as a means to demonstrate an effort to reduce future drug crimes, the Prime Minister issued this order indicating that drug users should receive extensive programming as an effort to reduce their recidivism (Kuratanavej, 2001).

On the other hand, similar to the selective incapacitation model that was discussed by Dr. Sintoppant in his personal philosophy on corrections, drug dealers are given severe punishments and are not afforded treatment (Kuratanavej, 2001; Department of Corrections, 2010). Further, drug dealers are not given leniency in their sentencing (such as community supervision or early credit for release) and they do not qualify for any type of pardon (Kuratanavej, 2001; Department of Corrections, 2010). This order has been thought to have a very strong impact on the drug offending population and it is thought to have reduced drug dealing significantly, due to the majority of them being incapacitated. Warden Sintoppant did note that the incapacitation of drug dealers did not eliminate drug dealing, nor did he or others think that it would completely eliminate this activity. As would be expected and has been seen among organized drug dealers in other areas of the world, there is always someone willing to fill in the vacancy created by a drug dealer who is imprisoned. But these efforts have slowed down drug dealing in Thailand and have also satisfied community desires to see them punished. For these reasons alone, this approach is seen as effective (Department of Corrections, 2010).

In Thailand, there has been increased use of inmate release programs, among those inmates who are eligible. Aside from the expiration of their sentence, there are other forms of release including good-conduct allowances, public work allowances, and parole. The conditions for each of these types of early release are often very strict. During the past decade, the Thai government has emphasized the need to use more prerelease programming as a means of reducing the prison population that is burgeoning with each passing year.

Inmates are able to earn good time by completing programs that an institution provides and that the DOC identifies as being of the caliber to award good time. Likewise, input from correctional administrators is used to consider the behavior and offense history of inmates, infractions and misconduct can and often does disqualify an inmate from acquiring good time. In other cases, misbehavior may simply reduce the amount of good time they are allowed to acquire during a given period of time during their sentence.

Warden Sintoppant noted again that on the responsibilities of prisons in Thailand is to prepare inmates to reenter the community. He noted that, at the base of it, humans are social animals. He indicated that it is his own belief that as social creatures, humans often have the need to live in some form of social grouping to which they must feel a sense of belonging. Because prison tends to limit who the inmate will socialize with on the outside and because it increases the amount of socialization that the inmate has with other offenders, there is a risk of *institutionalization*. Life inside prison tends to restrict the human developmental process as a social animal. Warden Sintoppant suggested that correctional officers have to remind themselves that inmates will one day return back to the community and, therefore, they need to ensure that inmates are indeed ready to be released and live productively outside the institution. Failure to do this will likely result in recidivism and the return of the inmate to the facility and, in the process, will simply generate more victimization of the public outside of the facility. This is, of course, what practitioners in the field of corrections wish to avoid.

Thailand Royal Pardon

One of the most unique correctional programs in Thailand is the Royal Pardon, which is connected to the constitutional monarchy of Thailand, in which the king is a chief of state. In granting pardons, there are two types that are used. The first is the individual petition and the second is the general pardon. The individual petition is, as the name implies, generated by the individual inmate and, for example, might consist of a circumstance where an offender sentenced to death may petition the king for mercy, requesting that the king commute the sentence to life in prison by virtue of granting a Royal Pardon. The general Royal Pardon is used on a more routine process for which most inmates are eligible to receive without filing a petition for the pardon.

According to the Ministerial Rules of the Ministry of Justice on Criteria and Execution Procedures (2003), it is the duty of the authorized prison official to inform the condemned person of the right to apply for a Royal Pardon (Finch and Tangprasit, 2012). The correctional official is required to ask the condemned person if he or she would like to exercise his/her right to request a Royal Pardon and, presuming that the offender wishes to pursue this opportunity, the prison official will then need to arrange for necessary support in the application process. After a prison commander (the prison warden) receives an application, he or she will forward the request to the minister of justice. At this point, the minister of justice will provide a recommendation to the King to either accept or reject the pardon. The granting of the Royal Pardon remains at the discretion of the King and no systematic or public rules are applied in this regard (Union for Civil Liberty, 2005). To be clear, a petition for a Royal Pardon is not limited to death-row inmates—other inmates are eligible to petition as well. However, only one application for a pardon may be made by an inmate.

General Assessments

Overall, Warden Sintoppant expressed satisfaction with the DOC and with his career in the correctional system of Thailand. While the work does require an individual to mix with a variety of malcontents and does include some dangerous encounters with these individuals, the overall experience is one that has been gratifying. Warden Sintoppant made it clear, also, that he felt that his work performs a public necessity but that he also has seen some successes among inmates who have refrained from committing future criminal acts.

He also commented on the fact that, unfortunately, some individuals believe that, in order to maintain respect and control within the institution, staff and administrators must be mean-spirited and callous in their approach to security. Warden Sintoppant has found that this is simply untrue, in his experience. In fact, what he has found is that when people are treated with respect, including inmates, it is much easier to gain their compliance. As a result, he makes a point to ensure that staff at his facility are professional, both in decorum as well as deed, and he has built an institutional culture where inmates expect this approach within the facility.

This is all in keeping with his belief that correctional work is a respectable profession of which staff should be proud. According to Warden Sintoppant, staff have to act in a manner that sets them apart and this helps to contribute to their sense of belonging to a profession. This is despite the fact that correctional officers in Thailand, like most other nations, do not tend to get paid as well as many other positions in the criminal justice system. For example, police officers, judges, or prosecutors are considered as a special type of government employees, and they have a superior pay scale to correctional officers.

Warden Sintoppant noted that many correctional officers view work in corrections as a family tradition because many of them come from families that have worked for the DOC for generations. One explanation for this tendency is the sense of loyalty that has been cultivated within the agency and among these families. This sense of loyalty is also a common attribute found among many Asian cultures, including the Thai culture, and this sense of loyalty and honor is passed down within families from one generation to the next. Another point regarding the generations-long involvement of family members in the DOC is that youth who grow up in a family where their parents work for the DOC tend to be familiar with the culture and context of correctional work. This makes them feel much more comfortable with working for the DOC when compared with other applicants who are not familiar with the correctional environment.

Generally speaking, people in the public do not have a very accurate picture of what occurs, on a routine basis, behind prison walls. In many cases, the public may have images of outdated prisons with staff who beat and torture inmates. Further, many people who are not familiar with this type work do not understand the stress involved with maintaining a prison facility, both psychological and physical. Over time, advances in communication and media technology have helped to mitigate some of the distance and isolation that are experienced in these facilities.

Perhaps most telling is that, in recent times, an increasing number of people have become interested in correctional work in Thailand. It is speculated that the global economy, as unstable as it has been during the past few years, has contributed to this trend. However, it is not just due to desperation and hard economic crimes that interest in this type of career has increased. Rather, there have been continued improvements in the DOC for employees, with an increase in benefits and other perks for persons willing to work in corrections. Improvements in working conditions, emphasis on professionalism, additional formal training, the growth of criminal justice programs in Thailand's higher education system, and increases in benefits have resulted in more interest in the field of corrections among young Thai candidates and job seekers.

Overall, Warden Sintoppant seemed optimistic about the DOC in Thailand. He noted that the organization is becoming increasingly modern despite budget challenges and he also indicated that the quality of applicants is getting better. He also noted that he has seen the sense of family among employees remain intact throughout the challenges that face the Thai correctional system and he considers this the mark of a healthy organization. When looking back on it all, he noted that though he did not initially desire to work in this field, his career in retrospect has been quite rewarding and most certainly interesting. It is this final observation that seemed to confirm his satisfaction in working in the field of corrections, along with the warm smile that emerged as he reflected on time past throughout his years of loyal service to the Thailand Department of Corrections.

Conclusion

From this chapter, it is clear that correctional systems and practices in Thailand are in a state of constant improvement, change, and evolution. The effects of technological advances can be readily observed in this prison system, in terms of both prison system operations and contraband that inmates use for criminal purposes. Thus, this field of work is dynamic rather than static, requiring administrators to be willing to adapt with the times. In addition, like many other prison administrators, working in the field of corrections was not Warden Sintoppant's first initial desire when entering the workforce.

Nevertheless, over time, he has come to regard his fellow staff and employees as family, in many respects, demonstrating the sense of loyalty that one can develop with others who work in this field. In addition, it is the nature of the work itself, with all of its corresponding challenges, that provides a level of challenge and responsibility that will pique the interest of most administrators. It is clear that this has been the case for Warden Sintoppant who, amidst his career-building efforts, obtained a PhD in criminology. When examining his career and the manner in which it has developed, it is clear that Warden Sintoppant is both an administrator and a scholar, working in a career field that is demanding but satisfying for individuals who thrive on challenge and the resulting opportunities that come their way.

Glossary

Association of Southeast Asia Nations (ASEAN): A political and economic organization that includes ten Southeast Asian countries: Brunei, Burma (Myanmar), Cambodia, Indonesia, Laos, Malaysia, the Philippines, Singapore, Thailand, and Vietnam.

General Prison Standards: This set of standards covers 10 aspects; namely, Managerial Administration, Qualified Staff, Physical Plants, Prisoner Classification, Custody, Work and Labour Force, Education and Vocational Training, Disciplinary Procedure and Punishment, Prisoners' Services, and Prisoner Activities and Privileges.

Institutionalization: When an inmate adapts so well to the prison environment that they become dependent on the facility and are unable to successfully reintegrate to outside society.

khuk: A facility that was designed to house offenders who received a sentence of 6 months or longer, prior to the reign of King Rama V (1868–1910).

Minister's Order on Treatment of Drug Offenders (1998): An order indicating that drug users should receive extensive programming as an effort to reduce their recidivism. This order also maintains that drug dealers do not qualify for leniency in sentencing, early release, or pardons from their sentence.

Prisoner's Living Standards: According to these standards, each prison facility is required to achieve a minimum of four out of five of these standards, namely Standard of Sleeping Material, Prison Kitchen, Canteen, Medical Centre, and Garbage Treatment.

Prisoner Transparency Standards: This set of standards emphasizes the transparency of prison administration and concern management including Standard of Rice, Food, Prisoner's Work, Welfare Shop, and Managerial Administration.

Royal Pardon: Granted directly by the King of Thailand, the vast majority of these types of pardons are given on special occasions or during national celebration. It has been long tradition of the king to grant pardons to express his compassion toward his subjects. The Royal Pardon consists of two types: the individual petition and the general royal pardon.

Selective Incapacitation: Identifying inmates who are of particular concern to public safety and providing them with much longer sentences than would be given to other inmates.

Tarang: A facility designed to hold inmates who received a sentence of less than 6 months, prior to the reign of King Rama V (1868–1910).

Conclusion

13

ROBERT HANSER, MARTHA
HURLEY AND DILIP K. DAS

This second volume of our *Trends in Corrections: Interviews with Corrections Leaders Around the World* series provides interviews with 12 correctional leaders from 10 different nations around the world. The selection of interviews was based on the availability of the interviewers and interviewees. Likewise, the interviewers for this volume were well-regarded scholars from a variety of locations around the world and were, therefore, well suited for the task of collecting and writing down the information and insights provided by each correctional leader interviewed.

When taking stock of these interviews, it becomes clear that there are many challenges that face correctional leaders, regardless of the area of the world in which they administer their facilities. Further, many of these challenges have similar themes and circumstances, despite the fact that these practitioners come from vastly different cultural backgrounds and disparate regions around the world. In all cases, these practitioners do consider it important to stay abreast of trends and developments in corrections around the globe, indicating that one can never be too informed on how other correctional organizations address challenges and generate innovative solutions to those problems.

As with our previous volume, we find that all 12 correctional administrators rose through the ranks over time and, in many cases, they also moved laterally from other areas of expertise or practice, eventually settling into their current area of expertise and attaining the positions in which they currently serve. For instance, Philippe Pottier in France (Chapter 1) started work in the field of juvenile probation, then worked at the Centre for Orientation, followed by a position where he supervised offender reintegration efforts. From there, he continued to work in a number of administrative capacities at the executive level.

Likewise, Sue McAllister of the Northern Ireland Prison Service (Chapter 7) initially began her career in England and Wales as an assistant prison governor trainee. She then worked at the organizational headquarters in a policy-related capacity, as the head of the security group for the system, then area manager with responsibility over a dozen prisons, eventually culminating that aspect of her career in the Public Sector Bid Unit. After retiring from the English prison system, McAllister went on to work in her current post as the director general of the prison system in Northern Ireland. It is clear that both of these practitioners moved up in positions of responsibility throughout their careers, but they also worked in several different areas of specialty in their respective correctional systems over the span of their careers.

The field of corrections, it would seem, is also one that was not necessarily the first choice for many of these practitioners. This is not surprising, as this area of the criminal justice system does not tend to be considered as prestigious as the field of policing and judicial work. Nevertheless, it is clear that these practitioners made the best of their careers and, once they had decided to stay in the field of corrections, they excelled in their commitment to that decision. For example, Keith Deville (Chapter 9), who retired from the Louisiana Department of Corrections and is now with LaSalle Corrections, really had not considered working in the field of corrections. As a young man, he had not sought or desired a career in the prison system. A conversation with his family, namely his father, who was also a Louisiana Department of Corrections employee, eventually led to his decision to seek employment with the prison system, where he served for more than 30 years in several prestigious capacities.

Another example would be Ayuth Sintoppant, from the prison system of the Kingdom of Thailand (Chapter 12). When he was young, this practitioner actually had hoped to be a pilot for Thai Airways or, alternatively, a career soldier for the kingdom. But his father was an employee of the Thailand Department of Corrections and wished for his son to follow in his footsteps. Due to a sense of family obligation and culturally based honor commitments, Warden Ayuth Sintoppant chose to work in the field of corrections. During the early part of his career, he did not enjoy this "chosen" vocation but, over time, developed a strong interest in this career path, moving up organizationally and in terms of his educational achievement. It is interesting that both Keith Deville and Ayuth Sintoppant were most influenced by their fathers, who were also correctional practitioners. As it turns out, this is not uncommon in the field of corrections, where generations of family members may be employed in a correctional system. For some families, prison work may be "in the blood," so to speak, serving as a common identity for the family. This may be the case even for those members who do not wish to work in this field initially but, for a variety of reasons, ultimately decide to follow suit with their kin.

Other administrators interviewed had even less incentive and less of a rationale for ultimately ending up in prison work. For example, Dušan Valentincic, director general of the Slovenia Prison System (Chapter 4), stated that he came to the prison system completely by accident. In fact, he noted that after obtaining much of his education, he was unemployed and simply needed a job; he had never envisioned himself working in a prison, especially as a guard. When he started, he considered this job only to be temporary until something else emerged. He went on to complete nearly 30 years of service and served as director general, culminating in several years of service in that capacity.

It was found that other administrators often had expansive career experience in other areas of expertise before coming into the field of corrections. Consider Michael Donnellan of the Irish Prison System (Chapter 2), who initially began his career as a psychiatric nurse working with youth. He eventually worked with the Department of Education as a psychiatric social worker in London, returned to Ireland, managed a detention center for youth, and, due to the desire to learn more and vary his expertise, landed the job of director of probation services in Ireland. Even then, Donnellan's diverse employment continued as he moved into the position of director general of the Irish Prison Service.

Likewise, Soh Wai Wah was a career police officer who is described as being "seconded" to the Singapore Prison Service (Chapter 11). This belies that less-than-prestigious role of corrections when compared to policing and is consistent with other practitioners who did not consider corrections their first choice of vocation. Ultimately, Soh Wai Wah would go on to implement a number of innovative changes in the Singapore Prison System, having a sense of vision that would motivate and mobilize many from throughout the organization to move toward expansive reforms. Thus, it is clear that while many of these practitioners may not have anticipated their careers to be in the correctional field, they became very competent and influential leaders and administrators.

It is also interesting that some of these administrators left one correctional agency to, eventually, work for another. For instance, Sue McAllister (Chapter 7) completed an entire career with the prison system, but after only 1 year of retirement she came back to work for the prison system. However, another correctional leader, Keith Deville (Chapter 9), worked for the public service prison system and then went to work for private prison companies after retirement from public service.

On another front, one other common theme found among several of these practitioners is that there was a tendency for most to take advantage of educational opportunities before and during their careers. For example, we refer again to Ayuth Sintoppant of Thailand (Chapter 12), who pursued studies while working, ultimately obtaining a doctorate degree in criminology. Thus, Warden Ayuth Sintoppant, PhD, is both a seasoned practitioner and a scholar. Likewise, Eduardo Enrique Gomez García of the Federal Penitentiary System in Mexico (Chapter 8) also became very well educated over the course of his career. Unlike many of the prior correctional administrators we interviewed, it was clear that General Gomez García had an interest in penology and corrections in his early years. Indeed, he had hoped to study penitentiary administration, but these types of specialized programs did not exist in Mexico at the time. He instead obtained a degree in public administration and ultimately obtained a doctorate in public administration. Thus, both Warden Sintoppant (Chapter 12) and General Gomez García (Chapter 8) obtained very high levels of education, differing, however, in their initial interest in corrections. The former was not interested in this field of work but eventually obtained a doctorate in criminology; the latter was very interested in correctional work but obtained a doctorate in another discipline. For both, these inverse outcomes were a matter of circumstances and availability of resources. This shows how random some of the career outcomes might be for many of these seasoned professionals.

The other correctional leaders interviewed in this volume also have noteworthy educational achievements. Consider Jaroslav Jánoš of the Slovak Republic Corps of Prison and Court Guard (Chapter 3), who continued his education throughout his career and, in 2004, completed his doctorate. Since that time, he has continued to work in a variety of academic capacities that address penitentiary and postpenitentiary issues. Other correctional leaders in this volume also have pursued high levels of education, including Gary Maynard (Chapter 10) of the United States, who holds a master's degree in rehabilitation counseling; Sue McAllister of North Ireland (Chapter 7), who holds a master of arts with honors; Philippe Pottier of France (Chapter 1), who holds a master's degree in social sciences and another master's degree in anthropology; and Soh Wai Wah of Singapore (Chapter 11), who holds a master's degree in criminal justice. Other leaders in this volume include Ramon Parés, who has a degree in law (Chapter 5), and Dušan Valentinčič, who holds a degree in sociology (Chapter 4).

It is clear that these practitioners did not only pursue higher education themselves, but also saw higher education as a vehicle for improving outcomes for offenders who return to the community and as a means of professionalizing the employees within their respective organizations. Consider Walter Troxler, who graduated in education sciences from the University of Fribourg, Switzerland (Chapter 6). His first work in corrections was as an educator of offenders. Later, Troxler would obtain a degree in systemic family therapy, which he would ultimately introduce as a primary program of intervention among juvenile correctional practices in the Swiss prison system. As the head of the Unit for the Execution of Sentences and Measures, Troxler found that his administrative duties tended to pull him from the more face-to-face experiences of corrections, his day being consumed with reports, computer readouts, budget issues, and the like.

It is interesting to note that many of these practitioners do not, necessarily, come from security backgrounds but come from the ranks of clinical practitioners in the treatment sector. As we have noted, Walter Troxler of Switzerland, with his background in family therapy, is one of these individuals. Michael Donnellan of the Irish Prison System (Chapter 2), with his background in psychiatric nursing and social work, is another such practitioner. Gary Maynard of the United States (Chapter 10), who has a long and distinguished administrative career in the states of Arkansas, Iowa, Oklahoma, and Maryland, also served as a psychologist for the Federal Bureau of Prisons. Further still, we should also consider Ramon Parés of Catalonia, Spain (Chapter 5). He began his career as a rehabilitation officer and, in his interview, made it clear that the goal of corrections in Spain is the rehabilitation and reintegration of the offender, citing the Spanish Constitution of 1978 as the prime reference for this justification. When asked about key challenges in future correctional operations in Spain, the former director of the Catalan Prison System indicated that addressing special needs populations, such as those who are elderly, have mental disorders, or physical disabilities, will increasingly be important. Thus, it is clear among these three practitioners that treatment and rehabilitation are seen as critical aspects to offender programming.

All of these correctional administrators sought to advance the state of correctional practice in their agencies through continued improvements in policy, programming, and resources, as well as the training of staff. For instance, Jaroslav Jánoš of the Slovak Republic Corps of Prison and Court Guard (Chapter 3) noted how legislative changes have made prison operations more humane and treatment oriented in nature and have changed the overall culture of the prison system in the Slovak Republic. Jánoš indicated that he had a primary role in writing many of the acts that ultimately constituted national policy on prison operations. Likewise, Soh Wai Wah (Chapter 11) of Singapore also pointed to the drafting of a new vision statement for that nation's prison system. The inclusive nature in which this vision statement was developed served to empower employees and, in the process, informed them of changes in the organizational mission so that revisions to future policies and programming would be understood among the various prison personnel throughout Singapore.

When considering the connection between theory and practice, it is clear that each practitioner believes that the two can be complimentary to one another within the correctional system, but their views on how and when these two aspects work together varies considerably. Warden Sintoppant (Chapter 12) provides a theoretical perspective that involves a form of selective incapacitation as the basic theoretical perspective behind the Thai correctional system, mixing this with a strong dose of social learning as the basis for the treatment and rehabilitation of offenders. Likewise, Keith Deville (Chapter 9) notes that there is a strong relationship between his correctional facility and a nearby university. Much of this has to do with the fact that his clinical director is also employed at that university and, as it turns out, this director is in charge of offender programming for the region. This programmer is also an evaluative researcher who binds theory and practice together. Further, the Louisiana Department of Corrections as well as LaSalle Corrections, with whom Deville is now employed, make a point to establish university partnerships around the state.

However, to some extent, many of these correctional leaders perceive a disconnect between theory and practice. For instance, Ramon Parés (Chapter 5) states bluntly that, when it comes to scholars at universities collaborating with prison practitioners, he thinks that universities are "not interested in the subject of prisons". Philippe Pottier (Chapter 1) also indicates that in France, there is little university involvement and he further adds that there are few research or theory articles available to practitioners who read and speak French. He notes that there is a seeming dearth of integration between criminological orientations of scholars with the practitioner population in France.

Others, such as Troxler (Chapter 6), indicate that there has been a lag in interest among university scholars to give research attention to prison work, though he is optimistic that change is on the horizon in the future. Dušan Valentinčič (Chapter 4) also states that integration between theory and practice is not yet present in Slovenia. As it turns out, in Slovenia, there are very few theorists who are interested in prisons, which is juxtaposed against the reality that the needs of the prison system are very different from the concerns of theorists. This makes it difficult for the two groups to establish some type of common ground.

The philosophy behind correctional work, for nearly every one of these corrections leaders, has some type of rehabilitation aspect attached to it. This was true for those who came primarily from security backgrounds as well as those who came from treatment-oriented backgrounds. In the process, some interesting examples were shared. For instance, Soh Wai Wah (Chapter 11) introduced the "Starfish Moral" as a theoretical perspective by which he notes the underlying idea that, in the Singapore system, human behavior can be changed and, in the process, people can be saved. While it may not be possible to save everyone, according to this viewpoint, saving just one matters. Soh further explains that the mission of the Singapore system is twofold: security and rehabilitation. He notes that theoretical perspectives are integrated into systemic operations to achieve both.

Many of the correctional leaders interviewed were able to comment on a variety of changes that have been experienced throughout their expansive careers. For Dušan Valentinčič, (Chapter 4) one of the key changes he observed was the shift toward a sociotherapeutic orientation for prison operations in Slovenia. For Dr. Jaroslav Jánoš in the Slovak Republic (Chapter 3), the Leopoldov massacre resulted in significant legislative change that included more emphasis on standards for custodial sentences, human rights, and the fair treatment of inmates, as well as treatment programming. In both of these countries, the eventual opening of borders between Western and

Eastern Europe led to dramatic changes for these prison systems, particularly as they began to adopt standards set forth by the European Union. In other cases, such as with the Slovak Republic, specific incidents that involved the media served as catalysts of change. Sue McAllister (Chapter 7) points toward the James Bulger incident, which impacted juvenile corrections in the United Kingdom, as well as the Pearson Review Team of 2008/2009, which was a scathing inspector report that followed an inmate suicide and profiled the Northern Ireland prison system as being heavy-handed, apathetic, and plagued by an insidious subculture. These circumstances prompted widespread change in the North Irish prison system, addressing the treatment of offenders within that organization.

Challenges and problems noted were many and were diverse among this group of correctional leaders. However, one key challenge emerged in nearly every case: problems with budgetary constraints, including cuts in spending that greatly limited the operational effectiveness of the correctional institution. Another challenge that seemed to be widespread was overcrowding. These two issues were universal among all 12 correctional leaders, though with varying degrees of concern. Related to these two issues was a desire for more community-based programs. Michael Donnellan (Chapter 2) indicated this, as did others, as these types of programs allow for more options in the offender reintegration process, are not as costly as prison, and also can help to ease the burden of prisons without compromising public safety.

These professionals have had many successes, but Michael Donnellan (Chapter 2) points out a particularly noteworthy success: allowing inmates to have small amenities while serving time. These practices have reduced riots, prison suicides, and a variety of other problematic behaviors. In Thailand, the professionalization of the correctional officer, through training and by instilling a sense of pride in this type of work, has been successful in shaping the organization, according to Ayuth Sintoppant (Chapter 12). Most of these correctional leaders observed improvement in the treatment of inmates, and this emphasis on humane practices has led to a constructive difference in the culture of their agencies.

In regard to evidence-based practices, all of these correctional leaders indicated the importance of such practices. Nevertheless, some, such as Jaroslav Jánoš (Chapter 3), General Gomez García (Chapter 8), and Warden Sintoppant (Chapter 12), indicated that while some data are available, the ability to track programs and determine effectiveness is limited. This means that, in reality, these countries should make improvements in their data systems and ensure that outcome results are shared among administrators throughout their system. On the other hand, Michael Donnellan (Chapter 2), Walter Troxler (Chapter 6), Gary Maynard (Chapter 10), and Soh Wai Wah of Singapore (Chapter 11) all have indicated that their prison systems maintain data and use data-driven processes to guide much of the policy and practice throughout the institution. The means by which this approach can affect policy and future outcomes cannot be underestimated, and each of these correctional leaders provided specific means by which their organizations utilize evidence-based approaches.

All of the correctional leaders interviewed in this volume note that transnational relations are important to operating within the correctional environment, though some find this to be more true than others. Warden Sintoppant (Chapter 12) noted that the Thai prison system has an influx of offenders from the various countries that are adjacent to Thailand. Likewise, General Gomez García (Chapter 8) also indicated that the Mexican prison system has been influenced by studies and visits to a number of countries in the European Union as well as other areas of the world. He also pointed to the problems of transnational drug syndicates within Mexico, Central America, and South America and the impact of these criminal organizations on Mexico's law enforcement process and its correctional system. Likewise, Philippe Pottier in France (Chapter 1) points toward the relationship that is shared between France and Quebec (in the nation of Canada) as well as France's role on various governing bodies throughout Europe to demonstrate that correctional practice in France does not occur in a global vacuum. These three as well as the remainder of correctional leaders in this volume seem to be well travelled and open to the idea of learning from other nations.

From the interviews provided, it becomes obvious that the functions and responsibilities of these correctional leaders are multifaceted and quite encompassing. Collectively, the correctional leaders in this volume show how correctional careers evolve, over time, among prison administrators around the globe. These leaders also show us that the field of corrections is demanding and ever-changing, requiring flexibility and innovative thinking to address the many pushes and pulls that are exerted upon a prison system. The ability to address issues within and outside the prison environment is fundamental for these administrators. Through it all, these leaders have vision and are forward thinking, possessing a transformative approach to leadership that has served to change the very nature of correctional practice. As with our prior volume, the leaders in this volume serve as exemplary role models for correctional professionals around the world. They give scholars and practitioners a unique inside view of the world of corrections from a variety of international settings, demonstrating that, regardless of the area of the world, effective correctional operations will always require competent stewards of organizational resources. At the same time, these correctional leaders must also understand and appreciate the unique social, political, psychological, legal, and financial demands that face this segment of the criminal justice system.

International Police Executive Symposium (IPES) www.ipes.info

The International Police Executive Symposium was founded in 1994. The aims and objectives of the IPES are to provide a forum to foster closer relationships among police researchers and practitioners globally, to facilitate cross-cultural, international and interdisciplinary exchanges for the enrichment of the law enforcement profession, and to encourage discussion and published research on challenging and contemporary topics related to the profession.

One of the most important activities of the IPES is the organization of an annual meeting under the auspices of a police agency or an educational institution. Every year since 1994, annual meetings have been hosted by such agencies and institutions all over the world. Past hosts have included the Canton Police of Geneva, Switzerland; the International Institute of the Sociology of Law, Onati, Spain; Kanagawa University, Yokohama, Japan; the Federal Police, Vienna, Austria; the Dutch Police and Europol, The Hague, The Netherlands; the Andhra Pradesh Police, India; the Center for Public Safety, Northwestern University, USA; the Polish Police Academy, Szczytno, Poland; the Police of Turkey (twice); the Kingdom of Bahrain Police; a group of institutions in Canada (consisting of the University of the Fraser Valley, Abbotsford Police Department, Royal Canadian Mounted Police, the Vancouver Police Department, the Justice Institute of British Columbia, Canadian Police College, and the International Centre for Criminal Law Reform and Criminal Justice Policy); the Czech Police Academy, Prague; the Dubai Police; the Ohio Association of Chiefs of Police and the Cincinnati Police Department, Ohio, USA; the Republic of Macedonia and the Police of Malta. An annual meeting on the theme of "Policing Violence, Crime, Disorder and Discontent: International Perspectives" was hosted in Buenos Aires, Argentina on June 26–30, 2011. The 2012 annual meeting was hosted at United Nations in New York on the theme of "Economic Development, Armed Violence and Public Safety" on

August 5–10. The Ministry of the Interior of Hungary and the Hungarian National Police hosted the meeting in 2013 in Budapest on August 4–9 on the theme of "Contemporary Global Issues in Policing". The 2014 meeting on "Crime Prevention and Community Resilience" will take place in Sofia, Bulgaria on July 27–31.

There have been also occasional special meetings of the IPES. A special meeting was cohosted by the Bavarian Police Academy of Continuing Education in Ainring, Germany, University of Passau, Germany, and State University of New York, Plattsburgh, USA in 2000. The second special meeting was hosted by the police in the Indian state of Kerala. The third special meeting on the theme of "Contemporary Issues in Public Safety and Security" was hosted by the commissioner of police of the Blekinge region of Sweden and the president of the University of Technology on August 10–14, 2011. The most recent special meeting was held in Trivandrum (Kerala, India) on "Policing by Consent" on March 16–20, 2014.

The majority of participants of the annual meetings are usually directly involved in the police profession. In addition, scholars and researchers in the field also participate. The meetings comprise both structured and informal sessions to maximize dialogue and exchange of views and information. The executive summary of each meeting is distributed to participants as well as to a wide range of other interested police professionals and scholars. In addition, a book of selected papers from each annual meeting is published through CRC Press/Taylor & Francis Group, Prentice Hall, Lexington Books and other reputed publishers. A special issue of *Police Practice and Research: An International Journal* is also published with the most thematically relevant papers after the usual blind review process.

IPES Board of Directors

The IPES is directed by a board of directors representing various countries of the world (listed below). The registered business office is located at Norman Vale, 6030 Nott Road, Guilderland, NY 12064 and the registered agent is National Registered Agents, 200 West Adams Street, Chicago, IL 60606.

President

Dilip Das, Norman Vale, 6030 Nott Road, Guilderland, NY 12084. Tel: 802-598-3680. Fax: 410-951-3045. E-mail: dilipkd@aol.com.

Vice President

Etienne Elion, Case J-354-V, OCH Moungali 3, Brazzaville, Republic of Congo. Tel: 242-662-1683. Fax: 242-682-0293. E-mail: ejeej2003@yahoo.fr.

Treasurer/Secretary

Paul Moore, 125 Kenny Lane, West Monroe, LA 21294. Tel: 318-512-1500. Paul@ipes.info.

Directors

Rick Sarre, GPO Box 2471, Adelaide, 5001, South Australia. Tel: 61-8-83020889. Fax: 61-8-83020512. E-mail: rick.sarre@unisa.edu.au.

Tonita Murray, 73 Murphy Street, Carleton Place, Ontario K7C 2B7 Canada. Tel: 613-998-0883. E-mail: Tonita_Murray@hotmail.com.

Snezana (Ana) Mijovic-Das, Norman Vale, 6030 Nott Road, Guilderland, NY 12084. Tel: 518-452-7845. Fax: 518-456-6790. E-mail: anamijovic@yahoo.com.

Andrew Carpenter, The Pier, 1 Harborside Place. Apt 658, Jersey City, NJ 07311. Tel: 917-367-2205. Fax: 917-367-2222. E-mail: carpentera@un.org.

Paulo R. Lino, 111 Das Garcas St., Canoas, RS, 92320-830, Brazil. Tel: 55-51-8111-1357. Fax: 55-51-466-2425. E-mail: paulino2@terra.com.br.

Rune Glomseth, Slemdalsveien 5, Oslo, 0369, Norway. E-mail: Rune.Glomseth@phs.no.

Maximilian Edelbacher, Riemersgasse 16/E/3, A-1190 Vienna, Austria. Tel: 43-1-601 74/5710. Fax: 43-1-601 74/5727. E-mail: edelmax@magnet.at.

A.B. Dambazau, P.O. Box 3733, Kaduna, Kaduna State, Nigeria. Tel: 234-80-35012743. Fax: 234-70-36359118. E-mail: adambazau@yahoo.com.

IPES Institutional Supporters

IPES is guided and helped in all the activities by a group of Institutional Supporters around the world. These supporters are police agencies, universities, research organizers.

African Policing Civilian Oversight Forum (APCOF; Sean Tait), 2nd floor, The Armoury, Buchanan Square, 160 Sir Lowry Road, Woodstock, Cape Town 8000, South Africa. E-mail: sean@apcof.org.za.

Australian Institute of Police Management, Collins Beach Road, Manly, NSW 2095, Australia (Connie Coniglio). E-mail: cconiglio@aipm.gov.au.

Baker College of Jackson, 2800 Springport Road, Jackson, MI 49202 (Blaine Goodrich) Tel: 517-841-4522. E-mail: blaine.goodrich@baker.edu.

Cyber Defense & Research Initiatives, LLC (James Lewis), P.O. Box 86, Leslie, MI 49251. Tel: 517 242 6730. E-mail: lewisja@cyberdefenseresearch.com.

Defendology Center for Security, Sociology and Criminology Research (Valibor Lalic), Srpska Street 63, 78000 Banja Luka, Bosnia and Herzegovina. Tel and Fax: 387-51-308-914. E-mail: lalicv@teol.net.

Fayetteville State University (Dr. David E. Barlow, Professor and Dean), College of Basic and Applied Sciences, 130 Chick Building, 1200 Murchison Road, Fayetteville, North Carolina, 28301 . Tel: 910-672-1659. Fax: 910-672-1083. E-mail: dbarlow@uncfsu.edu.

Kerala Police (Mr. Balasubramanian, Director General of Police), Police Headquarters, Trivandrum, Kerala, India. E-mail: JPunnoose@gmail.com.

Molloy College, The Department of Criminal Justice (contact Dr. John A. Eterno, NYPD Captain-Retired), 1000 Hempstead Avenue, P.O. Box 5002, Rockville Center, NY 11571-5002. Tel: 516 678 5000, Ext. 6135. Fax: 516 256 2289. E-mail: jeterno@molloy.edu.

Mount Saint Vincent University, Department of Psychology (Stephen Perrott), 166 Bedford Highway, Halifax, Nova Scotia, Canada. E-mail: Stephen.perrott@mvsu.ca.

National Institute of Criminology and Forensic Science (Kamalendra Prasad, Inspector General of Police), MHA, Outer Ring Road, Sector 3, Rohini, Delhi 110085, India. Tel: 91-11-275-2-5095. Fax: 91-11-275-1-0586. E-mail: director.nicfs@nic.in.

National Police Academy, Police Policy Research Center (Naoya Oyaizu, Deputy Director), Zip 183-8558: 3- 12- 1 Asahi-cho Fuchu-city, Tokyo, Japan. Tel: 81-42-354-3550. Fax: 81-42-330-1308. E-mail: PPRC@npa.go.jp.

North Carolina Central University, Department of Criminal Justice (Dr. Harvey L. McMurray, Chair), 301 Whiting Criminal Justice Building, Durham, NC 27707. Tel: 919-530-5204/919-530-7909; Fax: 919-530-5195. E-mail: hmcmurray@nccu.edu.

Royal Canadian Mounted Police (Helen Darbyshire, Executive Assistant), 657 West 37th Avenue, Vancouver, BC V5Z 1K6, Canada. Tel: 604-264 2003. Fax: 604-264-3547. E-mail: helen.darbyshire@rcmp-grc.gc.ca.

Edith Cowan University, School of Psychology and Social Science, Social Justice Research Centre (Prof S. Caroline Taylor, Foundation Chair in Social Justice), 270 Joondalup Drive, Joondalup, WA 6027, Australia. E-mail: c.taylor@ecu.edu.au.

South Australia Police, Office of the Commissioner (Commissioner Mal Hyde), 30 Flinders Street, Adelaide, SA 5000, Australia. E-mail: mal.hyde@police.sa.gov.au.

University of the Fraser Valley, Department of Criminology & Criminal Justice (Dr. Irwin Cohen), 33844 King Road, Abbotsford, British Columbia V2 S7 M9, Canada. Tel: 604-853-7441. Fax: 604-853-9990. E-mail: Irwin.Cohen@ufv.ca.

University of Maribor, Faculty of Criminal Justice and Security, (Dr. Gorazd Mesko), Kotnikova 8, 1000 Ljubljana, Slovenia. Tel: 386-1-300-83-39. Fax: 386-1-2302-687. E-mail: gorazd.mesko@fvv.uni-mb.si.

University of Maine at Augusta, College of Natural and Social Sciences (Mary Louis Davitt, Professor of Legal Technology), 46 University Drive, Augusta, ME 04330-9410. E-mail: mldavitt@maine.edu.

University of New Haven, School of Criminal Justice and Forensic Science (Dr. Richard Ward), 300 Boston Post Road, West Haven, CT 06516. Tel: 203-932-7260. E-mail: rward@newhaven.edu.

University of South Africa, College of Law, School of Criminal Justice (Prof. Kris Pillay, Director), Preller Street, Muckleneuk, Pretoria, South Africa. E-mail: cpillay@unisa.ac.za.

University of South Africa, Department of Police Practice, Florida Campus (Setlhomamaru Dintwe), Christiaan De Wet and Pioneer Avenues, Private Bag X6, Florida, 1710 South Africa. Tel: 011-471-2116. Fax: 011-471-2255. E-mail: Dintwsi@unisa.ac.za.

Guidelines for Interviewers

Call for Authors

We are currently recruiting authors to write chapters for Volume 2 of the *Trends in Corrections: Interviews with Corrections Leaders around the World* Series. Information will be presented on several countries using the personal views and experiences of a correctional leader in that country. Corrections scholars/researchers will be asked to conduct a comprehensive interview of the experiences and thoughts of a high-ranking corrections official in their country. The scholars/researchers will edit the interviews to emphasize personal experiences, ideas, and detailed examples of issues (both positive and negative) in their country's correctional system. The relationship between theory, evidence, and practice will be highlighted.

Brief Description of the Proposed Book

The main goal of the interviews is to capture the views of correctional officials. Your role should not be to criticize or interpret what the officials meant to say, but to write as accurately as possible what the officials told you. The chapter will be based on their views, experiences, and thought processes. We know what scholars/researchers think about corrections, but we know less about what the people who work in the corrections field think about and how they evaluate trends, developments, and issues in corrections.

The basic reason for doing the interviews is that we firmly believe that corrections officials possess a wide variety of information about the field and that practitioners can make significant contributions to our insight into the issues and problems of current correctional practices. The knowledge these individuals possess is not easily captured, but our goal is to describe their personal information in this book. The practical reason that we are asking scholars/researchers to conduct the interviews is because leaders in the field of corrections do not have the time to write and reflect on their experiences, views, opinions, and perspectives. We think in-depth interviews are one means to depict the knowledge of correctional practitioners, and this is why we are requesting scholars/researchers like you to record their views.

Goals of the Interviews and General Information

The general goal of the interviews is to present the views and interpretations of the developments, crises, and current issues in the correctional system *by experienced practitioners.*

Example questions include:

- What do those directly involved in the corrections profession see happening in the correctional system in their countries and internationally?
- How do they evaluate or interpret developments (either positive or negative) in corrections?
- Many books and articles contain analysis and interpretation of the state of current correctional policy, programs, and prisons by scholars and policy makers from outside the correctional system.
- What we would like to have are views and interpretations from within correctional organizations.
- What do leaders in the field of corrections who work in the jails and prison systems see happening in corrections?
- What are the issues they consider important?
- What changes do they see as successes or failures?
- What aspects of the system are likely long-lasting versus those policies or programs they see as more transient?

We want to emphasize one major point. *We do not want the official rhetoric (or the official success stories)* that high-level people sometimes fall back on during interviews; we want their *personal views and thinking.* If you have the sense that you are getting the formal language and official views on correctional policy and issues, see if you can get the officials to go beyond the official story and push them for their own views. The interviewer should seek to get the person being interviewed to move beyond simple answers, and get them to analyze and reflect on their experiences, ideas, and knowledge. Our trust in your interviewing skills is why you were asked to do the interview.

Topic Areas To Be Covered during the Interview

In this section, we discuss the desired content of the interviews. In some situations, there may be areas of importance in your country or community that are different from the questions posed below. In those cases, you should focus on these areas more completely and ask about these issues in addition to the questions listed. For example, questions for correctional leaders in transitional countries will likely deal more with changes in correctional philosophy and in organizations than questions for leaders in stable democracies.

Even in stable democracies, however, a particular area or locale can be in a state of prison crisis, and we hope that these specific issues will be addressed as well. Being familiar with the correctional policies and situations (such as any lawsuits) in your country will enable you to tailor your questions toward the dominant local issues that have had to be dealt with by the country's leaders. Be creative while sticking to the main issues at hand.

We have listed a number of general and specific questions that should be covered in the interview. Please try to cover the topics mentioned below as the flow of the interview dictates. Please add, elaborate, and use follow-up questions as you see necessary to clarify points, expand on ideas, and pursue an insight offered. All the topics below should be asked, but the specific questions listed for each main area are suggestions. Interviews have their own dynamics. Follow them down their most productive paths. Since each of you will be interviewing officials within different organizations, the list and sequence of questions will have to be adjusted for each interview. How you word each question is up to your own preference. When asking follow-up questions, please try to get specific examples or details of any generalizations made by the official. (Specific examples of overarching problems or situations in the leader's country are probably among the most useful and interesting pieces of information to readers.)

Eight Topic Areas (and Suggested Question Wording) for the Interview

1. *Career*: Tell us a little bit about your career: length, organizations worked in, movements, specializations, trajectories in your career that might differ from those expected, and so on.
   a. What motivated you to enter the field of corrections?
   b. Did the way your career developed surprise you?
   c. Did your work prove as interesting or rewarding as you thought it would?
   d. Do you have any regrets about an opportunity you pursued or chose not to pursue during the course of your career?
2. *Changes Experienced*: What do you see as the most important changes that have occurred in the field of corrections over the course of your career (philosophies, organizational arrangements, specializations, policies and programs, equipment or technologies, methods of rehabilitation, methods of community supervision, intermediate sanctions, personnel, diversity, etc.)?
   a. What changes in external conditions (support from communities, legal and legislative powers, relations with minority communities, resource provision, political influence, etc.) have had a significant impact on current correctional practices and policy?

b. Overall, has the quality of prisons, jails, and community supervision in your country/community improved or declined over the past 10 years? (For example, number of personnel per inmate ratio, amount and type of training offered, programs offered to inmates, rehabilitation strategies and the amount of money available to implement these programs, what percentage of inmates are able to have access to programs, how recidivism of both technical violations and new criminal activity has been affected, interagency cooperation, the effectiveness of top management providing quality control and directing managing and line personnel, inmate and staff safety, and inmate suicide rates.)
c. In general, is it more or less difficult to be a correctional officer (or supervisor, warden, regional management) now than in the past?

3. *Personal Correctional Philosophy*: What do you think should be the role of prison, jail, and community supervision officials in society?
   a. What should their job, functions, and roles be? What should be left to other people or organizations? What about line staff such as corrections officers? Prison/jail/community supervisors and wardens?
   b. Which organizational arrangements work and which do not?
   c. What policies does your country have in regards to relations with the community, political groups, and other criminal justice organizations? Do these policies work well? What hampers cooperation with other agencies and groups?
   d. How should corrections institutions be run? What programs should be provided, and how would you prefer sentencing laws to be modified so as to have prisons and jails include the individuals most deserving of incarceration? What are the best correctional strategies to ensure the safety and security of the inmates, staff, and community? What services should prisons and jails provide that are currently not offered? What services are provided that you believe should be cut?
   e. How should supervision post-prison or post-jail (or in lieu of prison or jail) be dealt with? Is the procedure used in your country working, or do you see an increased recidivism rate due to issues those supervised in the community experience? How would you improve this problem, or why is this process working in your country?
   f. Do you feel that your country uses appropriate intermediate sanctions when needed or is there a lack of such sanctions? Are intermediate sanctions such as treatment programs, intensive supervision, and electronic monitoring utilized, and do they

reduce recidivism while keeping those in the community safe? If not, what do you feel is the problem?

4. *Problems and Successes Experienced*: In your experience, which policies or programs have worked well, and which have not? Can you speculate for what reasons?
   a. What would you consider to be the greatest problem facing the correctional system at this time?
   b. There is a concern among some correctional officials that the global economic downturn initiated by the financial crisis that started in 2007 has significantly changed the nature of work in corrections. What consequences has the correctional system in your country/community experienced? Overall, how has the economic crisis impacted correctional practices in your country/community (e.g., have specific steps been taken to improve operating efficiency, to change release practices as a result of economic hardships, or to change to salary structures or benefits)? Are more people seeking careers in corrections?
   c. What problems in corrections do you find are the most difficult to deal with? What would be easy to change? Internal problems (culture of the organization, managerial deficiencies, allegations of corruption or gender related problems) or externally generated problems (resources, community support, parole or probation procedures, or lack thereof)?
   d. What is the most successful program you have worked with in corrections? What is the most successful policy in regards to the positive improvements that have been made to prisons, jails, or community supervision?
5. *Theory and Practice*: In your view, what should the relationship between theory and practice be? What can practitioners learn from studying and applying theories; and what can those who create theories of punishment gain from practitioners?
   a. What is the relationship between theory and practice right now? Does it exist? Does it work? What holds collaboration or interactions back?
   b. What kind of research, in what form, and on which questions would you find most useful for practice? If not very useful, what could or should creators of theory do to make their ideas more useful to you?
   c. Where do you find theory-based information? Where do you look: journals, professional magazines, books, publications, reports?
   d. Does the department of corrections you work for conduct research on its own? On what types of issues or questions?

6. *Evidence-Based Corrections*: In your experience, has your county's correctional system made use of various evidence-based programs? Do you feel that it is best to use evidence-based practices (or "what works") or that this focus is not important?
   a. What evidence-based practices are used now in prisons, jails, for intermediate sanctions, or in community supervision? Do you agree with the use of these practices? Do you feel that using more evidence-based practices would benefit the correctional system?
   b. Do you read information on evidence-based practices? Where do you get this information? If you do not have this information, would you be interested in having access to these practices? What programs have been proven to work best in your country?
7. *Transnational Relations*: How have you been affected by the following in your organization's work by developments outside the country: human rights demands, universal codes of ethics, practical interactions with corrections officials from other countries, personal experiences outside the country, programs developed by other countries, new sentencing laws, political strife, and war in your or neighboring countries?
   a. Have those interactions been beneficial or harmful? What kind of external international influences are beneficial and which ones less so?
   b. How have international relationships with other countries or other political influences had an impact on correctional policy or practice in your country?
8. *Role of Corrections*:
   a. How do you think the public views corrections in your country/community?
   b. Is corrections viewed as a tool used to maintain the existing social order and power structure in your society?
   c. What levels of public support does the corrections service in your country have?
9. *General Assessments*: Are you basically satisfied or dissatisfied with developments in the field of corrections?
   a. What do you think of the relationship between sentencing laws and public opinion to the functioning of prisons, jails, and community supervision?
   b. How do you view the release procedures in your country and do they contribute to or inhibit recidivism?
   c. What rehabilitative programs could be offered either inside or outside prison or jail that could decrease recidivism?
   d. How are intermediate sanctions (such as house arrest, ankle bracelets, rehabilitative programs in the community, and inten-

sive supervision, among others) in your country used, and how are they working or failing to work?

e. Which intermediate sanctions would you increase or create, and why?
f. How could changing the balance between intermediate sanctions affect prison and jail environments? Would that be an improvement?
g. What are the developments you see as most likely to happen in next few years, and which developments would you prefer to see happening?
h. What is most needed now to improve prisons, jails, community supervision, and the overall punishment process in your country?

Preparation for the Interview

Before the Interview

- Get a sense of how much time you are likely to have and what questions you will be able to ask during that time. No interview will enable you to ask all the questions you want, so it is best to choose your priorities based on who you are interviewing.
- You should, if at all possible, record the interview by audiotape to aid you in writing the chapter. Seek permission from the correctional leader before recording the interview.
- You will have space for about 6000–8000 words (on average) when writing your interview. It is important to pick the most interesting information that you have obtained (in your opinion). Our top priorities are the officials' reflections on the changes experienced during their careers, how they evaluate these changes, and the interrelationship between theory and practice. Thus, these areas are high priorities for the interviews.

Instructions for Writing Your Chapter: After the Interview

1. Please write a short introduction to the actual interview. The introduction should
   a. Briefly describe the basic structure of corrections in your country. You have to be the judge of how much an informed reader is likely to know about the country and how much should be explained.
   b. Briefly describe the interview itself. Where and when was the interview conducted, how long did it take, was there one or multiple sittings, and how honest and open do you feel the discussion was? What was the demeanor of the interviewee?

2. For publication, edit the interview to bring out the most important discussion and answers. You will likely have much more information from your interview than we will have space for in the proposed book.
3. Write a short conclusion about your impression of the interview. What were the major themes? Briefly describe how accurate the leader's views were in accordance with known literature, without being overly critical about any lack of knowledge.
4. Write a glossary of terms or events mentioned in the interview a reader might not be familiar with. For example, if you interviewed a California correctional official and the *Plata v. Schwarzenegger* lawsuit was talked about, please define this lawsuit so that readers without knowledge of a country's specific terms and laws might be able to understand what is being referenced.
5. We have had two basic styles that are used to write up interviews. Both are acceptable, but we prefer the second style.
    a. The first style is to simply transcribe the interviews—questions asked, answers given.
    b. The second style, which requires more work, is to write short statements about the topic of a question and then insert long excerpts from the interviews. The main point is to have the voice and views of the leaders being interviewed, not your own.
6. Construct short biographies of yourself and the correctional leader who provided the interview. The biography should include information such as educational degree(s), experience in the corrections field, and any notable positions/honors bestowed. These biographies will be included in the book.
7. Send the completed interviews and biographies to Martha Hurley (hurleym1@citadel.edu) and Dilip Das (dilipkd@aol.com). The total interview, including the introduction, body of the interview, conclusion, and glossary should be approximately 6000–8000 words. Biographies should be 100–200 words.

References

93/2008 Coll. of Law amending and supplementing Law no. 475/2005 Coll. of Law on serving of prison sentence of imprisonment and on amendments to certain laws. ACA (2011)

Act No. 475/2005 on serving of prison sentence. European Prison Rules, 2006.

Allen, H., Latessa, E., & Ponder, B. (2013). *Corrections in American: A Brief Introduction*. Pearson: Upper Saddle River, New Jersey.

American Correctional Association (2011). *American Correctional Association*. www.aca.org (accessed 14 February 2013).

Arroyo-Cobo, J. M. (2011). Health care strategies for mental health problems in the prison environment: The Spanish case in a European context. *Revista Española de Sanidad Penitenciaria*, 13, 100–111.

ASEAN. (2013). Overview of ASEN. Available at http://www.asean.org/asean/about-asean/overview.

Bartels, L., & Gaffney, A. (2011). Good practice in women's prisons: A literature review. AIC reports technical and background paper no. 41. Canberra: Australian Institute of Criminology.

BBC. (2011). Ronan Kerr murder "brutal and grotesque". April. Available at http://www.bbc.co.uk/news/uk-northern-ireland-12962723 (accessed 16 October 2013).

BBC. (2012). David Black murder: New "IRA" group claims it murdered prison officer. 12 November. Available at http://www.bbc.co.uk/news/uk-northern-ireland-20296702 (Accessed 16 October 2013).

Beaumont, G., & Tocqueville, A. (1833). *On the Penitentiary System in the United States and its Application in France*. Philadelphia: Carey, Lea & Blanchard.

Brägger, B. F. and Vuille, J. (2012). *Punir, prévenir et resocialiser: de l'arrestation provisoire à la libération conditionnelle. Aperçu général du droit des sanctions pénales et du système carcéral en Suisse*. Stämpfli.

Brinc, F. (1994). *Prostorske zmogljivosti kazenskih poboljševalnih zavodov in pogoji (standardi) za življenje in delo pripornikov in obsojencev v Republiki Sloveniji* [Capacities of correctional institututions, and living and working conditions (standards) of life for pre-trial detainees and convicts in the Republic of Slovenia]. Ljubljana: Institute of Criminology at the Faculty of Law Ljubljana.

Bushnell (2011a). El Temido Carcelero de Lecumberri. In *Altiplano: Organo de Difusion Penitenciario* 1, 9 (October).

Bushnell, 88-9. (2011b). Lecumberri: de "Palacio Negro" a Centro Cultural. In *Altiplano: El Personal, del Centro Federal de Readaptacion Social No. 1 "Altiplano"*... 1:5 (June 2011).

Bushnell, D., & Macaulay, N. (1994). *The Emergence of Latin America in the Nineteenth Century*. New York: Oxford University Press.

Caixal, G., & Roca, X. (1999). Addictive behaviors treatment therapeutic comunity in and out of penitentiaries. *En Trastornos Adictivos*, 1(3). Available at http://zl.elsevier.es/en/revista/trastornos-adictivos-182/sumario/vol-1-num-3-13000760.

Capdevila, M., & Ferrer, M. (2007). *Salut mental i execució penal*. Barcelona: Centre d'Estudis Juridics i Formació Especialitzada. Collecció Justicia i Societat.

Capdevila, M., & Ferrer, M. (2009). *Taxa de reincidència penitenciària 2008*. Barcelona: Centre d'Estudis Jurídics i Formació Especialitzada.

Carlson, P. M., Roth, T., & Travisono, A. P. (2008). History of corrections. In P. M. Carlson & J. S. Garrett (Eds.), *Prison and Jail Administration* (2nd ed.). Gaithersburg, MD: Aspen.

Castlebury, G. (2002). Texas youth offender program. *Corrections Today*, 64(6), 102–106.

Challis, J. (1999). *The Northern Ireland Prison Service: 1920–1990: A History*. Belfast: NIPS.

Cid, J. (2005). The penitentiary system in Spain: The use of imprisonment, living conditions and rehabilitation. *Punishment and Society*, 7, 147–166.

Cid, J., & Larrauri, E (Eds.). (2002). *Jueces penales y penas en España. La aplicación de las penas alternativas a la prisión en los juzgados de lo penal*. Valencia: Tirant Lo Blach.

Cid, J., & Larrauri, E. (2009). Development of crime, social change, mass media, crime policy, sanctioning practice and their impact on prison population rates. *Sistema Penal & Violença*, 1, 1–20.

Cid, J., & Tébar, B. (2010). Spain. In N. Padfield, D. van Zyl Smit, & F. Dünkel (Eds.), *Release from Prison. European Policy and Practice*. Cullompton: Willan.

Committee on the Administration of Justice (CAJ). (2010). Prisons and prisoners in Northern Ireland: Putting human rights at the heart of prison reform. Available at http://www.caj.org.uk/files/2011/01/17/prisons_report_web2.pdf (Accessed 22 October 2013).

Council of Europe. (1996). Report to the government of Slovenia on the visit to Slovenia carried out by the European Committee for the prevention of torture and inhuman or degrading treatment or punishment (CPT) from 19 to 28 February 1995. Available at http://www.cpt.coe.int/documents/svn/1996-18-inf-eng.pdf.

Council of Europe. (2006). European prison rules. Available at https://wcd.coe.int/ViewDoc.jsp?id=955747.

Crewe, B., Liebling, A., & Hulley, S. (2011). Staff culture, use of authority and prisoner quality of life in public and private sector prisons. *Australian and New Zealand Journal of Criminology*, 44(1), 94–115.

Criminal Justice Inspectorate Northern Ireland (CJINI). (2010). Northern Ireland prison service corporate governance arrangements: An inspection of corporate governance arrangements within the Northern Ireland prison service. Available at http://www.cjini.org/CJNI/files/3d/3ddfc1cc-64b9-43da-ad86-88950db136ee.PDF (Accessed 13 August 2013).

Criminal Justice Inspectorate Northern Ireland (CJINI). (2011). An inspection of prisoner resettlement by the Northern Ireland prison service. Available at http://www.cjini.org/CJNI/files/c2/c2d298bb-f13b-45ce-91e4-b040074e1383.pdf (Accessed 14 October 2013).

Criminal Justice Inspectorate Northern Ireland (CJINI). (2012). Report on an announced inspection of Maghaberry prison. Available at http://www.cjini.org/CJNI/files/b5/b561aa96-c6b8-417f-9c70-a736713315e8.pdf (Accessed 25 October 2013).

Criminal Justice Inspectorate Northern Ireland (CJINI). (2013). Report on an announced inspection of Ash House, Hydebank Wood Women's prison. Available at http://www.cjini.org/CJNI/files/e9/e919ac2b-4e79-4a80-b1f6-fb753bea3444.pdf (Accessed 22 October 2013).

Cullen, F. T., Fisher, B. S., & Applegate, B. K. (2000). Public opinion about punishment and corrections. In M. Tonry (Ed.), *Crime and Justice: A Review of Research* (pp. 1–79). Chicago: University of Chicago Press.

Cullen, F. T., Vose, B. A., Jonson, C. N., & Unnever, J. D. (2007). Public support for early intervention: Is child saving a "habit of the heart"? *Victims and Offenders*, 2, 109–124.

Dammer, H. R. (2002). Religion in corrections. In D. Levinson (Ed.), *The Encyclopedia of Crime and Punishment*, volume 3. Thousand Oaks, CA: Sage. Available at http://academic.scranton.edu/faculty/DAMMERH2/ency-religion.html.

Day, A., & Casey, S. (2012). Interview with Timothy Leo, chief psychologist of the Singapore prison service. In J. K. Singer, D. K. Das, & E. Ahlin (Eds.), *Trends in Corrections: Interviews with Corrections Leaders Around the World*. Boca Raton, FL: CRC Press.

Decree 368/2008 of the Ministry of Justice SR on regulations of imprisonment sentence.

Department of Corrections. (2005). Observation tours on Thai prison during the 11th UN Congress. The 11th United Nations Congress on Crime Prevention and Criminal Justice (Bangkok 18–22 April 2005). Available at http://www.correct.go.th/comnet1/un/pv1.html.

Department of Corrections. (2010). Prisons and correctional institutions. Bangkok, Thailand: Thailand Ministry of Justice. Available at http://www.correct.go.th/eng/prisons_correctional_i.html.

Department of Statistics Singapore. (2014). Latest data. Available at http://www.singstat.gov.sg/statistics/latest_data.html#14 (Accessed 3 March 2014).

Department of Correction. (B.E. 2555). A performance report of the Department of Correction to the public during B.E. 2555 budget year. Department of Correction, Ministry of Justice, Nonthaburi.

Department of Correction. (n.d.a) History of correction. Available at http://www.correct.go.th/correct2009/index.php?action=showcontent&c_id=3.

Department of Correction. (n.d.b) Authority, function, and division. Available at http://www.correct.go.th/correct2009/index.php?action=showcontent&c_id=8.

de Soto, H. (2000). *The Mystery of Capital*. New York: Basic Books.

Díez-Ripollés, J. L. (2004). El Nuevo modelo de seguridad ciudadana. *Revista electronica de ciencia penal y criminología*, 6(3), 1–34. Available at http://criminet.ugr.es/recpc/06/recpc06-03.pdf.

DiIulio, J. (1987). *Governing Prisons: A Comparative Study of Correctional Management*. New York: The Free Press.

Direcció General de Serveis Penitenciaris Departament de Justicia. Generalitat de Catalunya. (2012). Avaluació d'un any d'aplicació de la Circular d'Estrangeria. Available at http://premsa.gencat.cat/pres_fsvp/AppJava/notapremsavw/detall.do?id=164527.

Division of Corrections Annual Report Fiscal Year 2011. (2011). Available at http://www.dpscs.state.md.us/publicinfo/publications/pdfs/DOC2011AnnualRpt.pdf (Accessed 24 October 2014.)

Elias, G., The numbers game: Understanding staffing ratios. Available at https://nic.zendesk.com/attachments/token/wadxdqwhuuuhn7j/?name=The+Numbers+Game.pdf (Accessed 3 March 2014).

Farrington, D. P., Coid, J. W., Harnett, L. M., Jolliffe, D., Soteriou, N., Turner, R. E., & West, D. J. (2006). Criminal careers up to age 50 and life success up to age 48: New findings from the Cambridge Study in Delinquent Development. Home Office Research Study No. 299. London: Home Office.

Finch, J., & Tangprasit, N. (2012). Capital punishment in Thailand. Available at http://www.thaiprisonlife.com/prison-stories/capital-punishment-in-thailand/.

Fisher, M. (2012) A different justice. *The Atlantic*, 24 August.

Flynn, M. (2012). Reaction to St. Patrick's Report surprising for its mock shock. *Irish Times* (Accessed 20 October 2012).

Foucault, M. (1975). *Discipline and Punish: The Birth of the Prison*. Translated by Alan Sheridan (1977). New York: Pantheon Books.

Friedman, L. (1993). *Crime and Punishment in American History*. New York: Basic Books.

García Andrade, I. (2004). *Sistema Penitenciario Mexicano: Retos y Perspectivas*. Mexico City: SISTA Editoria.

García Luna, G. (2011). *Para entender: el nuevo modelo de seguridad para México*. Mexico City: Nostra ediciones.

García Luna, G. (2012). *A Discussion with Genaro Garcia Luna*. Washington, DC: The Woodrow Wilson Center. Available at http://www.wilsoncenter.org/event/discussion-genaro-garcia-luna.

García Ramirez, S. (1979). *El Final de Lecumberri: Reflexiones sobre la prisión*. Mexico City: Editorial Porrua SA.

Garland, D. (2001). *The Culture of Control. Crime and Social Order in Contemporary Society*. Oxford: Oxford University Press.

Gendreau, P., Cullen, F. T., & Bonta, J. (1995). Intensive rehabilitation supervision: The next generation in community corrections. *Federal Probation*, 58(1), 72–78.

General Directorate Collection Orders of the Prison and Court Guard. (2009). Order No. 86 on the treatment of inmates.

González, F. E. (2008). *Dual Transitions from Authoritarian Rule*. Baltimore: Johns Hopkins.

González Sánchez, I. (2012). La cárcel en España: Mediciones y condiciones del encarcelamiento en el siglo XXI. *Revista de derecho penal y criminología* 3ª Época, 8, 351–402.

Grayson, G. W. (2010). *Mexico: Narco-Violence and a Failed State?* (pp. 152–162). New Brunswick: Transaction.

Griffin, D., & O'Donnell, I. (2012). The life sentence and parole. *British Journal of Criminology*, 52(3), 611–629.

Grissom, B. (2013). Violence behind bars: Ties to mental illness. 22 September. Available at Panhandle Public Broadcasting System: http://www.panhandlepbs.org/news/texas-tribune/violence-behind-bars/.

Guerin, P., Harrison, P., and Sabol, W. (2011). Prisoners in 2010. US Department of Justice, 2011. Available at http://bjs.ojp.usdoj.gov/content/pub/pdf/p10.pdf (Accessed 24 October 2014.)

Hansard (Official Report). (2013). Prison Reform Programme: Prison Officers' Association briefing. Available at http://www.niassembly.gov.uk/Assembly-Business/Official-Report/Committee-Minutes-of-Evidence/Session-2012-2013/June-2013/Prison-Reform-Programme-Prison-Officers-Association-Briefing/ (Accessed 22 October 2013).

Hanser, R. D. (2013). *Introduction to Corrections*. Thousand Oaks, CA: Sage.

Hanser, R. D. (2014). *Community Corrections* (2nd ed.). Thousand Oaks, CA: Sage.

Hercik, J. M. (2007). *Prisoner Reentry, Religion, and Research*. Washington, DC: United States Department of Health and Human Services.

Hernandez, J. C., & Archibald, R. C. (2012). Blaze at prison underscores broad security problems in Honduras. *New York Times*. February 15.

House of Commons Justice Committee report. (2014). *Role of the Prison Officer*. Available at http://www.publications.parliament.uk/pa/cm200809/cmselect/cmjust/361/36103.htm (Accessed 3 March 2014).

Huntington, S. P. (1991). *The Third Wave*. Norman: University of Oklahoma Press.

Huntington, S. P. (2006). *Political Order in Changing Societies*. New Haven, CT: Yale.

Hurley, M., & Hanley, D. (2010). *Correctional Administration and Change Management*. Boca Raton, FL: CRC Press.

INEGI. (2013). Perfil sociodemografico, Estados Unidos Mexicanos: Censo de Poblacion y Vivienda 2010. Available at http://www.inegi.org.mx/prod_serv/contenidos/espanol/bvinegi/productos/censos/poblacion/2010/perfil_socio/uem/702825047610_1.pdf (Accessed 19 July 2013).

International Centre for Prison Studies (ICPS). (2013). World prison brief. Available at http://www.prisonstudies.org/info/worldbrief/ (Accessed 18 October 2013).

Irish Prison Service. (2012). *Annual Report 2011*. Dublin: Stationery Office.

Irish Prison Service. (2012). *Three Year Strategic Plan 2012–2015*. Dublin: Stationery Office.

Irish Prison Service. (2013). *Annual Report 2012*. Dublin: Stationery Office.

Irwin, J., & Austin, J. (1994). *It's about Time: America's Imprisonment Binge*. Belmont, CA: Wadsworth.

Johnson, B. R., & Larson, D. B. (2003). *The InnerChange Freedom Initiative: A Preliminary Evaluation of America's First Faith-Based Prison*. University of Pennsylvania, CRRUCS.

Johnson, B. R., Larson, D. B., & Pitts, T.C. (1997). Religious programs, institutional adjustment, and recidivism among former inmates in prison fellowship programs. *Justice Quarterly*, 14(1), 145–166.

King, R., & McDermott, K. (1995). *The State of Our Prisons*. Oxford: Oxford University Press.

Kuhn, A. (2005). *Sanctions pénales: Est-cebien la peine*? Grolley: l'Hèbe, Collection La Question.

Kuratanavej, S. (2001). *Crime Prevention: Current Issues in Correctional Treatment and Effective Countermeasures*. Bangkok, Thailand: Thailand Department of Corrections, Thailand Ministry of Justice.

LaSalle Corrections. (2013). About us—Our wardens, our services, our reach. Ruston, LA: LaSalle Corrections. Available at http://www.lasallecorrections.com/index.php?submenu=Home&src=.

Laub, J., & Sampson, R. (2003). *Shared Beginnings, Divergent Lives: Delinquent Boys to Age 70*. London: Harvard University Press.

Leibling, A. (2005). *Prisons and Their Moral Performance: A Study of Values, Quality and Prison Life*. Oxford: Oxford University Press.

Leo, T. (2014). Current evidence-based practices in the Singapore prison service. *Home Team Journal* 5, 44–52.

Liebling, A., Price, D., & Shefer, G. (2011). *The Prison Officer*. Cullompton: Willan.

Loh, K. (2013). Competency framework in the pipeline for CARE Network aftercare partners. *Home Team News*, April. Available at http://www.hometeam.sg (Accessed 28 August 2013).

Lohr, D. (2012). Remembering Attica Prison: The "bloodiest one-day encounter between Americans since Civil War". *Huffington Post*, 13 September. Available at http://www.huffingtonpost.com/2012/09/13/attica-prison_n_1880737.html.

Louisiana Department of Public Safety and Corrections. (2013). *Corrections Services—About DOC*. Baton Rouge, LA: LDPSC.

Luque, M., Ferrer, L., & Capdevila, M. (2005). *La reincidencia penitenciaria a Catalunya*. Barcelona: Centre d'Estudis Juridics i Formació Especialitzada. Available at http://www20.gencat.cat/docs/Justicia/Documents/ARXIUS/doc_11205211_1.pdf.

Mandeville, M. (2004). Leaving gang life behind in Texas. Corrections.com.

Martinson, R. (1974). What works? Questions and answers about prison reform. *Public Interest*, 35, 22–54.

Maruna, S. (2001). *Making Good: How Ex-Convicts Reform and Rebuild Their Lives*. Washington, DC: American Psychological Association.

Maryland State Administration. (2013). Department of Public Safety & Correctional Services. Retrieved from: http://msa.maryland.gov/msa/mdmanual/22dpscs/html/22agen.html#secretary. (Accessed 20 October 2013).

McEvoy, K. (2001). *Paramilitary Imprisonment in Northern Ireland: Resistance, Management and Release*. Oxford: Oxford University Press.

McKeown, L. (2009). An afternoon in September 1983. In P. Scraton & J. McCulloch (Eds.), *The Violence of Incarceration* (pp. 19–36). New York: Routledge.

McKittrick, D., Kelters, S., Feeney, B., Thornton, C., & McVea, D. (2007). *Lost Lives: The Stories of the Men, Women and Children Who Died as a Result of the Northern Ireland Troubles*. Edinburgh: Mainstream Publishing.

Meško, G., Fields, C., & Smole, T. (2011). A concise overview of penology and penal practice in Slovenia the unchanged capacity, new standards, and prison overcrowding. *The Prison Journal*, 91(4), 398–424.

Miller, J. (1989). The debate on rehabilitating criminals: Is it true that nothing works? *Washington Post*. Available at www.prisonpolicy.org/scans/rehab.html.

Morse, R. (1964). The heritage of Latin America. In L. Hartz (Ed.), *The Founding of New Societies*. New York: Harcourt, Brace and World.

National Institute of Justice. (2005). *Implementing Evidence Based Practice in Corrections*. Washington, DC: U.S. Department of Justice.

Norris, B. (2013). Comparison of per capita murder rates in Mexico and the US, 1990–2010. Unpublished paper, Midwest Political Science Association Annual Conference, Chicago, March 14.

Northern Ireland Prison Service (NIPS). (2013). Analysis of NIPS prison population from 01/07/2013 to 30/09/2013. Available at http://www.dojni.gov.uk/index/ni-prison-service/nips-population-statistics-2.htm (Accessed 14 October 2013).

Nur Asyiqin Mohamad Salleh (2014). More ex-inmates reoffend within 2 years of release, *Straits Times*, Singapore, February 12.

Office of the Inspector of Custodial Services Western Australia (OICSWA). (2009). Report of an announced inspection of Boronia pre-release centre for women. Report no. 62. Perth: OICSWA.

Pratt, J., & Eriksson, A. (2011). "Mr. Larsson is walking out again." The origins and development of Scandinavian prison systems. *Australian and New Zealand Journal of Criminology*, 44(1), 7–23.

Pravilnik o izvrševanju kazni zapora [Rules on implementation of the sentence of imprisonment]. (2000). *Uradni list Republike Slovenije* (102/2000).

Prison Reform Trust. (2012). Bromley briefings prison factfile: November 2012. Available at http://www.prisonreformtrust.org.uk/Portals/0/Documents/FactfileNov2012small.pdf (Accessed 15 August 2013).

Prison Reform Trust. (2013). Bromley briefings: Summer 2013. Available at http://www.prisonreformtrust.org.uk/Portals/0/Documents/Prisonthefacts.pdf (Accessed 25 October 2013).

Prison Review Oversight Group (PROG). (2013). First annual report March 2013. Available at http://www.dojni.gov.uk/index/ni-prison-service/prison_review_oversight_group_annual_report_2013.pdf (Accessed 22 October 2013).

Prison Review Team. (2011). Review of the Northern Ireland prison service: Conditions, management and oversight of all prisons. Final Report. Available at http://www.prisonreviewni.gov.uk/review_of_the_northern_ireland_prison_service-interim_report_february_2011.pdf (Accessed 9 August 2013).

Probation Service. (2012). *The Probation Service Recidivism Study 2007–2011*. Dublin: Stationery Office (see www.probation.ie).

Redondo Illescas, S. (2006). ¿Sirve el tratamiento para rehabilitar a los delincuentes sexuales? *Revista Española de Investigación Criminológica*, 4(6), 1–22. Available at http://www.criminologia.net/pdf/reic/ano4-2006/a42006art3.pdf.

Robinson, G., Priede, C., Farrall, S., & Shapland, J. (2014). Understanding "quality" in probation practice: Frontline perspectives in England and Wales. *Criminology and Criminal Justice*, 14, 123–142.

Ronel, N., & Segev, D. (forthcoming). Positive criminology in practice. *International Journal of Offender Therapy and Comparative Criminology*, EPub ahead of print. doi:10.1177/0306624X13491933.

Ryder, C. (2000). *Inside the Maze: The Untold Story of the Northern Ireland Prison Service*. London: Methuen.

SEGOB. (2013). Estadisticas del Sistema Penitenciario Nacional—Enero 2013. Available at http://www.ssp.gob.mx/portalWebApp/ShowBinary?nodeId=/BEA%20Repository/365162//archivo (Accessed 19 July 2013).

Slovenian Prison Administration. (n.d.) Prison administration: Bodies of the ministry. Available at http://www.mp.gov.si/en/about_the_office/prison_administration_bodies_of_the_ministry/ (Accessed 28 August 2013).

Singapore Prison Service. (2011) The prison story. Available at http://www.prisons.gov.sg/content/sps/default/aboutus/the_prison_story.html (Accessed 28 August 2013).

Smole, T. (2009). Analiza prezasedenosti zavodov za prestajanje kazni zapora Uprave republike Slovenije za izvrševanje kazenskih sankcij [Analysis of prison overcrowding in the National Prison Administration Slovenia]. Ljubljana: Prison Administration of the Republic of Slovenia.

Soh, W. W. (2010). The Yellow Ribbon Project Story (Singapore)— Reaching out and touching a nation. 12th United Nations Congress on Crime Prevention and Criminal Justice, Salvador, Brazil, 12–19 April 2010. Available at http://www.unafei.or.jp/english/pdf/Congress_2010/30Soh_Wai_Wah.pdf (Accessed 28 August 2013).

SPACE I (n.d.). Prisons and community sanctions and measures. Strasbourg: Council of Europe. Available at http://www1.umn.edu/humanrts/instree/g1smr.htm.

Standard Minimum Rules for the Treatment of Prisoners. (1955). Available at http://www2.ohchr.org/english/law/treatmentprisoners.htm.

Statistical Yearbooks of the Slovak Corps and Court Guard (2008) (Available at http://www.zvjs.sk/?rocenky).

Stohr, M., Walsh, A., & Hemmens, C (Eds.). (2009). *Corrections: A Text/Reader*. Thousand Oaks, CA: Sage.

Šugman Stubbs, K., & Ambrož, M. (2012). Recalling conditionally released prisoners in Slovenia. *European Journal of Probation*, 1(4), 99–111.

Texas Department of Criminal Justice. (2007). Security threat groups: On the inside. [Electronic version]. Huntsville: Texas Department of Criminal Justice.

Texas Department of Criminal Justice. (2014). Available at http://www.tdcj.state.tx.us/index.html.

Thailand Law. (2013). Royal Pardon in Thailand. Available at http://www.thailandlaw.org/royal-pardon-in-thailand.html.

Union for Civil Liberty. (2005). International fact finding mission: The death penalty in Thailand. Available at http://www.fidh.org/IMG/pdf/Thailand411-2.pdf.

U.S. Court of Appeals Fifth Circuit. (1980,). *Ruiz v. Estelle*. November 20.

U.S. Customs and Immigration Enforcement. (2013). 2011 Operations Manual ICE Performance-Based National Detention Standards (PBNDS). Available at ICE http://www.ice.gov/detention-standards/2011/.

U.S. Customs and Immigration Enforcement. (2014). Available at ICE http://www.ice.gov/about/overview/.

Uprava za izvrševanje kazenskih sankcij. (2010). Letno poročilo 2009 [Prison Administration of the Republic of Slovenia Annual Report 2009]. Ljubljana: Ministrstvo za pravosodje.

Vollmer, A. (1936). *The Police in Modern Society*. Berkeley: University of California Press.

Wahidin, A., Moore, L., & Convery, U. (2012). Unlocking a locked-down regime: The role of penal policy and administration in Northern Ireland and the challenges of change. *Howard Journal of Criminal Justice*, 51(5), 458–473.

Wahidin, A., Moore, L., & Convery, U. (2012). Unlocking a locked-down regime: The role of penal policy and administration in Northern Ireland and the challenges of Day, Andrew and Sharon Casey. Interview with Timothy Leo, Chief Psychologist of the Singapore Prison Service. In J. K. Singer, D. K. Das, & E. Ahlin (Eds.), *Trends in Corrections: Interviews with Corrections Leaders Around the World*. CRC Press.

Walmsley, R. (2011). *World Prison Population List* (9th ed.). London: International Centre for Prison Studies.

Whitman, J. Q. (2003). *Harsh Justice: Criminal Punishment and the Widening Divide between America and Europe*. New York: Oxford University Press.

Wilson, O. W., & McLaren, R. C. (1963). *Administración de la policía*. Mexico City: Editorial Limusa-Wiley SA.

Wood, D. (2013) Reforming the ranks: Assessing police reform efforts in Mexico. Woodrow Wilson Center. 12 February. Webcast available at: http://www.wilsoncenter.org/event/reforming-the-ranks-assessing-police-reform-efforts-mexico#field_speakers].

Worldhop.com Journal. (n.d.). A royal occasion. Available at http://web.archive.org/web/20060512194220/http://www.worldhop.com/Journals/J5/ROYAL.HTM.

Young, W. (1979). *Community Service Orders. The Development and Use of a New Penal Measure*. London: Heinemann.

Zakon o izvrševanju kazenskih sankcij, ZIKS-1-UPB1 [Enforcement of Penal Sentences Act]. (2006). Uradni list Republike Slovenije, (110/2006).

Websites

http://digital.library.okstate.edu/encyclopedia/entries/m/mc002.html.

http://doc.la.gov/pages/about/mission-and-goals/.

http://www.recercat.net/bitstream/handle/2072/90548/SC-1-076-09_cat.pdf?sequence=1.

http://www.sanipe.es/OJS/index.php/RESP/article/view/13/58.

http://www.tdcj.state.tx.us/documents/Security_Threat_Groups.pdf. Retrieved January 8, 2013.

http://justicia.gencat.cat/web/content/documents/arxius/justidata_46_3a_galerada.pdf.

Index

D

F

G

H

I

J

N

Q

T

U

V

W